Collect
1980

Collected Poems
1980–1990

GAVIN EWART

HUTCHINSON
London Sydney Auckland Johannesburg

© In this collection Gavin Ewart 1991

The right of Gavin Ewart to be identified as Author of this work
has been asserted by Gavin Ewart in accordance with the
Copyright, Designs and Patents Act, 1988

This edition first published in 1991 by Hutchinson

Random Century Group Ltd
20 Vauxhall Bridge Road, London SW1V 2SA

Random Century Australia (Pty) Ltd
20 Alfred Street, Milsons Point, Sydney NSW 2061, Australia

Random Century New Zealand Ltd
PO Box 40–086, Glenfield, Auckland 10, New Zealand

Century Random South Africa (Pty) Ltd
PO Box 337, Bergvlei, 2012, South Africa

British Library Cataloguing in Publication Data
Ewart, Gavin *1916–*
    Collected poems, 1980–1990.
    I. Title
    821.912

    ISBN 0–09–174756–2

Set in Bembo by 🅐 Tek Art Ltd, Addiscombe, Croydon, Surrey
Printed and bound in Great Britain by
Biddles Ltd, Guildford, Surrey

Contents

Acknowledgements

Some of the poems in this book have appeared in the following publications: *Ambit, Aquarius, Bananas, Britain Abroad, British Book News, Chronicles* (USA), *Country Life, Edinburgh Review, Encounter, Gallery, Grand Street* (USA), *Literary Review, London Magazine, Maledicta* (USA), *New Democrat, New Directions 33* (USA), *New Edinburgh Review, New Statesman, Nine New Poems* (USA), *Nova, Oxford Poetry, Poetry Australia, Poetry Durham, Poetry Ireland, Poetry London, Poetry Nation, Poetry Review, Quarto, Rialto, She, Spectator, Stand, Strawberry Fare, Thames Poetry, The American Scholar* (USA), *The Honest Ulsterman, The Listener, The Little Word Machine, The London Review of Books, The Paris Review* (USA), *The Salmon* (Galway), *The Sunday Times, The Times, The Times Literary Supplement, Tribune, Tuba, Words International*. Others have appeared in the anthologies *Light Year '84, Light Year '86, Light Year '87* (USA); *New Poetry 4, New Poetry 9, New Poetry 10* (Arts Council), *Summer Days*; and in the Poetry section of a PEN Broadsheet (ed. Fleur Adcock), *Larkin at Sixty* (Faber & Faber), Poetry Book Society Supplements 1980 and 1986 (ed. Peter Porter).

'Rugger Song: The Balls of the Beaver' appeared as a pamphlet produced by R.A. Gekoski for The Sixth Chamber Press. The limerick version of *The Importance of Being Earnest* was written for an anthology of such pieces, *How to Become Incredibly Well-Read in One Evening* (ed. Eric O. Parrott). The poem 'Gritty' was first published in *Chapter & Verse* (pamphlet, Mandeville Press). The extract from George Orwell's essay, 'Boys' Weeklies', is reproduced by permission of the estate of the late Sonia Brownell Orwell and Martin Secker & Warburg Ltd.

Poems have been broadcast by the BBC ('Not Now, I'm Listening', 'Poetry Now').

Introductory Note

Except for children's poems, this collection contains all my verse published in books since the appearance of *The Collected Ewart 1933–1980*.

Some of the poems in *The Ewart Quarto*, an illustrated collection containing only verse published in the magazine *Quarto*, were duplicated in other books and they have now been restored to them.

Gavin Ewart, December 1989

THE NEW EWART
(1980–1982)

Part One

The Wicked Uncle

Every prune-faced prissy straitlaced serious writer,
    as he sits with his goose quill in his ivory tower
    in the Land of Received Ideas, sipping Veuve Cliché,

dreams of that wicked uncle, the uninhibited natural
    man,
    down in the roaring bar drinking owl-tighteners,
    snapping the garters of the juicy serving wenches,

at home with the crude commercials, with statutory
    powers
    as a Philistine – whose tales of Art and Lance
    have nothing to do with Round Tables, Grails or
    Love.

Admired everywhere for his crude wit, one for the girls
    in every century, a gambler, irresponsible
    in a tweed suit, a prosperous Prospero,

numerate, in everything to do with golden shitlike
    money
    childishly an expert – simple music, simple jokes
    keep him happy, it's the Life Force surely

that pushes him up the board, a pawn of Freedom,
    the world his nursery, he is so enviable,
    so unlike his contemplative nephew, it's not true!

Exits

If you imagine life as a large room,
most of the Exits are marked Painful –
and this is what causes fear,
to get from here to there
the despot, the dandy and the duffer
all have to suffer.

But with the sudden atomic boom –
this is what makes some men disdainful
of death – or the slick quick knife
or shot, you're out of life
like that! bingo! couldn't be faster!
And that's no disaster.

It's when the slow darknesses loom,
the clouds look doom-laden and rainful,
that lightning hysterias fly
across the agonized sky.
Long illness brings dreams of funerals, hearses –
but sudden death: mercies.

Don't mourn them, like some stolid marble tomb,
those who go out like a light – gainful
it isn't, and they had luck,
missed what we all would duck
if we'd the choice: feeling iller and iller.
Long live the instant killer!

25A Norfolk Crescent

It's odd to think how
in that once-untenanted space
above our house
a man is having a bath,
a man and a woman are making love,
life is going on
in what once was air.

In that block of luxury flats
nobody knows now where
the nursery was;
it's so easy to blame
my father's 'I'm very disappointed in you'
for ambition
and the feeling lost.

Mothers comfort. Too much;
and in Cambridge Square
two twin boys
were learning to be queers.
'As the twig is bent', they say,
it's all written,
they say, or in the stars.

The intelligent children
understand the insults –
they suffer most.
The dim ones just grin.
If I had imagination – too much –
my father none,
that was my bad luck.

At this distance in time
the fear and hate exist
but can't be touched –
that house is now a ghost
within a house, where others now
live and suffer.
Tall in the anxious air.

Ode

'What the world needs are warmer hearts,
Not older poets.' – Auden and Kallman, *Elegy For Young
Lovers*

　　As wisdom percolates down
more slowly than water through coffee,
　　our Progress may seem to be back –

this century, three-quarters done,
has screamed *If you don't like it, kill it!*
and millions are mute as result,

in the water, the earth or the air
their particles rest or are wafted –
are we much better off than before?

Yet everything should be tried once,
aphoristic clichés are too tidy;
when murder's a way that's been found

no good, in the end, to win friends
and in general counter-productive,
we might even try something else?

No poet of sixty's a sage,
any more than a saxophone player,
he can't say *Do this!* or *Do that!*,

morals aren't his peculiar sphere,
his opinions are quite often silly.
In an age when some writers can't read,

so spontaneous it isn't true,
'gut reactions' get too freely mentioned –
but it all must go in through the brain,

no experience, none, can escape
when the senses flash messages light-speed
or reporterlike telephone in.

There is hope, while the human brain works,
SF addicts may turn out false prophets.
Selective or general culls

on the basis of colour or class,
by rampageous and wicked religions,
we might, in the end, quite avoid.

But the *heart*? Ah! Emotions so far,
as they sulk or play tag in the sunshine,
have been quite an unbiddable lot –

they '*won't* be told', that is the phrase,
or ordered about, they're haphazard,
      and they want some improbable things.

      Proud ladies in big flowery hats
dream of being held down, naked, and peed on
      by the whole of a rugger fifteen.

      Fantasies of such kinds are not rare
when the hormones, at home with the feelings,
      drink too much of our social champagne.

      As with weather, to forecast or hope
that our hearts grow perceptibly warmer
      is more or less all we can do –

      not giving up hope is the thing,
in the old-fashioned phrase, to be sanguine
      is the must for us creatures of blood.

Invitations

Invitations aren't easy.
When I was in my early twenties
I was giving a party.
I wanted to ask one friend – but not his wife.
My mother said: 'You must ask them both.'
But I was very loth!

She made me feel queasy.
Was she exactly *compos mentis*?
Oh, she shone like a Smartie
but I didn't want her – not on your life!
Now I know that it's not a party that one gives –
but drinks to relatives.

You can't leave out Josie
or really terrible Freddy
who's the boyfriend of a cousin,
your husband's family are all lining up.
There's something about the words *in-law*
that sticks in your craw.

11

It won't be very cosy,
but you must be ready
to take on at least a dozen
you'd not be seen dead with – let alone wine, dine or sup!
He has to be fond of parasites, that one who suffers most,
so rightly called the host!

Dickens and I *

After reading in a Derbyshire school, the fifteen and the
sixteen-year-olds are clustering round me (no fool like an
old fool), the clevers, the athletics, the shys, the bolds,
for me to sign their poem-photostats. I write 'Best
wishes to Clare; John; Clive; Maureen'. These are their
souvenirs – Bard Rock, Hippocrene beer mats – xeroxed
to help them sort out what I mean, like worksheets. I'm
the only worksheet on the scene!

Behind me I feel pressure from the girls, the gentle touch
of blouses, sweaters, blazers; felt but not seen. But
something feminine swirls into my brain. Young eyes
clear as lasers. It's like the scent of roses from a bed
where, still unpruned, the roses, jostling, cluster and of
the senses only one is fed but that's enough to soothe the
sensual luster – sex is that killing air, I tell you, buster!

But this is calm, I'm old. To jump about in goatlike joy is
something long gone by. Yet we have much in common,
there's no doubt, if you consider it – Dickens and I. He
came on Ellen Ternan crying backstage, a teenage girl
ashamed of wearing tights; he loved young women less
than half his age, he went round reading, liked his name
in lights. We'd be called tender, if we had our rights.

* *The prose of Dickens often contains iambic pentameters, unconsciously*
admitted. In these instances it should be re-named: prerse or vose. This poem,
consciously, is made up of rhyming lines printed as prose.

12

In the Restaurant

At the tables there is laughter, where executives are
   lunching.
'You're so beautiful!' a man says; there is holding hands
   (and footlove)
as the dishes and the egos, with experimental cooking,
so exaggerate the meetings and the matings of the
   twosomes.
All percentages and products are examined in the aura
of the wine carafes of redness that emblazon on the table
just the pinkness of the patches where white cloth is
   wobbled over –
as the sun that is our sovereign shines enticingly deep
   through them.

But the lovers and the agents, all of them demand a
   profit –
it may come in cheques, or simply the wet warmth of
   something fluffy.
For the laughter and the lovetalk are by no means, here,
   unselfish,
there is no one in the world who won't seek his own
   advantage
or seek hers (and I must say this); every altruistic action
is itself a conscience-soother and still has its private
   audience
of a God who sits in judgment, or more public
   approbation.
All the women stroke men's torsos for their own delight
   and sharing.

There's a two-way traffic running even in the kissing
   glances
of a girl who eyes a loved one over plates of fegatoni.
Even gold-diggers are giving, in a sense it's all a bargain.
See the black and busty hustle of the waitresses,
   good-natured
in the face of many orders; they are paid, of course, to do
   it.
It's so true we all want something – and that something

might be someone –
that the only problem left is: do we do it sad, or gaily?
Restaurants are no exception, and the whole of life
                                        is business.

The Big Hand

The big hand guides the hand to write an A,
the big hand guides the hand to write a B,
the big hand smacks the hand that writes a c
because all letters must be big letters,
only what is big can glorify the alphabet.

Small letters are shy and mean, the big hand knows,
they come out of hiding with what is coarse and
    common,
pinned to each day, knitted into each day,
eaten each day as so much necessary food.

The big letters are gods, they never eat or sleep
or clothe or copulate. Although they sound the same
they lie on paper in their pride of place –

anyone with eyes can see they're different.
The big hand made them in the time of giants,
there is no limit to their largeness,
they cavort in the sky, they rule the universe.

The little letters are like self-made men,
like men made out of stones, like useful ants
that swarm through letterpress; they never pretend to be big.
With them you can write loveletters or holy books
while the proud big letters are standing still in the sky.

Ballad

The kinky kisses
are near us in the night –
I cleared my brain of little girls
and tried to put it right.
The moon is bright.

The lurid lyrics
are sung beneath one's breath –
I put in gaol my dear desires
and sentenced them to death,
Elizabeth.

The naughty knifelets
shine with a sheen that kills –
I hospitalized my violences
and gave them sleeping pills.
The night wind chills.

The sexy singles
sell well in porno shops –
I dramatized my impulses
and told them they were flops.
The dark owl drops.

The randy razors
glint on, into my dream –
this one I cherish specially,
as you, perhaps, ice cream.
Oh, please, don't scream!

The blood runs blackly
under the blade's caress –
her life just hesitates away,
a shy girl to undress.
Oh, happiness!

The Semi-Sapphics

Oh no! Alcoholics don't dwindle into a happy twilight
like a permanent saloon bar between the wars, like
    something
beautifully written by old egghead P.G. Wodehouse –
        Mulliner's mildness

scouting for narrative, when a Large Gin and Tonic
tells a Small Brown Ale how it loved a girl and lost her
among the old beans and the aunts, where Lord
    Emsworth,
        the Efficient Baxter

and a loony doctor or two are the worst things you'd
    meet with.
Sociable, of course, the bars are – but also phoney
and the lonely women find disgusting faces on the
    pillows,
        waking next morning

with their simply putrid pick-ups from last night's
    drinking.
They are The Lost Girls (and Jean Rhys understood
    them),
the ones who have to live with only bottles for comfort –
        nobody loves them.

The Church is cold, perhaps, and very much less sexy,
but at least in physical terms it doesn't poison you.
It would be nice to say that, but of course you can't, of the
    Alehouse.
        Warm but waspish,

it has a sting in its tail; and the hung-over horrors
lead on to the hairs of the dog that bit them,
when they feel fragile and fear they are frigid,
        most unattractive.

Looking at mirrors never makes them feel much better.
The best you can wish them is someone to like them,
the frank confidence, the reciprocated cuddle.
        That might improve them.

War Death in a Low Key

This all happened in 1943, near Algiers.
I was at a base camp, waiting to be posted,
a Second Lieutenant in a Light Anti-Aircraft Regiment –
but my unit had dumped me (for a more efficient
                                    officer),
following an exercise where my map-reading had been
                                    faulty
(the maps were fairly old).
I had to start the whole thing. I had to lead the Troop off
and the road I was on wasn't even on the map;
consequently I took the wrong turning at the wrong
                                    crossroads.
'Understandable, but inexcusable,' the Assessor said
                                    later.

It was hot as hell. There was a donkey in the camp that
      brayed all day long,
a depressing sound. I was depressed, and felt like a reject.
There was a Captain with alopecia from the Eighth
                                    Army,
who wore his black beret all the time and made a very
                                    big thing
about being a Desert Rat (we, of course, were First Army) –
the war in North Africa was very nearly over
and the Germans and Italians were about to be pushed off
                                    Cape Bon
into the sea. This Captain was by way of being
a hand grenade instructor. Some of these junior officers
obviously worshipped him because of his daring,
and they would lob grenades about among each other.
One subaltern, one day, lobbed (or held) one once
                                    too often.
The top of his head was blown off, though his rimless glasses
stayed on his nose. Panic on the range.

I was told all this at lunchtime.
Later (because I'd known him? But I
hadn't really. I just knew which he was)
I was detailed to be part of the Guard of Honour at
                                    his funeral.

How many were there? Three or four of us? And
                                    the driver.
His body lay on a stretcher on the floor
of an open 15 cwt. We collected it from the Hospital.
There was no coffin. He was wrapped tight in a
grey army blanket (as I remember). Blood still
                              oozed through
at the top, where his head was.
Over-awed, I think, we sat in the truck with our rifles.

There was another burial, I remember.
A woman, a nursing sister. No coffin either.
She was wrapped from head to toe in bandages
like a rather plump, short mummy.
Somehow it was pathetic to see the mound of her breasts
and realize it was a woman. Young men's reactions
to such things are usually quite other.

The prayers were said, the red soil scattered on.
We fired, together, our valedictory volley.

We were quiet, but relieved, as we drove home empty.
His name began with an A? It's hard, now, to remember.
Someone that night slightly shocked me by saying:
'I knew him – but I'm afraid I didn't like him.'

Sestina: The Literary Gathering

At one end of the peculiar table Jeremy
sat, and talked about poetry to Carl.
He was a bit of a nutter. Next to him, Sheila
was eating a farinaceous dish. Lewis
listened intently to the words of Ursula.
They were all drinking cider. And so was Jane.

There was something quiet and achieved about Jane –
of course she was a good deal older than Lewis –
and she hadn't got the manic quality of Jeremy
nor did she understand engineering, like Carl,
or the details of catering, which obviously Ursula
had at her fingertips. They all liked Sheila.

They all agreed there was no one like Sheila
for lovability. Music to Jeremy
was the breath of life. Often, to Carl,
he would play his autoharp – this delighted Ursula
and certainly caused some pleasure to Jane –
sitting in the meadow with the cows and Lewis.

'Lewis?' said Jane. 'He's a dark horse, Lewis!'
'You never know what he's thinking!' cried Sheila.
'He's a very nice boy' was the verdict of Ursula;
he seemed more ordinary to Carl and Jeremy.
He was fond of Milton (he once told Jane) –
but only modern poets appealed to Carl.

There was a hint of dark Satanic mills about Carl,
a contained intelligence; no fly-by-night Jeremy,
he hadn't the open character of Ursula,
in this respect he was more like Jane
or the sheep and the cattle. And only Sheila
seemed to understand him – except for Ursula.

There was a bardic bravery about Ursula.
Not even Lewis, or Jane, or Sheila
had her bravura – in the words of Lewis
'She is the mother of us all!' For Jane
Ursula's writing was the tops, and Carl
confessed he was staggered, and even Jeremy,

though he liked Carl and respected Jane
and admired Lewis (and the work of Sheila),
said how he, Jeremy, really worshipped Ursula.

Circe I

Her Caliban cunt
was wild and woolly,
her nipples like
the ends of lemons,
she was an expert on
all kinds of pigfood.

For the rough sailors
she poured the wine out,
but for one man only
she plumped satin cushions,
spreading her bum,
inviting him in.

He felt so special,
a wonderful lover,
superior grunting
in bowers of vine-leaves;
pigs their background
and love their pigfood.

Circe II

It certainly is the smell of her cunt
makes you fall on your knees and grunt.

It certainly is the slope of her tits
makes your morality fall to bits.

It certainly is her incurved waist
makes you long for that truffle taste.

It certainly is her pubic thighs
makes your piglike prick uprise.

It certainly is her heavenly hair
makes you wallow and keeps you bare.

It certainly is her beautiful bum
makes you rootle and holds you dumb.

It certainly is her feminine hands
makes you the slave of glorious glands.

It certainly is the commanding eye
makes you happy to live in a sty.

Every Doggerel has its Day

The sun winks back from the back of the blade – John Arlott,
BBC commentary on the Second Test Match, England
v. Australia, 11 July 1977

The sun winks back from the back of the blade,
the commentators sit in the shade
and, however many runs are made,

it's a funny old game – sentimental too,
a ritual practised for me and you –
and Youth is the cause of the hullabaloo.

When the arm is strong and the eye is keen
the idea of old age is quite obscene.
But the County Cap (and the might-have-been)

lose the throwing arm and the timing sense,
however clever, however dense,
and the past, at last, is the only tense –

even the legendary W.G. Grace
at the very end couldn't stand the pace.
He vanished too – though not without trace –

and even a batsman as great as Hobbs
when he lay dead couldn't handle lobs –
this is what causes our sighs and sobs.

Old men with MCC-striped ties
lament lost vigour with watery eyes –
the active stroking of balls (and thighs).

Cricket for them's an escape from Life,
the worries of business, children, wife;
as Death stands by with his surgeon's knife

each fancies himself as a Peter Pan,
a young attractive cricketing man,
one of the fastest who ever ran

between the wickets or in to bowl,
a batsman with genius to lift the soul,
a merrier hitter than Old King Cole.

The game, as they sit and watch for hours,
reminds them of their longlost powers
until it's over – and *Send No Flowers*.

'Ce Petit Détail, Tellement Sexuel'

– Romain Rolland, *Le Six Octobre*

In the old days you were seriously worshipped,
carved on temples, always a prominent feature
of certain gods in gardens, propped in an upright position
on dead bodies of the Pharaohs;

secretly, the obelisks all celebrated you –
even the Victorians in Kensington Gardens
with the Speke Memorial obliquely remembered you –
and the spires of all the churches.

Jocular and lewd you exist at Pompeii
along with the scales and the Roman soldier
and all through the South small facsimiles of you
keep the Evil Eye from harming,

an Italian under-culture; and it's not surprising
that the word 'fascinate' (which belonged to the witches)
in the Greek and the Latin had its first meaning:
render impotent. Late Horace

used *fascinum* to mean you. You remain worrying
to all Puritans, and you can really frighten
bossy middle-aged busybodies. Like Armageddon,
truthfully they fear to see you.

Some religions impose a strict taboo
as rigid and inflexible as yourself; and detailed
representation in works of art, illegal,
is almost everywhere forbidden.

This is the bad news. There's a lot of it –
but I bring you too a modified message of hope.
As long as we exist, I think, in secret
your cult, enthusiastic twosomes

bowing down before you (as they always did),
will prosper; for the worshipping millions
in a real sense still owe their existence to you –
not quite a god, but a bold symbol.

Hunting the Badger by Owl-Light

The Elizabethans went stabbed to their death-boxes,
boys on stage squeaked like the Death's Head chrysalis,
gibbets like bus-stops in a land of death.

This was the start of something, life was death.
In deathly reverence divines like paper bags
exploded in sermons; *Death News* on every stand.

Death was a travel agent, crossing the Styx
was what the stoics fancied – the popular Death Special
was the Magical Mystery Tour the death-fanciers liked.

The Jokes of Early Aviation

The jokes of early aviation
were all about joysticks and cockpits –
the wartime ones, that rocked the aircrews,
were about pressing tits
and airscrews –

mechanical, verbal fornication,
and light relief for tomcat tomfools,
for dirty Dick and handsome Harry
(never, though good with tools,
would marry) –

as Mars, the god of masturbation,
held thousands there earthbound and grounded,
they praised with voices, not with bodies,
and seldom in a bed,
a Goddess.

In the Ninetieth Year

As my mother was dying
her head became skull-like,
her flesh left her bones.
She became more and more
like the skeletons they dig up,
curled, in hot countries.

Still alive, she was sleeping
more and more bone-like,
her heart's pounded thump
was all that distinguished her
from pre-history's burials,
the caves and the barrows.

Old bones are so neutral
and not really manlike,
for thought goes with flesh,
its lusts and its jealousies –
lose blood, and you're losing
the stuff of existence.

Cowardice *

Do you remember, in the Twenties,
the songs we used to sing,
reading our Westermans and Hentys,
before the days of Bing?
Gramophones were very sharp and tinny,
we could sit there and applaud
shows with stars like Laddie, Sonnie, Binnie,
Jack and Jessie, June and Claude.
We had no truck with opus numbers
or anything called Art –
and fox-trots (long before the rumbas)
gave us our happy start. . . .

This was our taste/ of the future,
we embraced/ that decade,
gleaming in glamour, with our hope not betrayed.
There lay Love – which our ten-year-old scoffing
felt above (girls with men!) – in the offing.

The sight of women set us giggling,
their bottoms broad and fat,
the Charleston and that sexy wriggling,
their bosoms not so flat,
as they jumped and bumped in that gay chorus –
though we watched the dance with scorn,
this was Life cavorting there before us,
and the reason we were born.
Of this we were just dimly conscious,
uneasily we'd sit
and judge, severe, like monks with tonsures –
soon to be part of it. . . .

It was all necks/ with arms round them,
grown-up sex/ on display –
a mystery coming our way.
We weren't too frightened,
we felt partly enlightened
in that faced-by-the-future far decade.

* Based on 'Dear Little Café', from Noël Coward's *Bitter Sweet*.
In 1926 (for the record) I was ten years old.

An Old Husband Suspects Adultery

I was just beginning to feel in the mood,
my desire was just beginning to harden,
as we lay cuddling like Babes in the Wood
or Adam and Eve naked in that Garden –
when the telephone started ringing.
She jumped out of bed (like Eve, naked)
and answered it – I could hear him darlinging.

She spoke to him coolly but she wasn't rude,
taking it in her stride with her long legs – flustered
she certainly wasn't. No thought of Bad or Good
grazed her. Domestic as custard
she talked, as if to a grocer,
like smooth-limbed Eve with a handset, naked,
standing there beautiful. I was feeling moroser

than I can tell you. A pin-up, a nude,
she'd made herself. Unreachable. She hung up
and climbed back into bed. Like Robin Hood
he'd robbed the rich – before he'd rung up
I'd really felt like doing it,
but now the thread was lost – Eve, so naked, couldn't
tempt me now into pursuing it.

Love Song

As you get old you begin to wonder –
what was all that lightning and thunder
actually about?
It was more than holding hands,
it had a lot to do with glands –
but now you're far out,

floating calmly in a lonely seascape;
passionate rose-garden, stormed treescape
very long ago
left behind – what they call Youth
seems now ridiculous, uncouth
(if you want to know).

As you settle into peace, or dourness,
that bitter-sweet, that sweet-and-sourness,
is a vanished taste;
yet those who never clasped and kissed
don't know exactly what they missed
or what went to waste.

Afrokill

1
The striped horse
is red inside
like sliced cake
There should be a notice
LIONS AT WORK

2
Pudgy plush muzzles
of faded yellow
of teddy-bear
show pinkness
from blood-nuzzle

3
They roll over
on invisible
beds, armchairs, divans,
sleeping so
foodful

4
The demon-faced
square pack-dogs
laugh at the banquet
brown snarling
lackeys

5
Last come the hopping
horrors
with big wings,
clean wavebreak
on shipwreck ribs.

Back

They come back, the terrible old words,
words like 'heart-piercing',
from the bad poems in the anthologies,
when I hear the voices of the children playing –
but not what they are saying.

I think back, ten or eleven years,
when we could hear sing
our own kids' trebles – the tree of knowledge is
apt to grow too fast in any London garden –
and soon our feelings harden.

They float back, like an archaic rhyme,
brightly transpiercing
parental minds, strong as old theologies,
sweet, that all too soon will grow both sour and flatter –
what they're saying doesn't matter.

MacNeice in Belfast 1938

Among the cranes and derricks
Herrick's verse seems odd,
and gantry, gull and gannet
span it, much as though God
(the poor old sod)
had gone off in hysterics.

A town hard, harsh, satiric.
Lyrics are out of place –
the only thing that's frisky,
whisky; whose golden face
shines through disgrace
and living that's empiric.

In many ways Satanic,
manic, and short of hope;
Noah might be left remaining.
Raining? Well, he could cope.
For Art, no scope.
But not much sign of panic.

A Contemporary Film of Lancasters in Action

To see them bombing up
and wheeling off into the dusk,
nose to tail, queueing, turning for the take-off,
like long-jumpers each one coming up
stationary
before they begin the run before the jump,
piloted by volunteer bank clerks.
Is my emotion bogus or inflationary?

I was never a hero,
the shark's tooth, boar's tusk,
seeming less frightening than this kind of flying,
for all kinds of courage rated zero,
admiringly
I admit they did what I could never,
sleepwalkers showing a sleepless courage –
long flights to firework climax, untiringly.

Obstinate, I survive
and, writing in this summer musk,
I say they were the patient venturing lions
and I the mean dog that stayed alive;
we owe them
every valedictory mark of respect
(bravery's facing such boring dangers)
that we can possibly, too late, show them.

A 14-Year Old Convalescent Cat in the Winter

I want him to have another living summer,
to lie in the sun and enjoy the *douceur de vivre* —
because the sun, like golden rum in a rummer,
is what makes an idle cat *un tout petit peu ivre* —

I want him to lie stretched out, contented,
revelling in the heat, his fur all dry and warm,
an Old Age Pensioner, retired, resented
by no one, and happinesses in a beelike swarm

to settle on him — postponed for another season
that last fated hateful journey to the vet
from which there is no return (and age the reason),
which must soon come — as I cannot forget.

Conversation Piece

I sit and hear my mother and my aunt
talking of dog-carts, of a century gone
I try to imagine (there are some who can't).
Their total age is 181.
Under the clothes, the bodies were the same
as those the striptease, shamelessly as cards,
deals to the watchers now. Just the same game
but played by different rules; *ripostes*, *on guards*,

masks of all sorts, the flirting with a fan,
a kind of fencing with an instinct. Who loved who
they had their ways of knowing, woman and man.
Something outside them told them what to do.
They weren't direct like us (are we direct?),
Victoria sat there like a monolith
but even nice girls knew what to expect,
how Zeus crept up on Leda in the myth —

without a visiting card, in fancy dress.
No lady left the house without her gloves.
Deafness makes meaning something they must guess,
arthritis stiffens Venus and her doves,
for four decades no lovemaking at all –
beauty was jolly, with a motoring veil.
There should be writing, writing on the wall:
All sex shall fail, but love shall never fail.

The Dwarf with Brass Teeth

*And the door closed, and the latch clicked, but the prince with
stars for his eyes and a new moon for his mouth didn't mind, for
he was young and strong, and though he wasn't handsome, he
had heard lots of doors close and click before this one, and didn't
feel at all frightened. But he would have been if he had known
who had closed the door. It was the Dwarf with brass teeth, who
was more dreadful than the most spotted of all things, and whose
ears were fixed on backwards.*

Even those who later become featured
as Success Stories, journalisted and preachered,
don't really have an easy time
as they grow to being a dollar from being a dime –

the fairy story Get Rich Quick is for the dreamers;
successful people can be mean, and schemers,
and to make a lot of dough
you must work at it, and be a hard-hearted so-and-so.

Those who make lots of money or you-name-it
are riding the tiger but can never tame it;
and the admired Great Lovers too
have to stop doing other things they'd like to do.

You must go at it monomaniac, whole-hearted,
know that you're bound to lose, before you've started,
and what you lose most is 'If . . .'
all the alternative lives you could lead before you're stiff.

The possibilities are fewer and fewer, as you get older
and the wind and summer sun strike that much colder.
When the door shuts in the vaults
you're shut in with your own limitations and faults.

Settling for less than the best is what is hardest –
hence God and the drugs and the fevered artist –
but for Madge, Maud, Kenneth, Keith,
for all of us, the Dwarf grins – with his sharp brass teeth.

The Death of W.S. Gilbert at Harrow Weald

Imagine that flat glassy lake in 1911,
a very Victorian part of the prosperous house
(architect: Norman Shaw),
a beautiful hot summer's day in 1911.

'The tiny island in the middle of the lake flames
                    with azaleas. . . .
The water's edge is fringed with golden iris and
                        forget-me-nots,
and beside the winding pathway there is white heather
                        for good fortune.
It is all set in a greenwood carpeted with half-uncurled
                        bracken ferns,
where the shadowy fading bluebells might be fancied
                            to ring
a muffled peal from fairyland.'

Into that water steps the white foot of a lady
and then, perhaps more timidly, the white foot of
                        another lady.
They wear commodious and decorous bathing
                        garments.
The water is very cold.
One lady is the pupil of the other lady
on that hot summer's day in 1911.

Gilbert has had lunch at the Junior Carlton,
he is teaching the more mature lady to swim. He is 74.

'My pupil was a much better swimmer than I,
and soon outdistanced me. We were both unaware
that the lake was deep further out,
and presently she tried to touch bottom and found herself
out of her depth. She shrieked out,
"Oh, Miss Emery, I am drowning!" '

A heavy body plunges into the water
like an old bull, like the leader of the herd,
with the scrotum tightened by that cold lake of 1911.
He swims to her, shouts advice: 'Put your hands on my
                                              shoulders!'
She feels him sink under her. He doesn't come up.
She struggles to the bank, he is dead of heart failure.

Is there a moral for old men? *Don't fool about with ladies?*
But all the same it's good to die brave
on a beautiful hot summer's day in 1911.

A Lyric of Love

As warm as a wasp's nest,
as cold as a key,
that is the way,
that is the worrying way
you've been to me;

as hot as a headache,
indifferent as ice,
that's what you've been,
that's what you've boringly been –
nasty and nice;

as jealous as ginger,
as neutral as knees,
that's how you treat me,
teasingly trap me and treat me –
fry me or freeze.

F For

As we fancy what is feminine and fimbriate
(as a farrier's familiar with fenugreek),
we fall friendly to those famous femmes fatales
whose fellatio
felled Field-Marshals freely.

For the female face is fabulous and fortunate
(and is favouring festivities and festivals),
far from fisticuffs and fiercely fatal fights,
felicific, its
fascination's forceful.

All those female forms are fleshy and fructiferous
(for us femiphiles so fitting, febrifugal)
and so full of femineity we feel
fine as feoffees, both
fuglemen and fulgent.

Property

In romantic fiction (which is women's pornography)
the heroine's hand, as it dives into the young man's zip
(though this is never mentioned),
is searching for a wedding ring;
though the books don't deal in physiological geography
it's always implied that marriage is the greatest trip
(to the romantic boss, who's well-intentioned) –
this is the one and only thing.

After the tables for two and the dances and car-petting
nail him down, they seem to say, to a beautiful house
where *everything* is beautiful,
with Old Masters all over the walls,
with every new gadget and deep-pile wall-to-wall
    carpeting –
where the wife is a kind of bossy ferocious mouse
and far more houseproud than dutiful,
where highborn neighbours pay calls

in a permanent paradise of chic materialism
and the sperm is just to produce a little bundle of love.
The thing that counts is status.
It's like a sentimental tune,
old-fashioned music in a time of discords and serialism.
So I am moved when I see the other kind of love,
lovers who touch in public (they may well hate us),
poor but not infected, entirely immune.

The Late Eighties

>   To her
> I am a coloured blur,
>   a just-heard voice,
>   as she sits there –
> she hasn't any choice.

>   Life fades
> like on-off hearing aids,
>   and in her sleep
>   the realler world
> is dreaming, long and deep.

>   This now
> needs living through somehow,
>   patience is all
>   and the time left,
> though slow, is surely small.

>   I touch
> the body changed so much,
>   she understands
>   some tenderness
> through bony arms and hands.

>   Contact
> is joining and a fact;
>   we once were one,
>   and touching's how
> all lovemaking gets done.

Infatuations

It's standard in our gossip to say
'I just can't think what he sees in *her*'
or 'I can't think what she sees in *him*'
and women are usually the sayers
(love is their game, and they are the players),

men don't seem to speculate in that way.
But it's striking how this thought can occur
in a different form, when the chance is slim
that two who have once been lovers
will ever join again under, or on top of, the covers.

They meet as different people always, they
find they've lost the flattering romantic blur
that blazed so strongly – that light is dim.
They, almost, think 'What did I ever . . . ?'
but hesitate, from pride. Admit such thoughts? Oh,
   never.

Down There on a Visit

Going is not straight in that cumbersome country,
molehills thick as molecules impede the pedestrian,
as the calamitous clay clings to his clogs.

Sight is not good in that land of apparitions
where at the eye's side trees tremble tremendously.
He wakes with his clock-watchers rimmed running
                                   with rheum.

Touch has gone shapeless in sweat-stained shivering.
The wonderful wines and the beautiful beers
are far-retchingly repulsive to the pasteboard palate.

Hearing has become almost equally horrible,
loud lout noises bang on his head-box
rattling around like parched peas in his brain-pan.

As he goes he mistrusts the gauche guiding locals,
interpreting mischief as mind-warping malice;
he is badly disposed to all, all beauty and boar-hunting.

To the Puritans who are the Gods of This World

It needed Cain and Abel too,
The brothers Murder and Incite
                              – C.H. Sisson

A Masturbating Mildred you,
or Would-Be-Fornicating Fred,
          not dead
but dying (as we all are too) –
          no shame
attaches to that age-old game,

but some to you! I see you both
as too-genteel Victorian types
          with pipes,
a lively dread of that giant Sloth,
          no votes
and bonnets, bustles, petticoats –

the man and woman of it. Still
you won't admit such dangerous acts
          as facts.
On the reverse side of the hill,
          you feel,
sits Satan, ready for a meal;

to have and be the entrée there
might be your destiny in Hell.
          The smell
of intercourse and pubic hair
          (God's toast),
the sin against the Holy Ghost,

burn in your brains like autumn leaves,
you reckon the venereal trap,
      like clap,
is sprung by this. Each one believes
      girls rammed,
badgered or rabbited, are damned.

You two have Envy as your friend.
Fear and Unkindness know you well,
      the bell
rings often at Enjoyment's End,
      where tea
is served to Pride, Unholy Glee;

Gossip and Bossiness, bosom pals,
are free to sit and to admire
      the fire,
can stretch their legs and smoke Pall Malls.
      Miss Hate
will stay particularly late.

Egged on by them, self-satisfied,
you tell us what we may not do,
      the coo
of pigeons is a switchback ride
      to Sin –
and the seductive violin.

Propriety in public! Write
only what nurseries think and need –
      your creed
is always this – and not what might
      (no!) stir
sex-feeling in a him or her.

And these are your instructions we
at our own risk refuse, deny!
      You sigh
that so much wickedness could be
      in life!
The standard husband, standard wife,

are all that are permitted in
your limited philosophy,
      the knee
is very naughty; whisky, gin
      are bad.
Thinking of such things makes you sad.

Without *you* to work out their will,
Pride, Envy, Hate and all that crew,
      Fear too,
could not force-feed their bitter pill.
      It's sweet
when 'Morals' make it fit to eat.

This is your function in our land,
you are the servants of a No,
      all so
prudent and pudent, underhand –
      I doubt
if we will ever throw you out!

On First Looking into Michael Grant's Cities of Vesuvius

In battledress, yes, I was there. That dramatic great
                              wartime eruption
      spewed out the red-hot shit; it looked very splendid
                              at night
crushing the villas and trees, and the ash came down,
                              a red-purple,
      to the depth of an old-fashioned foot. We moved the
                              trucks and the guns
for safety. But our letters home were security-minded.
                              No mention.
      You needed a four-wheel drive to churn through
                              that stuff on the road.
This was in March '44 (as the clubland talks would
                              remind you),

of Europe's one active volcano the last
        recorded display.

Before this happened, I took, on an outing, a party
        of gunners
    (we weren't operational then) to Pompeii; they
        wanted the church,
the wine-shops, the cheap souvenirs. I opted, alone, for
        the *Scavi*.
    I had one guide to myself – and paid with a tin of
        corned beef.
We covered a lot of the ground. His English was good
        but not perfect –
    I was pleased to hear of a king whose name seemed
        to be Charles the Turd.
Although I went there three times – with a friend on
        two visits –
    and the guide remarked with a grin, as we looked at
        the rough plaster thighs,
how it was obvious enough that the body we saw was
        a woman.
    We went round the brothel as well. He lit up the
        paintings on walls
with a candle held high; you could see where each girl's
        speciality, pictured
    above the door of her room, enticed you inside to
        her skill.
He unlocked for us, too, with his key, that famous and
        frivolous fresco
    which shows the soldier who weighs his huge
        uncircumcised cock
on the scales, and the gold goes up – for pleasure's more
        precious than money.
    Behind us, by accident, there (for this is inside a
        house door)
an American nurse walked by. She gave a great 'Oo!' and
        fled, shaken.
    I don't know what it's like now. But *Off Limits*
        would, then, be the words;
and the delicate souls of the girls were protected, the
        brothel was banned; though

plain enough in the road you could see a large
                              bas-relief tool
to point the vernacular way to the house dedicated to
                              Venus.
    With a naked foot, on dark nights, it must have been
                              useful, at that.
Herculaneum wasn't so good. The best thing of all was
                              the statue
    that shows Pan at work on a goat. This was our
                              verdict, at least.

So, Grant, you swim into my ken. With your writing, so
                              large and clear, telling
    of thirty-three years ago now – more or less, give or
                              take, to the day
when the boil on the neck of the land burst, on the
                              warlike eighteenth
    and we stood with our drinks, there, to watch, on
                              the roof of the officers' mess,
how the lava rolled down in the dark, a slow raw mass on
                              the skyline.
    We didn't think so much, then, of the suffering; how
                              those who died
choked in the chemical fumes – like the brave and
                              inquisitive Pliny,
    like the dog at the end of its chain. That's one of the
                              things about war.
The dying was commonplace, then. It was interesting,
                              more than distressing.
    And of course you're entirely right, the gladiatorial
                              shows
were disgusting (as Seneca said); more so than the
                              drinking and fucking.
    Dr Arnold, the father, who wrote that the Bay of
                              Naples was one
long drama (and 'fearsome' too) of Sin and Death, and,
                              yes, Pleasure,
    got it wrong in his Puritan way – and so did his
                              talented son.
Why should there be shame? No one lived (as you say) to
                              be much over forty –

over most of the world, to this day, that's an average
                                                    life.

We are exceptions, aloof and well-dressed in our
                        self-conscious cities.
     If any small British town, perhaps a resort like
                              Torquay,
were quickly hermetically sealed, volcanoed and covered
                                              for ever,
        would archaeologists find such a high standard of
                                                     art?
Architecture, as well. I think you make a good point
                                                 there.
        I know they crucified slaves. There was cruelty, but
                              easiness too;
the easiness of a land where the passions could be quite
                                              volcanic
        but with the blue sea and sky there was always
                          benevolent sun.

The Doll Made by my Dead Sister

A doll 33 cm high
made throughout of felt –
I prop her up in front of me as I write –
dressed in Victorian clothes
(pieces of women's dresses)
with a full skirt reaching to the ground.

But this doll is a lie –
and that mouth where butter wouldn't melt –
turn her inside out, she's as black as night,
as black as sloes,
confounding all guesses,
turned upside down, skirt over head . . . There, aproned
  and gowned,

stands a plantation slave
and under her ballooning skirt
is the head of the other (red wool hair, green eyes),
invisible; so each
is an opposite in a way . . .
though neither has legs, neither has private parts –

amateur psychiatrists would rave
and knowingly dish the dirt,
saying 'Escape from sex!' with excited cries,
two girls with no breech . . .
that's what they used to say,
but there's more to it than that, even in these simple crafts
   and arts.

The Moment

There are even photographs of it:
the moment when, for the first time,
in that tense, expectant landscape,
the enemy troops appear.

There they are, advancing –
Germans from World War One
running with rifles.
As, from far back in time, so many others.

You are the opposing infantry –
this means you.
Your brain falters. *This
is it*, you think,

*these are the ones we've heard
so much about*. Like old people
when, for the first time, they confront
the unambiguous symptoms.

The Doggerel of Life

Yeats, who admired Robert Bridges
and his poems about linnets,
who wouldn't have lasted five minutes
at their Menin Gates and Vimy Ridges,
cut out from his great Ox Book
the Owens and Rosenbergs. But look,

Dorothy Wellesley is there, crazy,
and Flecker, whom iambics tempted like houris;
nothing could be more vacuous than Rabindranath
     Tagore is;
or, than W.J. Turner, more romantic and hazy;
or more of an ugly rhyming zombie
than that great genius Lascelles Abercrombie.

So what he missed was the vivid actual factual.
In a way he emerged from his youthful Celtic Twilight,
gazing at the moon through a Dublin skylight,
but he was very selective, describing what was tactual –
the copulation of the nymph and gland-boosted satyr.
The hot blood of a machine-gunned friend was a very
     different matter.

Kipling's Imperialism and Ours

(The Light That Failed)

If you call a spade a spade,
those wars were really trade
and the box-wallahs had it made.

As trade follows the flag
the guy with the carpet-bag
brings dollars and jet-lag.

Right Wing strong-arm regimes
help the market, it seems,
in those Latin American dreams.

Red satellites gather round
like sheep in a pound
and applause is the only sound.

The massacres, black by white,
are an artistic sight
in the African day or night.

In Kipling's Sudan, war dead
made patterns of colour, he said,
decomposed composition, and led

his artist-hero to rave
of the multichrome deaths of the brave,
while the Queen they were out to save

sat there and loved John Brown
as he drank the whisky down
and the beauties went on the town.

The Animals in the Adelaide Zoo

The animals in the Adelaide Zoo are very comfortable.
It's a small zoo but very well organized.
The elephant stands in a small space but seems happy.
The black-backed jackals run; hunting, hunting,
    hunting.
A slow loris moves quiet in nocturnal lighting.
The black panther is a melanistic form of the spotted
    leopard.

The animals in the Adelaide Zoo are not rhetorical.
The zebras are not torn apart by lions.
The hippopotamus is in happy water.
The giraffe's sex organs are as high as your head.
The jaguars and ocelots attack nothing.
Everything is as it should be in the Adelaide Zoo.

The animals in the Adelaide Zoo are already in Heaven.
Their children are born lucky, nobody hates them.
They are surrounded by love and regular food.
Their lives are without drama, they show no fear.
Eviscerated on a path lies a tiny indigenous mouse.
In their cages, they show no concern, in the Adelaide
  Zoo.

Ode on the Death of the Air Commodore

For E.J. Thribb

Oh, Commodore!
You will never drink anything any more!
No more beer, gin, brandy, whisky or wine
that made you feel so fine
and roll down the street lurching out of bars
and causing consternation among cars!

Oh, Commodore!
You have flown to God on that further shore!
You lived in gin with Lady Blank,
drinking like two fishes in a fish tank –
this made your brain soften and your arteries harden
and when she locked you out you slept in the garden!

Oh, Commodore!
Alcohol is a deceiver and a most conspicuous whore!
Perhaps I should mention
that every week you drew an Air Commodore's pension
and poured it into the glasses in local pubs,
an old bad-tempered lion and far from its cubs!

Oh, Commodore!
That once-goodlooking head must often have been sore!
You might easily have choked on your own vomit
but, as it happened, far from it –
far quicker and cleaner, a heart attack
as you lay there, completely pissed, on your back!

Oh, Commodore!
Were you once a pilot in Korea, or in the Second World
    War?
Did you fly bombers or fighters, incredibly brave,
before something gave
and to this one drug you became such a terrible slave?
What went wrong? The Devil is very possessive –
he blotted you out, aphasic and aggressive!

Oh, Commodore!
Believers say there is Mercy, God doesn't shut the door.
You often had to be helped home,
and all roads lead to Death, as they once did to Rome,
and indeed your life can't have been very funny –
far too much drinking, too much spare time and money!

The Lovesleep

In an exciting world of love-bites, nipple-nipping,
unbuttoning and unzipping,
kisses that are
the highest kind of communication,
the lovers experience their timeless elation;

perhaps they reach those peaks where, like a bomb
    exploding,
the angels sing, encoding
ecstasies that
our language can never really deal with –
its nouns and its adjectives that no one can feel with;

but when the woman lies in the man's arms – soft,
    sleeping,
in perfect trust and keeping
faith, you might say,
that is the truest peace and disarming –
no one can sleep in the arms of an enemy, however
    charming.

Rape of the Fly

These sausages are blood-bespattered pigs,
these eggs from jungle fowl. These naked chickens
are hornbills only fit for making soup.
The critics are the natives, words like stones,
that make derisive gestures but don't kill,
canoes all round, but I pursue my course.
The lovely ladies, birds of paradise,
flirting the tops of highest mountain trees!
Like the uncritical women of the tribes
they lie there, opening admiring legs.
The weighty letters to the *Herald*
are monstrous droppings of the cassowary.

The speeches and the books, the late Awards –
the rivalry, who's best and who's next best –
the Medals for the sailing through the swamp.
Our sex-mad novelists, gigantic genitals,
hopping aboard with elephantiasis!
Grossly inflated reputations! Only we
whose dysentery, malaria, beri-beri
proclaim us obstinate and purposeful,
deserve this world, so like the one we left.

Still in my dreams I visit that great Island,
I mapped it and I know it, mile by mile.

I miss the mosquitoes and the arrowheads,
the shrivelled corpses wrapped in bark, the skulls
trophying a longhouse – 150 yards –
navigating the tireless looping sandbanked river,
pushing upstream against the current's flow
with engine power that scarcely made us move.

This was my one achievement, my reward
a country where the missionaries are savage.

NOTE *Rape Of The Fly* is an account of the exploration of New
Guinea in the 1870s, written by John Goode. The Fly is the main
river. The poem is supposed to be a reminiscence by Lawrence

Hargrave, the engineer, who later fell out with D'Albertis, the leader of the Expedition. He makes a comparison with the 'civilization' of Sydney.

The Little Girl Writes a Sonnet about her Dead Cat

I do not hope to see my cat again
or look upon that friendly furry face
in some imagined, altered, other place
where there is never ice or hail or rain
or bitter wind or cutting of the sleet
or falling, drifting, animal–hating snow
that slants down drearily, both fast and slow,
to gem his coat or wet his feline feet.

That there's Cat Heaven, kitten-having-fun,
I don't believe – where any cat can lie
stretched out like streaky bacon, always fed,
happy and purring in perpetual sun.
I'm sorry for my cat, he had to die –
but I still love him, even though he's dead.

Tears are Round, the Sea is Deep: Roll them Overboard and Sleep

Though I am old and dirty
it wasn't always so
my face looked very different
forty years ago

I know you can't own people
though the law thinks you can
a man is a man is a man is a man
but not a married man

They can't be forced to like you
by anything you do
you can't make love by willpower
and women know this too

It's only by behaving
with no thought for effect
that we become attractive
escaping that neglect

which hugs the constant lover
the worshipper of tears
who attracts nothing to himself
except the fate he fears

I don't say be indifferent
just don't expect defeat
or else that tragic programme
will head for a repeat

To think one's lovable or nice
is always very hard
this is the province of the cad
and the fast-talking card

But still a man is something
you can't deny he's there
don't put him down or sit on him
he isn't like a chair

for folding up to put away
in garden shed or loft
and women too are human beings
and more than sweet and soft

they have their thoughts and feelings
behind their bobbling fronts
it isn't all beauty beauty
and sex and silly cunts

So though I'm old and dirty
and funny in the head
I think I've learned a thing or two
before I drop down dead.

O Yongë Fresshë Folkës, Hee or Shee

They look so beautiful, that's how they look –
but none of them has been into a book.
They look so fresh and innocent (because they've got to)
however hard they try (they do try) not to.
Yet evil's there, unseen or just subliminal,
a baby face can be that of a criminal.

While we look full of woe, and vice untold,
simply because we happen to be old.
Tired eyes, a stoop, a neck so like a vulture's –
these are the hallmarks of our silver Cultures.
They have the Force, testiculate or clitorate,
we – for our pains – the joy of being literate!

The Owls are Leaving

The owls are leaving town, in a strong procession.
They stream into the side streets, to the squares,
They fill the squares and block the avenues.
They move in silence. They are eight feet tall.

The owls are leaving town, with a sure precision.
Their eyes look straight ahead, they do not turn,
Their features clothe them in a secret wisdom.
No looking back. Each one is three feet broad.

The owls are leaving town, with no hint of passion.
They shuffle forwards, they are calm and good,
Their feet expect the texture of the roadway.
They never loved us. They are birds that go.

The Deaths

On the plains the lions walk among the herds of
wildebeeste like policemen or soldiers among the
citizens, not using their power, peaceful and not
destructive. Occasionally they run them, get them
going. Perhaps they don't kill, but in the galloping herd
the running tires a weak one. Next time round, he is
singled out, isolated and caught. The catcher throttles –
then the tearing. The pride lopes up, it's a family picnic.
Hyenas, vultures, tidy all the scraps.

Surely our deaths are like this, surely the deaths walk
round with us; at home, on city streets? Not showing
their claws, since they need only wait, they trot beside us
like obedient dogs. The old, the tired, the ill are run to a
fall – a date is at their throats, the deathday date. They
wear it like a collar. They too are dogs.

Self-knowledge

Why does it always come as a surprise
to realise there are people who dislike you,
when an uncomplimentary word (like *shit* or *bitch*)
is reported as used to describe you?
They are fierce against you as hawks, undovable –
and you always imagined you were so lovable!

Of course they may have got you wrong;
or they may hate you simply because you're English
or French or American; there are many stereotypes.
Instant hatred is very easy.
Class can bring it on, perhaps, your way of speaking –
what *you* think's refined *they* consider a twitlike
   squeaking.

But remember, even murderers don't think they're wicked.
Hitler, for example, thought he was helping Germany
by killing all those horrible Jews and subversive Reds.
He never regarded *himself* as ghastly.
So that might comfort you. *Let there be light!* Be
glad to learn you're not as nice as you might be!

Pian dei Giullari

Never go back, they say. Never go back.
I went back.

With my twenty-one-year-old daughter
I walked through the Porta Romana,
up the Erta Canina,
round the curved Giramonte
and high beyond the city.

I was twice as old as then.
A lot of it I didn't recognize,
I thought we were lost –
till a name startled me into recognition:
Pian dei Giullari.
A small hilly road
but there, as in sentimental dreams,
was the straight drive through the olive orchard,
the house in faded orange with barred windows,
our once Headquarters.

And there, almost opposite,
the entrance to her villa
where 28 embraced 16.

Was this sad or happy?

Our weak, nice Major died
(I saw his obituary by accident),
the love affair came to nothing.

In those days we were careless –
as the war was careless of us.
Nobody thought very far ahead.
Girls were like wine for the drinking.

53

The landscape that we saw from our windows
in a time of cicadas and nightingales
stood there unaltered.
I looked at it and felt the warm lightness
of khaki drill on my shoulders.

Montale

As I stood among the wild lettuce
in that desolate sexlandscape
with the autumnal green of late August,
I thought of Montale,
of the bits and pieces of the past
that keep us hermetic.

Somewhere there was a river,
a tidal river
sluggish with low water.
With its help, I knew,
woodbits and old bottles
had climbed the concrete bank.
It was all mud and concrete
but I couldn't see it.
It had, even, its complement of sailors.
It handed out driftwood.

But I stood alone in wild lettuce,
a plant that doesn't exist,
clumping the rough fairway
to an overgrown golf course,
distant neutral buildings
and the figures of cricketers,
open land – and its name was Sadness.

There were paths, but vague ones,
I could have stayed, I could have
gone in any direction.
I went to the river.

A Punk Turkish March for Christopher on his Giving Paintings by my Dead Sister to my Children

(terkib-i bend) *

Not since the reign of Bayezit the Thunderbolt
and the days when the Beloved was moon-faced,
almond-eyed, eyebrows two bows, eyelashes arrows,
has a poet been given such a pleasing emotional jolt,
a kind of mental orgasm (let's not be strait-laced)
in a life whose perspective inevitably narrows!

I'm overjoyed to hear what you did –
giving one of *her* pictures to each kid.

So much feeling attaches to an artefact
(all art is imperfect, this doggerel most
of all perhaps – you can't rival God,
said the Moslems, who botched every creative act),
good or bad, her painting haunts us like a ghost
and means more than Be-Bop, Rock, Reggae or Mod.

This is because we all understand
each brush-stroke was made by a once-living hand.

We see her physically there, in front of the easel,
each canvas is a presence as real as her face,
more charged than the instant smiling photograph
(like a happy rabbit unaware of the weasel)
and proves she didn't vanish without trace,
though Time, in our philosophy, has the last laugh.

And even Shakespeare, one day, will be gone.
The clocks like policemen are crying *Move on!*

---

* 'Metrical lines could also be grouped into stanzas, or *bend*, of from
four to ten lines, though the longer groupings are very rare. The *terc-i
bend*, where the stanzas are separated by a repeated rhyming couplet,
and the *terkib-i bend*, where the rhyming couplet changes each time,
are forms used for philosophic or contemplative poems.'
– Nermin Menemencioğlu: *The Penguin Book of Turkish Verse*

We can't remember her as a statue on a plinth
or frozen in the fixed epithets of the old *divan* poet –
though you *could* say that once her cheeks were rose
and her hair *could* be described as hyacinth,
her teeth as pearls (court verse, wouldn't you know it!).
The things we remember her by are not those.

The visual images blur and grow faint –
but her pictures are still there, as fresh as paint.

The Dying Animals

The animals that look at us like children
in innocence, in perfect innocence!
The innocence that looks at us! Like children
the animals, the simple animals,
have no idea why legs no longer work.

The food that is refused, the love of sleeping –
in innocence, in childhood innocence
there is a parallel of love. Of sleeping
they're never tired, the dying animals;
sick children too, whose play to them is work.

The animals are little children dying,
brash tigers, household pets – all innocence,
the flames that lit their eyes are also dying,
the animals, the simple animals,
die easily; but hard for us, like work!

'And Female Smells in Shuttered Rooms'

Short square fingers stuffing pipes
and Kilpeck witches in the streets,
all the Apeneck Sweeney types
riding women, staining sheets!

Sensitives wince into the world,
it seems to them so rough and coarse;
French poets, filigreed and pearled,
are better than a wingèd horse

and perfumes floating round an arm
than the crude odours of the groin –
foul Circe with her porcine charm
and Charon with his deadly coin!

★ ★ ★

Once, Eliot, I was shy as you
and impotent as you (I guess);
I failed at what I tried to do,
my sex-life was an awful mess.

But Stephen, Wystan, Christopher
enjoyed themselves with loads of boys,
they did not hesitate, demur,
or shrink from treating them like toys.

The lad is sad who masturbates.
It's good but not quite good enough –
though (once) was good enough for Yeats.
The wet warmth of that furry muff,

the girlish kiss, attracted still,
tiptilted tits, the big-eyed gaze –
I ended feeling rather ill;
I missed my homosexual phase.

A forest, round about, of cocks
grew up, a sexual Sacred Wood,
to flaunt Eternity, mock clocks;
and there, alone, I weeping stood.

Those others kicked the gong around –
Tom, Dick (especially Dick) and Harry
gave them the bliss I never found.
They even took time off to marry.

A nightmare (you could call it) and
the worse because I was so young –
Love seemed a Never Never Land.
Like Keats, infected in the lung,

I yearned for Light that never was
(there's not much fun in lonely yearning)
and this was made much worse because
I wasn't in a job and earning.

So unemployed and unenjoyed,
I sipped my bitter, loveless cup –
until, like Fathers out of Freud,
the bloody Army took me up!

Homeric Hymn

When Apollo's about
a brightness is all around,
it shines and shines on the ground,
a comet that stares you out,

you know a remarkable god
is helping to bend your mind
and you will unerringly find
it isn't a con or a cod

but a genuine daylight ghost,
an undeniable fact,
telling you how to act –
and more demanding than most.

He'll grant the half of the prayer,
but it will be only the half,
not the cow but the calf –
you mustn't ask more than your share,

nothing is quite all right
and nothing goes all your way,
Apollo may rule the day
but he can't put a stop to night,

granting a prayer entire
is something gods seldom do,
the ones that are happy are few
and you risk the Olympian fire

if you protest too much
or boast in your human pride –
the roughness of the ride
is surely reserved for such;

so make it a modest plea
for fame or fortune or love –
Venus might come, with a dove
or two, from the sexy sea –

and say to yourself 'That's fine!'
when blessings come in disguise.
The gods, with ironical eyes,
are devious, but divine.

The Crumbs of Sex and Comfort

The crumbs of sex and comfort
that fall an old man's way
are for a rainy day,
demand judicious hoarding –
they're few and far between
but valuable, I mean,

and love is rare, and rarer
as energy grows faint.
The patience of a saint
is needed in a lifetime
of waiting for the joy
that every girl and boy

is taught is round the corner.
Romance! deluding word!
imaginary bird
that flies out iridescent
in adolescent dreams!
Soft flesh (like chocolate creams)

although we grow maturer
won't quite lose its appeal
(the two ways that we feel),
the taste, perhaps, of childhood
but in our late decades
never entirely fades

and vanishes for ever –
there still is nothing much
the ecstasy of touch
won't better in the moment
of the triumphant cry
that love is honoured by.

Women Over 40 Are Perfect

The respectable ladies who think it's so
disgusting
that teenage girls should sink so low
as lusting
for the goodlooking companionable boys
have not been, in their time, averse to such joys;

many of these saints have had one (or two)
abortions –
nobody speaks of them (well, would *you*?),
distortions
of an instinct, the kind of mistakes
that an innocent girl very often makes,

hushed-up, of course, it's understood,
and private,
in the best conditions money could
contrive it,
victims of the rich alcoholic sperm.
But these young ones must go to the full term,

because they've surely got to be taught
a lesson,
sluts that they are, and *caught* –
you'd guess an
unholy public nuisance had come to light
from the pure drivel that those moral madams write.
60

Part Two *The So-Called Sonnets*

Sonnet: Danish Blue

From Copenhagen reports come in
of an American film marked 'Genuine Porn';
it all takes place in a hospital (a favourite scene)
where pretty nurses with glasses fellate male patients
(artificial masturbation?) and there's some joker
who keeps putting Spanish Fly into the drinking water
so that meetings of the Management Committee end up
   as orgies
and the woman President (with all the other girls) loses
   her knickers.

In particular, and this film is called *Sweet Freedom*,
the Doctor with the very biggest organ
is ramming it (in the interests of Science – orgone
   research)
into a really permissive dark-haired naked beauty.
As he does so she cries (male fantasy): 'Oh, fuck it, fuck
   it, fuck it!'
A real woman, as anybody knows, would cry: 'Fuck *me*!'

Sonnet: The Greedy Man Considers Nuclear War

I suppose you all realize we shall lose the sizzling sausages
and the mild mountains of mashed potatoes!
Boiled silverside with dumplings, raspberries and cream!
We shall vanish from the pecking order of the tikka
   chicken,

trout with almonds will swim away from us,
little lambs no more will jump into our mouths,
fragrant with rosemary; all the good wholesome food
will vanish just as surely as sophisticated dishes!

And what shall we be left with? Some assorted politicians
not very good to eat, some dispirited root crops,
tinned food perhaps – everything else burned up,
the culture of the kitchen, the chef's wisdom of the ages
vanished in a flame like the bread in a toaster!
The end of eating civilization as we know it!

Sonnet: The Red Fairy Book

I remember as a child I used to be terrified
by the illustrations to those stories that Andrew Lang
    collected,
where Princes were likely to be chopped into little pieces,
something nasty lived in the lake, and nine-headed Trolls
were decapitated by some good-hearted simpleton.
There was also a horrible Japanese animal
that spoke when it was cut into joints that hung from the
    ceiling
and because of its pleading was finally reconstituted and
    dangerous. . . .

But in fact the real world, now that I know it,
turns out to be quite a good deal more horrible –
where men are skinned alive and castrated,
where various emblems are stuck into women,
there's self-righteous torture (electric chairs and
    hanging).
And nothing can be remedied, as in fairy stories.

Sonnet: The Hymn-Singers

We're officer cadets in 1940 –
and some of us won't get out of this war alive.
There's snow, and ice, on the gun park. With freezing
   hands
we bring the gun into action (so many seconds flat).
Later, in pubs, we sing the rugger songs,
establishing the warmth of wartime camaraderie,
like women's sewing bees, one sex together,
making a joke of love we're frightened of. . . .

Years later will come the impotent polymaths
to say we shouldn't have sung them. Though very young
   men
think women and battle are equally tests, they'll say
it's homosexual. But we were a Congregation,
hymn-singing in that darkness – so would you!
Those sex-linked Spartans knew a thing or two!

Sonnet: The Light and the Dark

You say: Why are all the poems about the dark side of
   marriage?
About the rows, the screaming, the differences of opinion.
I say (because I like arguing?) that very few of them are –
but in any case poems are general and not to be
   interpreted literally
and they're also a kind of cure for the bad parts of life.
Stating a problem is itself, in a way, a solution.
Happiness is the one emotion a poem can't capture,
there are very few sonnets that purr with contentment.

But here goes! To be in a warm bed with somebody
   friendly,
to be looked after, cooked for, cared for; these are not
   nothings.
Conversation and fun, companionship, Twenty Questions,
humming the Verdi, Puccini, Bellini. . . .
Do I have to write it out in words: *I love you*,
after the fondness of a quarter of a century?

Sonnet: Comics

The comics know their way about (they always have),
they know they can raise the giggling laugh by saying
'He has very heavy commitments', 'He's got a large
    overdraft'
or 'Take down her particulars!' It's standard,
oblique references to cocks, balls, breasts, even (by way
    of pussies)
cunts. And this is how the Puritans like it,
it's exactly like scratching something that itches
(hence prurience); it's sly and not direct. Though
    pleasurable.

But if you use the words, describe the actions, they go up
    in flames.
Somehow they are not easy (we are not easy)
about being sexual creatures. They won't accept
that at best we're thinking animals. So keep it dark.
The preachers and the comics are in league.
Creating and dispersing thoughts of guilt.

Sonnet: Cat Death

But how, they seriously say, can you ever compare
the death of your mother to the death of your cat?
I answer: easily. After she had the pin in her hip-joint,
as she haltingly pushed her walking-frame towards the loo
she simply foreshadowed his slow limping progress,
with the bone-cancer distorting his harmed right
    shoulder,
towards the cat-pan, the cat-tray (whatever you call it).
Both of these, to see, were equally pathetic.

And as she lay in the hospital, with noisy breathing,
hardly eating, seldom conscious; and as *he* lay,
in unhappy lethargy, not touching his food,
drinking a little, liquid intake only – surely he deserved
equally the drug that pushed him into unconsciousness
and it was good that both were separated from pain?

Part Three

Dreams

So I have this recurring dream. My publisher tells me that a new Editor has been put in charge of me and all my works; and I go along to the publisher's office and there, lo and behold! the Editor turns out to be an Editress, and she is sitting there ready to discuss my new book of poems – which lies in typescript before her.

She is a neat, tidy, well-turned-out lady of fifty or so, with gaudily rimmed spectacles and an owl-like look, blue rinse hair. She explains that the Poetry Readers' Association, of which she is President, will not like a lot of the poems in this book (which she has photostatted and circulated to all her membership). She quotes a letter received from a housewife in Esher, which says: 'This book is sheer filth. I tremble to think what would happen if it were left lying about the house for young children to read!' A domesticated Professor has written: 'This kind of pornography is anti-life.'

The Editress picks up a big blue pencil, about a foot long, and begins – with the utmost savagery – to score great diagonal lines through the poems not approved of. In the end one poem only is left, its innocence established. This is about feeding a horse with lumps of sugar. I leave the office feeling I am lucky not to be arrested.

The other form of the dream (for this is a serial dream and exists in two parts) is exactly as above except that the Editor turns out to be a very serious smartly dressed American. He is called Chuck. 'Glad to meet up with you!' and 'I'm mighty pleased to have the opportunity to talk with you!' he says, and 'Hopefully, now, we can get some place!'

His view is that all the poems should be rewritten by him and then re-presented to me for a joint consultation. He starts to go through them: 'The end of this one ought to be at the beginning!' he says, and (when he comes to the word 'expedient') 'The kids'll never understand this!' He explains to me that in Iowa nobody has ever heard of Telemann or Ronald Firbank – nor has he ('Who they?' he asks). He criticizes the poems for lack of positive thinking. 'These are all *negative* poems, Gavin!' (we have been on first name terms since the first moment of meeting). In the end no poems are left unscathed; they are all bowdlerized, simplified, run through the cliché-machine. No one line is more than two words long.

As in the first dream, I wake drowned in sweat, with a feeling of criminal inadequacy.

Elegiac Verses for a Dead Headmaster

'I would prefer' was your name (if you translated it out of
the Latin),
appropriate in every way, a Classical Scholar like
you
should have been very well pleased. You enunciated so
clearly
no syllable ever escaped. blurred, unincisive or
vague,
'the circle' (you said) 'of the teeth'. From Homer, the
ἕρκος ᾿οδόντων.
You had a robinlike stance as you stood there
before the whole school
telling us, humorous, firm, about the Speech Day
arrangements –
'two tents with the singular appellations: Tent A
and Tent B',
confident, twitched your black gown; our laughter was
cautious and servile,

for halolike over your head your Power hung – to
beat and expel.
When the strong rulers relax, it could be a very good
omen
but nobody likes to take risks. We giggled a bit at
the hymn
we sang in the Chapel, that said 'in constancy follow the
Master'.
You were a poet, though, too – at Marlborough
wrote a School Song,
'The Wind That Blows Over The Downs', and, later,
light verse was your forte.
In Canada you wrote a piece that comically
mentioned Moose Jaw
and equally Medicine Hat; a Conference, this, of
Headmasters?
(that seems the fittingest term, as lions have their
pride and the geese
their gaggle and virgins occur in a giggle when nouns are
collective).
You read this aloud to the school, an 'ego trip'
someone might say,
but after all, where is the harm? There certainly were
some Headmasters
whose views were unpleasantly pi – you were
more liberal than that.
'I don't like' you once said (not to me) 'this young man
D.H. Lawrence!'
two years after his death; we smiled at this
Philistine view.
His *Letters* I had as a prize I didn't ask you to sign – you
probably wouldn't approve. Your wife to a
musical friend
explained how you never should shut, not ever, the top
of a piano.
If you shut it, she cried, damp air is shut in with
the keys!
At some educational moot you sat (so he said) next to
Auden –
he was surprised you were such a peaceful,
scholarly man,

not major-generally or given to military bluster,
        as one could surely expect, knowing the name of
                the school.

You lived to be terribly old and when you died you were
              ninety,
      forgetting the names of the boys and even the
          names of the staff.
You frightened me when I was young, but I was a
          nervous young shaver.
      In the Elysian fields this is a form you will know
(you told me once that my name, grammatically, ought
             to be Thouart).
      It isn't Latin or Greek; but a tribute, nevertheless.

Jubilate Matteo

For I rejoice in my cat Matty.

For his coat is variegated in black and brown, with white
   undersides.

For in every way his whiskers are marvellous.

For he resists the Devil and is completely neuter.

For he sleeps and washes himself and walks warily in the
   ways of Putney.

For he is at home in the whole district of SW15.

For in this district the great Yorkshire Murderer ate his
   last meal before he entered into captivity.

For in the Book of Crime there is no name like John
   Reginald Halliday Christie.

For Yorkshire indeed excels in all things, as Geoffrey
   Boycott is the best Batsman.

For the Yorkshire Ripper and the Hull Arsonist have
   their horns exalted in glory.

For Yorkshire is therefore acknowledged the greatest
   County.

For Hull was once of the company, that is now of
   Humberside.

For Sir Leonard Hutton once scored 364 runs in a Test
   Match.

For Fred Trueman too is a flagrant glory to Yorkshire.

For my cat wanders in the ways of the angels of Yorkshire.

For in his soul God has shown him a remarkable vision of Putney.

For he has also trodden in the paths of the newly fashionable.

For those who live in Gwendolen Avenue cry 'Drop dead, darling!'

For in Cambalt Road and Dealtry Road where the Vet lives there are professional people.

For Erpingham Road and Danemere Street and Dryburgh Road include the intelligentsia.

For in Clarendon Drive the British Broadcasting Corporation is rampant.

For the glory of God has deserted the simple.

For the old who gossiped in Bangalore Road are unknown to the dayspring.

For there is a shortage of the old people who adorned the novels of William Trevor.

For in the knowledge of this I cling to the old folkways of Gwalior Road and Olivette Street.

For I rejoice in my cat, who has the true spirit of Putney.

Double Dactyl: Emily Dickinson *

Stay-At-Home-Fey-At-Home
Emily Dickinson
Wrote – in a Kind of Un-
dotty – Clipt – Morse –

Capital Letters – God –
Lucifugosity –
Dashes – a Cart before
Such a Dark Horse!

* This poem was a winner of a *New Statesman* Competition.

An Old Larkinian

When I think of the crumby poetry
    people turn out to honour some pseuds
and Old Pretenders (and you must know it!) – *re*
    Art, alas, there are always such feuds –
so many whom Kingsley would simply call shags
or, if female, could be regarded as hags
    or old bags,

are enshrined in collectors' items, *Festschriften*,
    that others think give verse a bad name.
So it's like taking sides, saying 'I was at Clifton'
    or 'I'm an Etonian', no one can blame
poets for being admirers well-versed in one another
like a worshipping schoolboy younger brother
    or a mother

proud of the son's or daughter's achievements,
    sticking the pins of the journey into the map,
following them through loves and bereavements,
    seeing them off each morning in a school cap,
more than terribly pleased when they make the team,
celebrating the Knighthood with a joyful scream;
    a sunbeam

indeed he seems, or she! I'm a Larkinian
    and glad to acknowledge it to all;
though I know that death has a lot of dominion
    my admiration for your verse is not small,
you are far the best of the lonely scullers
and I'm proud to wear, among solemners and dullers,
    your colours.

Preserved

In the blurbs of the old slim volumes
they used to write:
'These are all the poems that Mr Stringfellow
wishes to preserve.'

At once there is an image of flat
copper preserving pans bubbling away
in a big kitchen, and of Mr Stringfellow
pouring, stirring, sealing the Kilner jars.

In fact there may be as much difference
between real living experience and his verse
as there is between the fresh beautiful raspberries
and the artificiality of jam.

Mackintosh Madrigal

My purple face, my yellow teeth,
    My little tiny eyes,
My snuffling and my nightly snores,
Unpleasing even to the whores,
    No longer prompt a young girl's sighs
    As she lies soft beneath, ho ho!
    As she lies soft beneath!
    Ho ho!

My pursed-up mouth, my aching back,
    My memory half gone,
My eyes walked over by the crows,
Unfashionable, ill-fitting clothes,
    Will never bring a Great Love on –
    Me in my dirty mac, ho ho!
    Me in my dirty mac!
    Ho ho!

The Lively Arts?

Bohemian Life goes on, the same as ever, untiringly.
'She threw a full bottle of wine at the wall!' they say,
    admiringly.
At the parties they all behave violently or insultingly.
'He poured his whisky all over her!' they say, exultingly.
'I love passionate people like that!' they say, adoringly.
But it follows a pattern (besides the waste of alcohol)
    really quite boringly.

In a bar with muzak once, I was told (unless I'm
     dreaming)
a neurotic wife said 'If you don't turn that music off, I
     shall start screaming!'
and they didn't – and she did; it was high-pitched, very
     effective.
To deduce the chaos this caused, you don't need to be a
     detective.
But those parties! A critic in a corner is bringing his lunch
     up
and two poets are getting ready for a first-class
     punch-up.

In the fifties once, a man introduced somebody as Dylan
     Thomas
(a pure mistake, in all good faith) and, without dotting i's
     or putting in commas,
this fellow clocked him – knocked him flat as a kipper.

He thought he was taking the mickey. So begin to hunt
     for your glass slipper
and slip away before midnight, is my advice to the
     literate.
Avant-garde behaviour (when it's pissed) is never very
     considerate.

The Victorian Husband
(Before the Murder)

Each morning, coffee cold as ice,
His thoughts to one thought carried:
How nice to be happily married,
To be married to somebody nice!

With mangled muffins and bad tea,
As insults were being parried,
He thought: To be happily married,
To be married to someone like me!

If I were rich – that would suffice!
I should not be so harried.
I should be happily married
To somebody really nice!

A Little Traditional Song: Of Love

They say women don't go for
pure sex
as men go for it.
Men are less fussy –
put their arms round the necks
of the housewife *and* the hussy.

They say women don't welcome
bed games
like men, don't welcome
that Pink Intruder –
like to know lovers' names,
only loved ones can get ruder.

They say women love people
not parts.
The love's for him, *him*,
(touch goes with emotion),
not for his loving arts,
lips and hands like soothing lotion.

They say women, etc.
They say!
No, no, not always!
Films, books, get bluer,
there's the Pill, day by day
all such women are fewer!

Hear the Voice of the Bard!

The Poet likes to float down from the sky,
complete and comfortable from on high –
    he knows he's in a state of Grace,
    making his Kingsley Amis face,

bringing the Word to the hopeless proles
who've never had (and who won't have) souls,
    flighting in from Olympian blue
    to show them all a thing or two,

and for the girls with the better looks
he's quite prepared to sign his books
    (refined slim volume or weighty tome);
    he'll read and read till the cows come home,

mind and attention flag and drop
but he won't ever want to stop.
    He knows that what he calls his 'work'
    shines bright as stars in the general murk.

The rhetoric that the Poet brings
is far above terrestrial things,
    booming with symbols, myths and signs,
    improving Nature's dull designs.

As well as genius, he may be high
on several glasses of rum or rye –
    but that inspiring drunkard's slur
    is the genuine, true Impressionist blur

that shows contempt for the mean exact
of men who are timid and talk with 'tact'.
    And, later, when they gather round
    to say 'How lovely!' and 'How profound!'

and some confess themselves nonplussed
and 'influences' are discussed
    and 'Which living poets do you admire?'
    he warms himself, as at a fire,

among the Englit this and that,
and stretches and purrs like a basking cat –
    and winks a conspiratorial eye
    at the naked Muse in the English sky.

Strange how Potent Cheap Music is! *

When I began to care,
movies with Fred Astaire
could soften both the heartache and the shock;
romantic public song
could right my private wrong,
a healing and permissive Dr Spock.

For love (sex isn't meant)
is always slightly bent
and never seems to go quite straight ahead –
if Venus were the boss
we all should suffer loss
and end up very firmly in the red.

In those days She could croon
a simple woozy tune,
and this confirmed us in our feeling that
LOVE was the only thing,
long as a piece of string,
inscrutable, indefinable Cheshire Cat.

And even now, though rogue
ballads are not in vogue,
a few can still be found there in the charts.
It's a relief to sing
this, that or anything –
in pop the trumps are very often hearts.

* Noël Coward (*Private Lives*)

Most people like a beat,
the musical élite
cannot deny Beethoven's cosmic thump –
Stravinsky too (I guess)
liked rhythm more than less,
and with their works the joint will really jump.

So, music (highbrow, low)!
Like water let it flow!
Strong feeling is remembered in those notes,
a sad and sexy past
made bitter-sweet at last;
let Venus Polyhymnia have your votes!

Literary, Residential

Neurotic ladies
who go on courses
are often unable
to hold their horses.

Disturbed Humpty-Dumpties
of spite and fear,
it's not long before
the cracks appear.

They sit there like
a witch's curse
and giggle when rivals
read their verse.

Asked an opinion
(the foolish may),
'I think it's terrible!'
they'll say.

As alcoholics
like seeing double,
what they like is
causing trouble.

Disrupters from
the neat front parlour,
they're lonely/sad
like the tunes in Mahler.

You can't help them
(their poems might)
on their long, long journey
into night.

On the Menu

Coming very shortly are the following:
my wonderful cricket story *The Nattrass Overthrow*,
praised by all the critics as the best short novel
this century about a freak run-out;
Confessions Of A Muffdiver, flash autobiography
('I always loved that soft warm wetness with the fuzzy
    surround!'), banned and enjoyed
by everybody, a piece of smart revelation;
Did They Go Back To Felixstowe?, an Edwardian saga
trolloping through the Home Counties, full of fake
    history
and semi-under-housemaids, hierarchical,
fit to induce a television coma, with marvellous dialogue
like 'Goodbye, darling!' and 'So you both saw fit to . . .'
a winner of the Booker, apotheosis of the bogus.
All these are coming. But I shall sit at home
and write unacceptable epigrams about the status quo.

A Newly Discovered Poem, Written by Mr William Wordsworth in his Madness

It is some Book of Famous Fidgets
That He holds within His digits.
Some Tract that transcendental grows
Is what He traces with His toes.

Huge He is and looks quite weird
With His grey almighty Beard,
And there's something truly frightening
In the way He throws out lightning.

As He sits upon those Hills
Where we like sheep digest our Ills,
He is Lord of Place and Time –
The Egotistical Sublime!

Marry a Lord!

Saw a well-dressed woman on a train –
she was going to London for personal gain.
She was going to:

>   dramatize her drawers,
>   popularize her panties,
>   make notable her knickers!

It was plain
she was on the make –
and no mistake!

I knew she was going to:

>   marry a Lord –
>   then marry another Lord –
>   and then marry another Lord –

and get as much alimony
as they could afford!
With her low cunning
and her loving arts
and the private enterprise of her private parts!

I knew she was going to:

>   marry a Lord –
>   then marry another Lord –
>   and then marry another Lord –

I knew they'd be bamboozled
but never (never) bored!
Breaking up homes
and breaking hearts
by the private enterprise of her private parts!

I knew by instinct,
without rhyme or reason,
she was heading for
the mating season!
I knew what she wanted,
what she had in mind –
and what she wanted
she would surely find!

I knew she was going to:
                    marry a Lord –
                    then marry another Lord –
                    and then marry another Lord –
They'd all worship her,
she couldn't be ignored!
With her great beauty
and Cupid's darts
and the private enterprise of her private parts!

Miss God

*My dear, of course it's a sin. All we can hope for is that
Miss God will forgive us. –* W.H. Auden to Chester
Kallman

The sex-lives of the poets!
And Miss God flounces in!
Who cohabits and who coits
And with what sense of Sin –
This is her one big worry
And can't be worked out in a dreadful hurry.

In good moods she excuses
And turns a smiling face,
It's okay if it amuses –
She likes a bit of lace
And (an unmarried mother)
She's partial to a little of the other.

Often, when she is shaving,
She thinks 'Am I a *man*?'
(The angels would be raving)
But, flirting with a fan,
She ogles her creation –
And knows it's good, monogamy to masturbation.

The Meeting

In the long and boring meeting,
in the hot and boring meeting,
there was shouting by the Chairman,
bullying almost by the Chairman,
people rose on points of order,
caused chaos with points of order,
argument became emotive,
all the words used were emotive,
and this was the obvious reason
passion overcame all reason.

Everything was twice repeated,
sometimes more than twice repeated,
as they worked through the agenda
(it seemed elastic, that agenda,
becoming longer, never shorter),
their utterances grew long, not shorter,
it was just like spreading butter,
words went further, like spread butter,
covering each subject thinly,
covering almost nothing thinly.

People talked about resigning,
disgruntled talk was of resigning,
accusations in a covey
flew like partridge in a covey,
yet this was not entertaining –
it sounds like drama, entertaining
as the TV scenes in courtrooms –
this was *not* like scenes in courtrooms,
it contrived to be quite boring,
really quite immensely boring.

It was more like scenes where children
shout insults at other children,
it was like a verbal punch-up,
more long-winded than a punch-up,
but the bitterness and anger
brought out words like knives in anger,
it was more like verbal murder
if there's boredom in a murder –
any moderate survivors
in the end *felt* like survivors.

Like being rescued from a snowstorm,
or blinding words whirled like a snowstorm;
they could only cry for brandy,
go to pubs and order brandy,
they felt they deserved some medals
like the Army's campaign medals –
through the tumult and the shouting
(quiet was strange after the shouting)
they achieved the peace of something
through the meeting – which was something.

It was like peace after beating
heads on walls, like hours of beating
heads on walls and never stopping –
till at last the joy of stopping
seemed a truly great achievement,
lack of pain, a great achievement,
it's so lovely when you stop it!
Negative delight, to stop it,
flooded through them after meeting
at that long hot boring meeting!

81

A Coy Maiden Solicits Aid
from a Critic

Porter, published Porter,
hear my plea,
be a big help to
little me!
Bring me succour
and bring me aid,
help me to call a
spade a spade,
make my adjectives
fit and apt,
you're an enthraller,
I am wrapt!
Take what's archaic
from my verse,
make it better –
at least not worse –
what's inverted
turn around,
save me from the
Liverpool Sound!

Porter, published Porter,
wave your wand,
get me out of
my Slough of Despond!
Make my rhymes for
ever true,
all my metaphors
sparkling new,
get metaphysics
into my lines,
I want fresh grapes
on my old vines
but I'd be glad if
you could stop
my love songs sounding
like last year's Pop –

not like a tatty
overblown tart,
I'd like you to make them
into Art.

A Ballad of the Good Lord Baden-Powell

(Companion Piece to Lawrence Durrell's *Ballad Of The Good Lord Nelson*)

If Lord Baden-Powell ever had a stand,
sex in the head or sex in the hand,
he fixed his mind on Matabeleland
      (till he pumped it all into a Lady)

He hadn't heard about white slave trafficking,
the only relief he had was Mafeking,
he liked war and the crying and havocking
      (till he jumped it all into a Lady)

He was a virgin who married late,
he told all the lads not to masturbate,
of blindness and madness this could create
      (till he bumped it all into a Lady)

In *Scouting For Boys* he clearly said
if temptation raises its ugly head
don't sleep in too warm or soft a bed
      (till he lumped it all into a Lady)

Never, he said, play fast and loose
with the pure male fluid, it's a vital juice –
cold baths will save you from self-abuse
      (till he flumped it all into a Lady)

On Brownsea Island the first Boy Scouts
were quite as green as Brussels Sprouts
and tied in knots by love's ins and outs
      (yes, he humped it all into a Lady)

But Puritans marry and fall in love,
Venus can coo like a well-born dove
and love is below as well as above
        (how he clumped it all into a Lady!)

When he wrote *Rovering To Success*
he'd seen a woman without a dress –
which once he would have thought sheer wickedness
        (and he rumped it all into a Lady)

So now his Gospel for ever abides,
proof against changing times and tides,
it's plainly written: *Boy scouts, girl guides*
        (wow! he dumped it all into a Lady!)

A Victorian Enigma

It was indeed an impenetrable type of being. A thick
growth of what a trichologist would have called hair
adorned the portion that might be described as the head;
and this was attached by a tubular structure consisting of
bone, musculature and other medical matter, covered in
skin, to what in some of our more popular murder cases
is inevitably headlined as the torso. From this depended
or protruded two upper limbs, having prehensile
attachments, while to the lower part of the body were
attached two longer and as it were smoothly extruded
features, used as supports during locomotion. The
attachments to these were almost completely lacking in
the prehensile quality above-mentioned.

   From the front of the upper part of the body projected
two large soft protuberances, centred on which, as the
bull's eye on a target, two pink excrescences could be
seen. It was not hard to determine that the tissue of which
these last were constructed was of an erectile nature.

As the head boasted two adornments that might be said to be eyes, one olfactory organ, and movable mouth-parts, so the torso could be described as 'adorned' by a pink and mouth-like generative organ (as we later discovered it to be), situated between the two lower limbs. To this, indeed, a crisp overgrowth of comparatively short hairs added an air of importance – and even of mystery.

The creature seemed, as we gathered round to inspect it more closely, almost oblivious of our scrutiny. We learned later that it was in all probability silently contemplating its own uniqueness; the eyes had a far-away look, and one of the prehensile attachments to an upper limb was partly inserted in the organ situated at the junction of the legs, which it gently agitated with a mild strumming motion.

Both Professor Doyle and Mr Wells were transported by their contemplation of this primitive organism. 'Only to think,' cried Professor Doyle in tones of rapture, 'that I should be privileged to see with my own eyes this prehistoric phenomenon, known to us hitherto only from the writings of the Greek and Roman poets and philosophers!'

Stripping a Teenage Wall

This wall is a palimpsest,
a parchment written on twice
(under the shirt lies the vest).
Images – nasty, nice –

have been cut out, copydexed,
some in the name of Tesco
commercially oversexed
and some Old Masters, fresço

and easel painting, photos
that once appealed to my daughter.
Offered to Art, ex-votos
and lambs to the slaughter,

clipped from the Supplement page –
like the temples of Mayas
they remind of an earlier age.
I descend through the layers.

Beneath Michelangelo's 'Night'
a priceless Korky The Cat
and Minnie Mouse, black and white,
under some four-colour tat

advertising a wine,
all evening-dress slinky.
Days when Mick Jagger seemed fine
and Rupert Bear kinky!

Sophisticated! Joined hands
of a Florentine martyr
cover the rollicking bands
(geological strata)

of the pre-teen comic strips
where the nippers are nipping
in a child's world without hips
or strippers stripping.

Using a thing like an adze
I peel them away from the wall –
a young woman's fashions and fads,
innocent Eve and the Fall.

My Children's Book

So I sit down and create a few characters:
a horrible rabbit called Big Bunny Biscuits,
who tortures little children by means of arithmetic,
snapping off their arms and legs when they can't add up;
a buccaneering dog called Billy Barker,
whose terrifying growl makes little girls deaf
at a range of half a mile; a sinister sheep
who treats little boys' heads as pasture
and crops them down to a velvety crewcut.
Its name is Capillary Phlogiston.

All babies, at birth, are forcibly inducted
into the Anti-Saccharine Society.
In the Great Jungle are child-eating orchids
(Rhodesia-Boysonia); there are world-beating snakes
and a very bad pop group called *Chrys an' the mums*.

In my book even the jokes will be bad.
Everyone will live in a state of disgrace
and have misadventures. No angels or fairies
will be able to stand the atmosphere for more than a
    minute.
Real life (of any kind) will seem a blessed relief.

Burlesque: Auden in the Forties

Deftly, admiral, from your fly
    Draw the huge unwilling cock,
Let unlettered lovers sigh,
    Love can fade and time can mock,
But you are Venus' prey
    From head to toe
And twice as gay
    As any well-hung, bell-bottomed
    Matelot.

'Hello, sailor!' is the cry
   History greets you with in bars,
The pink cadets scream 'Me, oh My!'
   While mad Furies in fast cars
Drive past but not away,
      Whatever you
May think or say,
         They're ready, hell or high water,
      To pursue.

Barbarians drink castles dry,
   Darlings live and die in bed,
All our futures are a lie,
   Truth invests the past instead:
Pretty blossoms on the may,
      Louche blackbirds urge
You not to stay –
         The fateful poem, well-written,
      Is a dirge.

The Ballad of Erse O. Really

(A Nonsense Of Ireland)

Oh, sure ye'll have heard of that witwandering scholar
that was in for a penny and in for a pound and in for an
   almighty dollar
how he opened the eyes of the foculties with his don's
   donnees like valerian
antispasmodic and clumping about with his bad rhymes
   like a megatherium

         Chorus Jim McJoyce's silly sanitarium
                  full of delirium!

He was the boyo for all the accredited academicals
Arragh! they tested every sinful syllable with their
   syllabub syllabus chemicals
but he wron away from them still catcalling teasily
Let the rabbit see the stoat! They were woeful and weaselly.

Chorus He sang breezily
　　　Hell Comes Easily!

For the Muse had him by the horn and no Englit sanitary
　　Deportment
could prise them apart, it was synthetic and a seamless
　　garment
she let him feel the weight of her Titfield Thunderbolts
　　surely
it was a game with spatial rules, it was educated hurley

　　Chorus Short and curly
　　　　she loved him dearly.

So they never gat him, though they brought in a true bill
　　of damages
and put a spectral scanner onto his sob-standard
　　Skandiknavian languages
He was one too much for them, in Cameforth,
　　Oxbritches and Iowa
they never neutered his nastiness with Festicles of Light
　　at Rhayader

　　Chorus Take a short ride on her
　　　　with a girl guide on her.

Homage Comforts Exiles. He sang like an aviary.
This is his Celtic abbreviated breviary.

For the Ghost of Nancy Mitford

Hear the haughty highborn ladies,
dancing through their marble halls,
lovely in their silks and satins,
gay from evensong to matins –
talking balls.

Hear the sporting shooting ladies
crossing moors of grouse and rock,
much preferring hares and pheasants
to the humble local peasants –
talking cock.

Hear the gambling bosomed beauties,
chips in each delicious lap,
full of cognac, gin and vinos,
when dice roll in rich casinos –
talking crap.

They Flee from Me
That Sometime Did Me Seek

At this moment in time
the chicks that went for me
in a big way
are opting out;
as of now, it's an all-change situation.

The scenario was once,
for me, 100% better.
Kissing her was viable
in a nude or semi-nude situation.
It was *How's about it, baby?*,
her embraces were relevant
and life-enhancing.

I was not hallucinating.
But with regard to that one
my permissiveness
has landed me in a forsaking situation.
The affair is no longer on-going.
She can, as of now, explore new parameters –
How's about it? indeed!
I feel emotionally underprivileged.
What a bitch!
(and that's meaningful!).

Dialogue Between the Alcoholic and his Better Self

A Would you like a gin and tonic?
B No, I'd rather have bubonic
                                        plague!

A Try a Haig

or a dark and sexy Guinness?
Your idea of getting thin is
                                        out.

B Please, no stout!

A Are you partial to a lager,
as Slavonic as a saga?
B   No!
Donne-moi de l'eau!

A Why not have an iced Campari?
It's as basic as a Maori
                                        dance.
B Not a chance!

A Many people fancy ouzo
as Man Friday fancied Crusoe.
B   Greek?
Not this week!

A Try the calming glass of claret
that the poet in a garret
                                        sipped.
B Man, you've flipped!

A Could you down a pint of bitter?
B Please excuse me if I titter!
                                        Ale
in the Holy Grail

wouldn't tempt me – nor would cider!
I'm quite fly (though you're a spider).
                                        Tea

is for me!

A   Frisky whisky, sherry, brandy
    can contribute to a randy
                            lay.
B   GO AWAY!
    You have plenitude and foison
    of these drinks, the purest poison
                                known –
    leave me alone!

    I'll turn cartwheels when you've gone, the
    truth is I'm happy on the
                            shelf.
    Drink them yourself!

A Male Chauvinist Celebrates
International Women's Year *

It's been a particularly good year
for women
(I should like to raise a true connoisseur's cheer
for women),
a Vintage Year – 1975 –
and women can make one glad to be alive.

They've all matured particularly well
in the hot sun,
developing good contours, skin colour and smell
in the hot sun –
they're at their very best with music and wine.
Try one tonight. You can have one of mine.

* This poem was a winner of a *New Statesman* competition.

Asked to Write a Poem on the Subject 'Who Am I?' by the Magazine Nova, 1975

Once I was an ovum, and At Home to a sperm.
Soon I wore a prep school cap for term after term.
For most of my twenties I was busy with a War,
in a mud-coloured uniform I didn't much adore.

Then I worked in agencies, in a dark office suit,
at ads too full of adjectives, much fruitier than fruit,
copywriting. After that I was a freelance next,
shabby in my casual clothes, a plain straightforward text.

'Role-playing' is the word they use; and one certainly can
think of more than Shakespeare's seven ages of man –
the baby, the bully, the boyfriend and the bore
are simply variants of the apple, all with the same core?

There's a cupboardful of costumes – what would I want
    to be?
What would I like the world to think the quintessential
    me?
Anthologize! The best of each unsatisfactory stage
might make a compound flattering to me in my old age.

The teenage vigour, as it were, the bright and youthful
    looks
could be combined with wisdom (gained from reading
    all those books).
Oh, so clever and attractive! That's man's (and woman's)
    wish,
who in the womb once had the nature of a fish.

Human beings' pretensions are the braying of an ass,
It's right our dissolution causes, mainly, gas;
and our feeling so important doesn't, either, get us far –
for a vast amount of nothing is what we really are.

The Germanic Day

I wake the wifehag in the marriagebed
She makes quickcoffee in the breakfastcups
We wake the girlchild in her sleepingroom
I take the hounddog for a pavementwalk
We eat the cornflakes and the baconegg

I drive the smallcar to the officeblock
I read the newmail on the clear desktop
My giggling girlclerk takes the shorthand down
Reports from salesmen take up workingtime
My brainpan rings with what the farsound says

I mealeat in Directors' Diningroom
The Chairman tells me of his own forecast
The afternoon has salesfigures for food
Salesareas talk in the meetingroom
A wellshaped lovegirl brings the teacups in

I end the workday with campaignplan talk
My girlclerk tells of farcalls from outside
I drive the smallcar to the privatehouse
I take the hounddog for a pavementwalk
I kiss the wifehag in the marriagebed.

Rooms Must be Vacated Before Noon
on Day of Departure

At the end of an Irish tour, in a town that could be called
Trevorstown after William Trevor, who lived here
before he changed his name and became a famous
novelist and lived in Devonshire, a town whose name
some of the natives of the country pronounce as though

it were the sound made by an English crow –

94

but I pronounce it like the name of the thing that gets stuck in the neck of a bottle – in the Glenvera I enjoy a sausage-egg-and-tea delicious breakfast, modifying thus the slight hangover induced by mixing St Raphael with Cork Dry Gin,

and I have almost no sense of sin.

Why should I? Literary tours and excursions are meritorious endeavours and those who engage in them deserve well of the creature comforts and should never creep about crying *Peccavi!*, as they rattle in trains across the centre of Ireland, which is very flat –

but that's enough of that.

I don't want to talk about guilt and I won't talk about guilt because this, although it is work of a kind, is also a kind of holiday and I have a sense of release drinking Guinness in Montenotte – where the sun shines down in a very Italianate way

and work seems very like play.

For Patience Strong

A wife is like a court jester (but without a sense of humour); she's there to make a grape fruit feel like a satsuma – to cut her husband down to size, to make him feel small, or as though (like Hitler) he had only one ball. A monorch, not a monarch, and by no means a king, and not really very much good at anything. This is the course of action that a wife pursues, when she's not moaning low or singing the blues. There's not a lot that a husband can do, although in so many cases this is true, and success may not crown even a determined attempt – because, as well as children, familiarity breeds contempt.

Gritty

(A Subaltern's True Story, 1942)

Driving a tractor towing a Bofors gun
in the early morning (ice on the road?)
Gunner Gritty slid into a tree.

Crushed in his cab in that cold winter sun,
he later died, 'shedding his earthly load'
the Padre might have said. To me

(a junior subaltern), the BSM,
the man of God, there fell the routine task:
to represent the unit at his grave

up in North London, London's suburb hem,
and, duty done, what more could we three ask
than the deserved pub lunch? Alcohol gave

comfort, food warmed our thoughts of pity.
The Sergeant-Major, quite seriously, said to me:
'I shouldn't have the pudding if I were you, Sir.
It's gritty.'

Part Four

Crucifixion

Suppose they came along one morning and said 'Right! To-day we're going to crucify you!' It would come as a shock, to say the least; and particularly if they had already set up a brand new wooden cross, handmade, in your back garden, and had the hammers and high quality nails ready, no expense spared, to do the thing in style. After the first numbness of the shock, who would be able to resist shouting and screaming, completely hysterical or even technically mad? There would certainly be fainting and falling about. We forget too easily how such cruelty was once commonplace, no more regarded than (nowadays) a starving lost dog in the harsh streets of a big city. The man or woman who could contemplate the endurance of such torture – for they would not hesitate to crucify women, and even children – with the calm and philosophical courage advised by the Ancients would be rare indeed.

Dirty Weekends

Dirty weekends. Something so soiled, snide, sly and now (Venus be praised!) so old-fashioned about these words; from the days of frustration, puritanism and secret meetings. Faked hotel registers and a general feeling of dirty knickers and used French letters. And yet such encounters and companionships can be as full of true love (in the baleful words of the song-writers) as the arranged and church marriages that reoccur in photographic colour in photographers' shops in provincial towns; He and She both decked and smiling, the little bouquet of bad-taste bridesmaids, a tortured god in the background. For what is touched and what is felt, in both cases – the union for two days or for a lifetime – is not pink flesh only; the emotions too are

97

engaged. Those erections that cause sniggering among schoolboys and schoolgirls are spiritual things. The nipples, to the lover, are not just utilitarian and of the laity, but holy. The girl shines in the dark like an angel or the Virgin Mary, and the word 'worship' is not in the church service only, but in reality.

Romeo Addresses his Poperin Pear

You've been inside Juliet, you lucky little thing! You've been part, temporarily, of an extraordinarily beautiful person. When we were together, you belonged to her and she belonged to me. Although my wise uncles say that no person can or should 'belong' to another person; and in a love like ours, where everything is freely given, there is no question of one being the property of the other. My wise uncles also say that, just as most men do regard their wives as their property, a large number of girls regard a boyfriend as a personal possession and wives, even more so, regard their husbands as belonging to them like a carved chest or an embroidery frame.

You look, now, so coy and bashful. So innocent, so incapable of that brazen effrontery, that stiff resistance in the face of love, that ardour in the armed encounter! And yet you know a thing or two, an adept in the mysteries of women, designed to tear the veil of the temple and penetrate to the holy of holies, the Grail, the womb, that tidebound inward sea. . . .

How could this lamb be so like a lion, so rampageous, so rampant, storming the ramparts, effecting a breach, received in the citadel with joy, a relieving army?

You are indeed a two-face, both shy and shocking, in your two wildly different moods. I'm watching you, you cyclothyme! Juliet is watching you too. She has a small smile on her face and she is sending you a message of congratulation: 'Well done, my good and faithful servant!'

98

Love Difficulties

In my time the whores have said to me encouraging whorelike things – such as 'You're putting on weight!' and 'Nice and hard!' – while women engaged in it more for love than money have remarked 'You underestimate yourself' and 'That looks to me remarkably like an erection'. But never (and for this kindness I shall always be grateful) when there was impotence or difficulty did any of them taunt me with the contemptuous insults that young men so much fear: 'You're not a man!', 'Tie a pencil to it!' etc. etc.

It's too easy to equate sexual performance with masculinity. Not lack of maleness but the fixating mothers and the castrating fathers are to blame. Many thoroughgoing homosexuals are able (I mean the male ones) to have intercourse with women – but they're not much interested in it. On the other hand, men who love women are more likely to be afraid of failure; and even perhaps because of their anxiety to do well, to lose potency for that very reason. Specific anxiety over the outcome is allied to the oedipal fears and guilts.

From all such depressing sadnesses, may Venus deliver us!

A Glastonbury Cricket Match

Frottie Fridges was the next person in, the very last person to bat for the Wookey Hole cricket team. Frottie Fridges was a complete and perfect rhombus, with the look of a squeezed square. Nature had made her four feet high and not very much thicker, reckoned from back to front, than the big front door at the Vicarage. In her pads and batting gloves this mammalian repository of local wisdom had indeed the appearance of a very wide deformed cricket bat herself.

As she approached the wicket her shrewd Quantock brain was occupied with intense rustic thoughts, concerning for the most part the Vicar and his lover, the beautiful Nuttie Zetland. She was thinking, as she took guard: 'He do masturbate she, and she do masturbate he. But 'tis a girt mock to reason how none o' these wold sinners do never masturbate *me*!'

So saying and thinking, with great female complacency, she settled down to await the next ball of the over. Meanwhile all the blades of grass on the cricket pitch were striving with a kind of communistic solidarity, to take a decisive part in the game. They were at one with the thirteen players exercising themselves there, and far more deeply engaged than the two umpires. As the ball struck them they did their very best to divert it towards the wicket, since all pitches do their utmost to assist the bowler.

Mad Lekker, as he walked slowly back before turning to bowl again, sniffed viciously as he passed Nuttie, who was the batswoman at the other end. His little bear's eyes narrowed as they rested on her classic breasts. Imaginative lust carried him forward, flooding into the remotest portion of his consciousness. He became a wave in the Bristol Channel, a crystal in a Mendip stone wall, a black-striped perch in the Brue under Pomparles Bridge. On his right as he walked, dogsplurge burgeoned and the ratsfoot spread its purple patches evenly over the outfield, awaking in him atavistic affiliations. On his left the vivid green of the cat's crocus attracted his wandering gaze as he turned on his heel and hesitated, 'alone and palely loitering', before beginning his run-up to bowl. Only slightly distracted now by Nuttie Zetland's perfect breasts, in their rough cheesecloth cricket shirt, he broke wind and began to gallop towards the crease. The dark earth beneath him seemed to him then, under its covering of grass, like a vast wild-maned horse, upon whose back he was being borne through space! A poignant smell of musk rose up from where his heavy white boots pressed against that huge living creature. From that fragment of white mystery there slid across land and water into the soul of Mad, as he approached and passed Nuttie's earthy presence and released the leather sphere, the curt voice of the umpire, Lord M.'s bastard: 'No ball!'

– J.C. Powys, Captain Somerset Second XI, 1933

100

THE EWART QUARTO (1984)

A Pindaric Ode on the Occasion of the Third Test Match Between England and Australia, Played at Headingley, –16–21 July, 1981

Well, GATTING was batting and YALLOP came in at a
gallop to save a single . . . we could mix and mingle
with the loud crowd, on our telescreens we saw the
   best match ever to be called a Test Match . . .

Don't be abrupt, don't interrupt,
just keep quiet, don't riot, sit still and listen,
hear the Umpires' bell – I'm ready to tell
a story of glory and the unfading laurel crowns
   that glisten . . .

THURSDAY
Australia went in first, they were soon grinding
   away on a day
when England were finding it hard. I tell you, mate,
the English bowlers didn't bowl very straight,
it was like watching a coffee-grinder or standing
behind a cement-mixer, as those batsmen went
through the motions, they knew they had oceans of
   time. Their slowness was a crime
and didn't produce standing ovations – but justified,
buildings don't stand up without foundations . . .

FRIDAY

203 for 3, and a catch dropped by GOWER, the power
and the glory seemed as though it had really
   deserted BREARLEY.
OLD bowled quite well; but all this day
the Australians seemed well on their way.
DYSON didn't charge at the ball like a bison;
but he made 102, and 102s, like the 89 made by HUGHES,
and YALLOP's 58, meant a good score – and a lot
   more. Confidence.
They declared at 9 for 401 – for England not much fun,
though BOTHAM bowled straight and moved the ball
   both early and late,
the one ray of light in the gloom (6 for 95). Still,
   England's doom
could be seen to loom. BOTHAM seemed to prove it –
if he could swing it, the Australians too would
   certainly move it,
by seam and flight.
But no untoward fright. No English wicket fell
   that night.

SATURDAY

Yet England didn't rise again on that third day.
GOOCH out for 2. The thing to do seemed to be to
mooch around, BOYCOTT 12, BREARLEY 10, even
GOWER only very briefly came into flower.
24. Again some light from BOTHAM – where others
   were thrifty
he was prodigal, with a well-struck 50.
LILLEE, ALDERMAN, LAWSON bowled well – at the stumps.
Far better than the English bowlers. A bad night,
   with grinding molars
and all England's supporters down in the dumps.

MONDAY

England 174 all out and, following on,
GOOCH, with the score at zero, had already gone.
The radio mentioned odds of 500 to 1
for an England win. But this wasn't the Oval, there
   weren't any LAKERS,

and, with regard to these odds, there can't have been
    many takers.
Would Australia even have to bat again?
The most sensible thing seemed to be to pray
    for rain.
227 to avoid the innings defeat.
BOYCOTT played straight, calm and unflappable (46),
some of WILLEY's more aggressive strokes (33) were
    very clappable.
But 4 down for 41! Even 5 for 105,
there didn't seem much to keep our hopes alive.
It was like the tide inexorably flooding in over
    the sand,
seven wickets had gone for 135. No sign of a stand,
like King Canute, nobody could send the sea back
    with a cricket boot,
92 runs still needed for Australia to bat again, the
    steep hill of the follow-on
and only three wickets left,
any English laugh must have been a hollow one!

But BOTHAM, looking like a lion on a British egg,
seemed to be willing to have a brief, glorious thrash,
pulling, driving, cutting and sweeping to leg,
with (once) something not much different from a
    tennis overhead smash . . .

and, slowly but surely, we realized that he knew
    what he was doing
and although it was very clear that he was riding
    his luck
the ball met the meat of the bat, this wasn't just
    cause for booing
or irresponsible (like the slogger who's out for
    a duck).

The next day's papers compared him to
that six-hitting fabulous Croucher, Jessop –
and indeed he jumped down the pitch like a gressop
(the Old English for what James Joyce with his Irish
    voice called a gracehoper

and most ordinary people call a grasshopper).
One particular six, a tremendous one, parabola-tall,
made one feel pretty sorry for the ball.

DILLEY, too, turned agressive. 56 runs, and all made
   with style.
Someone shouted 'Why didn't you bowl like that?'
He was out at 252. A century partnership.
The Australian bowlers, even LILLEE, began to
   look ordinary.
BOTHAM's hundred. BREARLEY gave him the *stay there!*
   signal, very clearly.
From then on he shielded OLD, running singles at the
   ends of overs
and scoring in fours only (twos were difficult).
OLD was bowled for 29, a good innings.
Then it was WILLIS. 351 for nine
at close of play. Fine. A commentator was heard
   to say:
'They need a hundred runs to bowl at!' These
   they had.
It still looked hopeless, but not quite so bad.

TUESDAY
BOTHAM hit one more four, ALDERMAN got WILLIS.
356 all out. When they went in
Australia needed only 130 to win.
It all went quietly ahead, though BOTHAM got WOOD
   for ten.
DYSON and CHAPPELL looked as firm as rocks,
   and then
DILLEY went off to have a boot repaired. WILLIS
   took over –
and from then on the Australian batsmen were never
   in clover.
That wild Goose flew in like a bat out of Hell –
3 wickets in 11 balls, without a run being scored!
Surely the batsmen to come must have prayed to
   the Lord!
CHAPPEL, HUGHES and YALLOP – the names say it all.

This was the kind of bowling you can't play at all!
OLD had BORDER for a duck. MARSH didn't have
    BOTHAM's luck
and DILLEY boundary-caught him at fine leg, one of
    the hardest blows struck.
Before that DYSON went. 68 for 6. Soon just 75 for 8.
Only LILLEE at the end, with BRIGHT, showed any
    kind of fight.
BRIGHT 19, LILLEE 17 (DYSON made 34
and this was very easily the top score).
55 runs needed. Two wickets to fall.
WILLIS had LILLEE caught by GATTING, a mishit hook
    off a less straight ball.

BREARLEY said afterwards, in a sort of magnificat,
'I didn't think WILLIS could still bowl like that.'

BOTHAM came back. OLD dropped ALDERMAN twice
    in an over.
If that had been FLETCHER
that Yorkshire Chauvinist crowd would have made a
    meal of it, you betcher
life, as one of the commentators said.
Still, though everyone was tense, under his beard
    OLD's face must have been a bit red . . .

Finally, though, WILLIS knocked out BRIGHT's
    middle stump,
and everyone jumped for joy, a really
    unbelievable jump!
111 all out. They'd done it by 18 runs . . .
And this is an ode to Cricket, Cricket and its white-
    robed sons!
Like the bounce of a rugger ball, you can't tell which
    way it'll go,
it's totally unpredictable, if it's like anything at all
it's truly like a game of soccer played with a
    rugger ball!
But of course you must praise WILLIS (8 for 43)
and BOTHAM's magnificent innings – 149 not out.
Goose and Guy the Gorilla

were the two favourite flavours, like (say)
    Strawberry and Vanilla –
but MIKE BREARLEY also deserves praise,
as a first-class Captain in a good many
    different ways.

This tribute that mangles the epic and the lyric,
this rough populist Pindaric panegyric,
this dithyrambic doggerel is here to make the claim
that since STODDARD did it in Sydney in 1894
no other Test side in history has ever followed on
    and still won the game!

On the 100th Birthday of
P.G. Wodehouse

(15 October 1981, also the Centenary of the Chinese
poet Lu Xun)

Like most of us (Time's temple's architrave)
he spends his hundredth birthday in the grave
(the squiggly bits in architecture, we
are not important to Eternity)
but here was something, happy to be 'light',
that shines like Shakespeare, just as bravely bright!

The words that cozen us, the ancient ploys!
The fairy-story worlds – where girls and boys
face aunts and alienists, the dragon seed,
and ritual attire (without, they bleed)
must save them (ties! oh, ties! oh, waistcoats, spats!)
and sweet flat-chested girls in floppy hats!
Where love is love, without its sexy smell,
and there's no stroking at the bearded well.

It's true the working class, the vast majorities,
and women in their sharp oppressed sororities,
don't ever find him really all that funny.
Perhaps to dig him much, you must have money?

Even war's spillage, its seepage and its ullage,
didn't much disturb his dreams of Dulwich
(there's not much doubt that his idea of heaven
was just to watch the Dulwich First Eleven).
He kept his innocence, exploited when
the Nazis said they too were gentlemen.
O'Casey called him a performing flea,
there to amuse applauding bourgeoisie –
quite right. But more, much more, to it than that!
He only understood one kind of bat.
The Draculas of politics flew by,
he hardly knew that they were in the sky.

Perhaps he was to blame – he should have known –
a good man, without malice, on his own
he much increased the gaiety of nations
by serving Art with daily ministrations,
as much as Wilde's or Yeats's, Seamus Heaney's . . .

Lounge lizards have a bifurcated penis
(but did I know what people did in bed?)
one of my father's (medical) students said –
a joke I treasured (at the age of ten) –
I was well into Wodehouse, even then.
No, surely I was older, more like twelve?
Walt Whitmanlike, I contradict myself –
I take the books down – 1928!
But still a sexless pre-pubertal state.
Leave It To Psmith, A Damsel In Distress,
Ukridge, the Mulliners, *Money For Nothing*, yes,
beans, crumpets, Jeeves, a soulful poetess . . .
On those foxed pages and the thoughts they house
I was well sluiced and quite content to browse!

Before him, Richmal Crompton filled my shelves –
two first-class writers, a class by themselves
(Doyle, Haggard, Henty, Westerman and Wells
had no more humour than *The Book of Kells*).

But what makes Wodehouse leader by a mile
isn't his thought but his pellucid style,
clear and colloquial. The thought (and lots)
went into all those complicated plots,
worked out like early musical comedies.
Reality? Oh, no! far from it! Is
there any backtrack, short cut, sideways twist
that labyrinthine Wodehouse ever missed?

Those characters more addictive than the bottle!
Gussie (newt-fancier), the young Fink-Nottle.
Lord Emsworth, Tuppy Glossop, Bertie Wooster,
even Aunt Agatha's a morale-booster!
Anatole ('God's gift to the gastric juices'),
Percy Pilbeam, Chimp Twist, both foul abuses,
snakes in the grass, whose moral turpitude
would make a moralist throw up – or burp
    (it would!),
Rosie M. Banks and martyred Bingo Little,
the forceful female and the male, more brittle . . .

Duet for Aunt and Nephew. Critics say
each novel is a musicless musical play.
I'd go along with that. But still the story
isn't exactly his great crowning glory –
we know the Efficient Baxter will retreat
and dithering Lord Emsworth find his feet,
all Aunts be foiled, and True Love find a way,
Jeeves work his magic, for ever and a day
the steel-willed girls will have their silly asses,
with not much mention of the toiling masses
(O'Casey, down!). Blandings is Eden. Waugh
was right too. This is Alice's door.
Soon lost forever, Innocence is the key
to Never Never Lands where all are free
in pastoral joy – a humorous Brideshead
(nostalgia for childhood, not wine and bed).

He has his century. Now clap him in!
And send Sir Roderick Glossop howling to the bin!

And Art A Ruminant

'but wonder
If in fact art is better than life.
ROY FULLER: *Bagatelles*

Strange that I still a parlous chorus croak,
Alarmingly at variance with art!
Curious the enormous distance that the heart
Must cover in some worn old buffer's joke,

How now I must fumble what I once could poke –
The Muse's groin, she being a bright young tart
(Strange that!). I still a parlous chorus croak.
Alarmingly at variance with art,

How odd that she should sip her vesper coke
And that her gaze, as one feared from the start,
Should pierce us, eye a veritable dart
Thrown in a pub by some young beer-loud bloke!
Strange! That I still a parlous chorus croak!

Auden

Photographed, he looked like Spencer Tracy
or even Danny Kaye –
in the late Forties. But later it was wiser
to look the other way.

A Bit Of A Ballad

(Scotland v. Australia, Murrayfield, 18 December
1981)

Oh, broken, broken was the play!
And blawn the half-time whistle!
The Wallabies hae scored tries three,
Four penalties the Thistle.

109

The second half now gars begin,
On the snaw-stripit green,
And but twelve points the braw Scots hae,
The Wallabies fifteen.

But 'tis the bonny Andy Irvine
That kicks the penalty
That levels a', 15–15,
As level as your e'e.

And they hae ta'en the whisky malt
That stand to see the battle,
And syne they harry the Scottish team,
As drovers harry cattle!

The lions on the standards roar,
And Scotland scores again!
'Tis the muckle Rutherford –
A drappit goal, ye may ken!

'Hauld fast! Hauld fast!' Clerk Irvine cries,
'My bonny lads, wi' me!
We'll weill withstand, on either hand,
The assaults o' the enemie!'

The Wallabies are ravenous,
They sling the ba' aboot –
The Scots defence stands firm as rock,
They dinna care a hoot!

There's but five minutes' playing time,
Australians leap and rin,
And 'tis gowd jerseys everywhere,
Like a rugby loony-bin!

But 'tis the muckle Rutherford
Has ta'en the ba' in's hands
And kicked it full high i' the freezing air
And higher than the stands.

The ba' has landed on its point,
The ba' has bounced full high –
And 'tis the wee Renwick has caught it and
'Tis an inescapable try!

Oh, wae, wae, were the Wallabies,
Baith here and owre the faem,
Tae see the braw wee Renwick rin
And bear the victory hame!

For now 'tis 15-22 –
Australia does trail,
A score that hurts. Irvine converts,
Like driving in a nail!

And so rejoice in Embro toun,
The final whistle blaws,
Mak merrie, 24-15!
All Scots, they hae guid cause!

The Phantom of the Opera

In a world full of Thomas Hardy-type ironies
what could be properer
than that a Literature Director should be
a man who only cares about music –
Charles Osborne,
the phantom of the opera.

Contemporaries

Well, to begin with, you must know
Shakespeare was called an 'Upstart Crow' . . .
and now we find from poets' letters
what they thought of bardic betters.

Graves liked Lawrence (mad T.E.).
D.H. (a poet too if he
wasn't so obsessed with sex!)
sent no current through his flex.
Graves, an engine in a siding –
shunted there by Laura Riding –
thought all Auden's verse was 'fake'
and Willie Yeats a big mistake.
He loved Skelton and E. Rumming's
tunnings – and (save us!) e.e.cummings!
Pound was crazy, vain though vital,
no poet – hadn't earned the title.

Another part of that same wood:
and here, too, things are not so good,
Professor Lucas, no wild zealot,
calls Eliot a 'drunken helot',
D.H. calls Joyce '*Olla podrida*'
(a putrid cabbage, yes, dear reader!),
while V. Woolf thinks him middle class
or lower, and G. Stein, alas!,
knows she's more 'advanced' than him
(though Stan supports his brother Jim).
Wyndham Lewis (first name Percy)
sternly watches, without mercy,
what a crew without a cox!
Hemingway – a big 'dumb ox',
Virginia too, he says, somehow,
is less a woman than a cow!

And all the while the *famille* Sitwell
goes for the foes whose throats would slit well –
does it get better, does it worsen?
Edith calls Enright (D), 'a person',
while Geoffrey Grigson causes pain
by naming *her* as 'that Old Jane'
and shouting loud, without duplicity,
that she's an expert at publicity!
And Spender: 'Who *is* Peter Porter?'
Campbell, reactionary snorter,
whose afternoon's a Fascist faun day,
attacks the Leftist team, Macspaunday.

(But Byron, once, recall, gave Wordsworth
a most unpleasant nickname: Turdsworth.
Romanticised and Jeffrey Farnol'd,
Shelley was called by Matthew Arnold
an 'angel', yes, but 'ineffectual',
and Aldous too, that intellectual,
flew mothlike from a Bloomsbury rug
to put him down – a 'fat white slug'.)

And so, we know, the bad opinions,
throughout Her Majesty's Dominions
and places where she holds no sway
like the big-headed U.S.A.,
are even now being written down –
this moment as a clot or clown
you and I are being described
in private letters, diatribed
outspokenly (no halfway hints)
in all the highbrow public prints,
but most of all, by butch and camp,
firmly thumbed down with a stamp!

On Being Asked by My Daughter to Lend Her My Father's Leather Motoring Coat of 1930

No, no, I couldn't! Not for an hour or a minute!
Dan would be off on his motorbike, straightaway,
    in it!
It would very quickly be covered in grease or oil –
the very things that most incontestably spoil
a coat of such a kind, a genuine collector's piece
but most vulnerable (as McGonagall would have
        said) to oil and grease!

In fact, most of Evelyn Waugh's highborn friends
had coats like that;
they came to them naturally, like cream to
    a prize cat.

113

Or, if you wore it, with its true soft leather feel, it
wouldn't be long before your local criminals set out
        to steal it.
Because a real leather coat, buttoning to the neck,
with a broad leather belt (suitable now for
   a discotheque),
was Hitler's Choice in 1938, the year when the Czech
was sold down the river by a Conservative regime
that thought itself (they all do) the cream of
   the cream.

So I must refuse. And if you ever see
that coat walking around, inside it will be *me!*

The Locative

'The Locative. The names of towns, small islands,
domus, humus and *rus.*' KENNEDY'S LATIN PRIMER

The names of towns are so evocative
they have to go into the locative –
Pompeiis, Adelstrops and Selbournes,
full of the peasants and the well-borns,
where the curates had misgivings
about exchanging rural livings.
Small islands? Procida or Ischia –
Latin freedom was much friskier,
at home on that volcanic soil
(Ibsen and Auden on the boil),
no birth control – sex too was rural,
a tergo, interruptus, intercrural!

New! (a Pam Ayres)

It was the Fourth of January,
The New Year was very new!
I got on the train at Putney,
To take me to Waterloo,

114

I had to hop on quickly –
British Rail won't wait –
Seven in the compartment,
I was number eight.

I settled in the one empty seat,
Me basket on me lap.
On me right was a woman,
On me left was a chap.

I saw how he held his paper
And glanced now and then at his feet –
The news was less new than his shoes were,
My, they shone bright and neat!

The woman on me other side
Cradled a shiny bag,
Dusted the black patent leather,
As new as a store's price tag!

Opposite me was a fellow,
And there at his feet on the floor
Was a beautiful newborn briefcase,
Set there for all to adore!

Accidentally I'd kicked it
As I struggled onto the train,
He looked as though he could kill me –
then kill me all over again!

On his right was another man,
A wine-coloured scarf round his neck,
New and noticeable – there he sat,
As proud as Gregory Peck!

Three in a row, on his right again,
An umbrella man sat erect,
Twirling a new umbrella,
Superior and select!

Upright and perfect between his feet,
He leaned on it like a sword,
Like a symbol of knighthood,
Well-bred and just a bit bored.

Away to me left a woman sat,
Next to the lad with the shoes;
A pair of gloves lay in her lap,
Uncreased, with no sign of use.

From time to time she stroked them.
It was like shouting aloud,
She and the others, how Santa
Had certainly done them proud!

But there was a seventh person,
Next to the briefcase man –
He sat there wedged in his corner,
Pale and haggard and wan.

From his feet up, he was shabby,
Worn shoes and a cuff-frayed shirt,
Nothing of his was smooth and clean,
He looked rough and acquainted with dirt.

He truly did look scruffy,
There by the NO SMOKING sign.
He had nothing new about him
That I could guess or divine!

I saw he was frantically chewing,
He had a brown-stained right hand,
And as I looked for *his* newness
I began to understand!

He'd made a New Year Resolution,
And one that isn't a joke!
What was new with him was his new resolve
Never again to smoke!

This poem is based entirely, in every detail, on a journey made
by my wife – an example of the poet using another person's
experience as his raw material.

The Most Famous Poem of J. Strugnell

Say not the Strugnell nought availeth,
    The biro and the beer are vain,
Poetic craft wherein he baileth
    Lost on the vast illit'rate main!

If odes are dupes, verse plays are liars,
    Where meaning lies in tropes concealed,
The High Sublime is looking pious
    And something silly is revealed.

For while the poets, proudly reading,
    Don't entice the prettiest girls,
Faber and Faber, both, are speeding
    To smother them in gold and pearls.

And not by magazine sales only
    Or playing trumpets, all that jazz,
Shall Strugnell cease from feeling lonely –
    Slim volumes give him what he has!

The Beginning of an Ode on Who's Who

I'm terribly excited –
I have been invited
to join that great bunch of nonentities
who have the inflated identities,
such as Lord Leatherhead and Viscount Foxford
(who knew all the right – or were they the wrong? –
people at Oxford),

metallurgists, musicians,
phenomenologists, physicians
(and almost anyone in Debrett is
sure to be in with the celebrities –
but it's not so common for the neglected scribbler
to get into this exclusive club before he's senile
or a dribbler);

though there you might someday find it,
when you were halt, lame and blinded,
your name – is it really a good dropping one?
Though once one's in there's no stopping one,
one can drawl, like MacBeth★, 'Oh course I'm in
    Who's Who now,'
one's poetic specific gravity is certainly multiplied
by more than two now!

I'll be there with the great ones,
the truly honoured-by-the-State ones,
in that Never-Never-Land fathers
never reached (though both my grandfathers),
with conservative academics, donnish and prudish;
among the old women of both sexes my name
    may seem
a tiny bit rudish?

But the military, the Naval, the flying
(who don't mind people dying),
the Earls and the epistemologists,
the dentists, divines and Catholic apologists,
those who in stately homes discuss a *cru* or
    a crumpet,
though they won't like it at all, I'm sure, will just
have to lump it!

★ It may seem that George MacBeth has been unfairly singled
out. Indeed I could equally well have used the names of any of
the included poets: Dannie Abse, A. Alvarez, Kingsley Amis,
George Barker, Patricia Beer, Sir John Betjeman, George
Mackay Brown, Charles Causley, Robert Conquest, Patric
Dickinson, Ronald Duncan, Lawrence Durrell, Sir William
Empson, D.J. Enright, Roy Fuller, Robert Gittings, Geoffrey

Grigson, Thomas William (Thom) Gunn, Ian Hamilton, Seamus
Heaney, John Heath-Stubbs, Geoffrey Hill, David Holbrook,
Ted Hughes, Clive James, Elizabeth Jennings, Thomas Kinsella,
James Kirkup, Philip Larkin, Laurie Lee, John Lehmann. Peter
Levi, Christopher Logue, (George MacBeth), Norman MacCaig,
Adrian Mitchell, Kathleen Nott, Harold Pinter, Ruth Pitter, Peter
Porter, Kathleen Raine, Peter Redgrove, Henry Reed, Anne
Ridler, Alan Ross, Howard Sergeant, Penelope Shuttle, Jon
Silkin, Stephen Spender, Julian Symons, R.S. Thomas, Anthony
Thwaite, Charles Tomlinson, John Wain, Sir John Waller.

These are all there, with Rev. Canaan Sodindo Banana
(President of Zimbabwe), Leonid Ilyich Brezhnev, the Brodie of
Brodie, Barbara Cartland (with a list of novels as long as your
arm) and Sir Walter Scott (twice). Wot, no Tambimuttu? No
David Gascoyne? No (separate) Lady Wilson?

THE YOUNG POBBLE'S GUIDE TO HIS TOES
(1985)

Part One

The Young Pobble's Guide to his Toes

Everything comes, everything goes.
Some day you must say goodbye to your toes –
all bitten off by the beasts of the sea
or fading away by a gradual degree,
vanishing into an elbowless night
all blurred and dim in your elderly sight.
The sun goes down and the eyes give up,
your toes will fade, kerflip, kerflup . . .

The moral shines bright as a mermaid's hair.
Count them and keep them while they're still there!

Lights Out

With each new book the old poet thinks:
Will this be the last?
Biros, pencils, typewritters, pens and inks
whisper to him: Get going! Move!
Get it out fast!

Cram the poems in like a herring glut –
two, three to the page!
Randify your writing, riot and rut,
time's short, get out of that groove
they call old age!

Write it all down, write it fast and loose,
it may be sad stuff –
and you were never a golden egg goose –
but shout it out, coming too soon you've
got silence enough!

Singable

Maimed personalities make the best poets still,
with flaws all over the shop,
opium and alcohol, no one could say of them
they never touched a drop –
and there's a strain of reclusive old ladies too
who hardly go out to tea,
agoraphobes, with a murderous loneliness –
not jolly, like you and me –
all the neurotics, the Muse will quite welcome them,
yes, *and* their queerness and quirks,
what does it matter? It turns out so singable,
it doesn't gum up the works!

Acts of Love

*Emily, in reply to Tabby's remonstrances, declared that, if
he was found again transgressing, she herself, in defiance
of warning and his well-known ferocity of nature, would
beat him so severely that he would never offend again. In
the gathering dusk of an autumn evening, Tabby came,
half triumphantly, half trembling, but in great wrath, to
tell Emily that Keeper was lying on the best bed, in
drowsy voluptuousness. Charlotte saw Emily's whitening
face, and set mouth, but dared not speak to interfere; no
one dared when Emily's eyes glowed in that manner out of
the paleness of her face, and when her lips were so
compressed into stone. She went up-stairs, and Tabby and
Charlotte stood in the gloomy passage below, full of the
dark shadows of coming night. Down-stairs came Emily,
dragging after her the unwilling Keeper, his hind legs set in*

a heavy attitude of resistance, held by the 'scuft of his neck', but growling low and savagely all the time. The watchers would fain have spoken, but durst not, for fear of taking off Emily's attention, and causing her to avert her head for a moment from the enraged brute. She let him go, planted in a dark corner at the bottom of the stairs; no time was there to fetch stick or rod, for fear of the strangling clutch at her throat – her bare clenched fist struck against his fierce red eyes, before he had time to make his spring, and, in the language of the turf, she 'punished him' till his eyes were swelled up, and the half-blind stupified beast was led to his accustomed lair, to have his swelled head fomented and cared for by the very Emily herself.

– Elizabeth Gaskell, *The Life of Charlotte Bronte*

1 Traditional

What loving punishment the Lord could give,
a dog's life in the Parsonage, dark graves
where, in the typhus black, their Death could live!

Slab-sided judgment on the dismal tombs!
Drear hopeless hymns, a stern-faced God that saves,
the actual shrivelled flesh they rhymed with – wombs.

They were so little, childlike, small and bent,
large noses, crooked mouths – the 'dear remains'
fitted a child's neat coffin, one long Lent

of self-denial all three sisters kept,
killed by consumption and their dreadful drains.
The words alone flashed out where rainstorms wept!

2 Political

They really loved the Duke of Wellington,
they were a nest of tiny troubled Tories –
as colourful as parakeets and lories,

flaming with passion and 'Thy Will Be Done'.
Yet in that free-for-all, that *fritto misto*,
they didn't truly relish an *aristo*.

The cultured, polished people at the Grange,
the 'plaid silk frock', the 'burnished shoes', 'white
                                    trousers',
meant nothing to these cats – they were all mousers

out on the moors and wild, far out of range.
They never were lukewarm, or smooth, like lotion,
what they liked best was fierce untamed emotion.

Charlotte was adamant in saying how
Jane Austen was all right, after a fashion,
but very superficial, short of passion,

not 'spitted on the horns of a mad cow'
(a very telling phrase of Emily's)
but quite at home in high-born femilies,

without 'fresh air', 'blue hill' or 'bonny beck' –
instead the fenced-in flowers, the fine 'neat borders'.
Almost, all three preferred the lower orders.

3 Personal

Branwell alone, with the greatest regularity,
filled the old Black Bull with Hibernian hilarity,
just the coarser sex with convivial vulgarity –
        they called him Patrick easily
            when drinkers filled the inn!

Branwell alone, taking opium with civility,
quickly overturned all his painterly ability,
oh, wasn't he the quare one, with his talkative virility –
        they called him Patrick openly
            when drinkers filled the inn!

124

Branwell alone, in that gloomy old sorority,
broke out in a male and a masculine minority,
chasing after tail, with a fig for all authority –
        they called him Patrick drunkenly
          when drinkers filled the inn!

Branwell alone, with a drinking man's proclivity,
shining like a star as an agent of activity,
acted out the dreams they repressed in their
                        passivity –
        they called him Patrick praisingly
          when drinkers filled the inn!

Don't Make Me Hate You!

Foxtrot Song with Introduction

Your jealousy and bad temper –
oh, keep them under control!
What they do to my love for you
is to redefine it and undermine it
like a mole!
I know you're not a phoney,
a pseud or a slut –
so please don't make me
say to myself:
I'm very fond of you BUT . . .

Don't make me hate you!
I'm not happy to hate you!
Please just try to act
with a little . . . tact,
a lass can make a lad
feel so very sad!

Don't make me hate you!
I don't want to hate you!
When those things you say
make my heart turn away
or make me get mad
I feel oh, so sad!

I don't want to leave you –
so don't make me go!
Oh, I won't deceive you,
it's only when you're acting like a
so-and-so
that I want to go!

Don't make me hate you!
I just hate to hate you!
It's when you behave
as though I were your slave –
then I do feel bad,
so depressed and sad!

Aros Castle

I first saw Aros Castle when I was ten, in 1926 –
a ruin with a great ruined window like an eye.
My father took me shooting rabbits. I can fix

all that in my mind. There was a man with a ferret,
the rabbits lived under the rocks, quite near the shore.
I shot my first-ever rabbit. I was proud with acquired
                                        merit.

And on the small headland the Castle sat still,
looking like a picture postcard view from a window.
After that summer I didn't see it again until

I came to Mull in 1937 (I was twenty-one),
I was reading *Present Indicative*, I'd just finished
                                        Cambridge,
I had no job in prospect, a lot remained to be done,

it was hot and we drove Margery's car round the
                                        island roads,
Calgary, Gribun and so on, a lovely summer,
and the Castle still sat there like something with loads

of time on its hands. The eye never blinked or
                                        shifted.
It stood there clear. If it vanished, it would come
                                        back –
as soon as the rain stopped or the mist lifted.

When (in 1967?) I saw it again
I had Margo with me, it was Easter,
a huge rabbit popped up and eyed us with disdain

outside the window, at breakfast. The world had
                                        carried
on with its wars and its worries, the Castle
                                notwithstanding,
and I had been eleven years married.

That eye never closed. It wasn't designed for sleeping.
It seemed (perhaps this is the pathetic fallacy)
as though it had Time or something in its own
                                        safe keeping.

In 1968 we brought the kids before its unchanging
                                        face.
Jane had to dive into Tobermory Bay from a boat
among a lot of jellyfish. It was part of a race.

And this year, 1981, was (so far) the last time.
I once walked to the Castle – its base is smothered in
                                        nettles
and walking round it isn't much of a pastime.

I think it's nearly 500 years old, but I might be
                                        wrong.
Obviously someone once took trouble to destroy it –
it's a long time since, as a castle, it was really on
                                        song!

Man and boy, you might say, I've been there and
                                        seen it,
as tourist and time-traveller. If they holocaust us
(if Reagan and the Russians really mean it)

I bet that crumbling picturesque dump outlasts us!
Meanwhile it's into thoughtfulness, if not depression,
that that non-seeing picture postcard eye creepily casts
us.

The Good Companions

They stand behind you and whisper:
Fill your glass! and *Fill your plate!*
Now they are nameless, but later you'll know their
names,
fiends and familiars with eating and drinking games:
Big Belly and Red Nose and Brain Damage.
They'll find you, sure as fate!

Tip-tankards, they jog the elbow:
Let's finish it! Have the other half!
They'll be your companions throughout your later
life,
the Knights of the Blissful Bottle, the Knavish Knife,
Lord Blood Pressure, Lady Redvein-Cheeknet,
the lewd litre, the loud laugh!

I could do with a drink! they whisper,
Oh, for a knife! Oh, for a fork!
Though they're refined gourmets and eat a lot of
French
you'll know them by a very piglike kind of stench,
Lady Burper, Bad Breath, Fartwell –
all dying for the popping of a cork!

A Wordsworthian Self-Apostrophe from the Fourth Floor of the Hotel Admiral (Copenhagen)

Relax. Relax. It's 8 o'clock. The gulls patrol the
                                    harbour.
It's a perfect Danish winter morning.
A man is fooling about with a snow-machine,
a brush that whirrs a pathway on the quay.
A little snow-blizzard looks to be blowing,
but you're inside and warm; with loved ones far
                                    away,
Margo, Jane, Julian, the family names –
Victorian sentimentality, but still are loved ones
and absence makes the heart grow fonder,
though some say out of sight is out of mind.
Wordsworthian thoughts! And soppy Richard Jefferies
prosed of the fine physiques of 'dearest Greece'
(*The Story Of My Heart*, your journey book).

Relax. Relax. The gulls float by the window.
So much of life is so repetitive.
Breakfast comes up, five kinds of bread and coffee.
The roll is hundreds-and-thousands in caraway seeds –
I love the little buggers – remember what Churchill
                                    said
when Admirals plonked Traditions of the Service.
The joy of caraway seeds and coffee!
And you reflect that this is a blue city
and Wordsworth wouldn't have liked it.
Apparently, the sex-shows need a hush,
cathedral silence, solemn and complete –
the man cannot maintain his proud erection
in face of ribald cries, or shouts, or laughter.

Relax. Relax. Baby, it's cold outside!
Life below freezing. The Danish word for scissors?
Your nails need cutting. Such minutiae
aren't part of the egotistical sublime –

but they're important to the traveller.
Long poems spread the inspiration thin
like Danish butter on the varied bread.

And in the night a fucking great ship ties up
(to use the language of sailors) – the *Prinsesse*
                              Margrethe –
perhaps about fifty yards from the hotel window.
It looks huge and reminds you of Newhaven.

'Hills that purify those who walk on them'
I read in Jefferies. You might as well write:
'Ships that purify those who sail in them'.
The snow keeps up. You mean, keeps drifting down.
All prepositions are a wayward race.

Hot news comes in – a Right Wing coup in Spain.
Young Wordsworth wouldn't have liked it, the old
                              one wouldn't have cared.
It makes *you* feel quite sick. You're back once more
in 1936, and twenty years old. Spain, a Republic.
You can't do much about it (you couldn't then).
Franco didn't end upside down, like Mussolini.

Abortive – comes the news. Long, sighed relief!

Freedom a topless bar where tits are swinging –
the bad régimes are bras to crowd them in.

Your Copenhagen Guide says 'Topples Girls',
with Spanking, Animal, Rubber, Urine, Chains.

Jefferies gets better – on the Victorian vice of work
and how many millions slave to keep alive –
a kind of blue sky socialism. He didn't believe in God
but neither did he credit Evolution.
In ways, a Lawrence before his time –
in 1883 the legs were limbs.

Oh, such limp verse could limp right on for ever –
as Wordsworth in his garden paced up and down
                              composing,

to spout it all out to Dorothy, a kettle on the boil
and she receptive, humble as the teapot,
ready to write it down.

Relax. Yours is a similar domestic brew.
Drift lazy like the gulls. Sex, love and politics
won't stop for you, an engine idling.
Those gulls bring a message too: relax, relax.

23 February–2 March
revised 28 April, 1981

In Another Country

Our bodies have changed
and are no longer the same
as those that had connection
a quarter century ago;

the scar by the nipple
where the cancer was excised,
the blotch where radiation
burned sore the tender skin;

the womb quite removed;
and a grey white streak
badgers your forehead –
though you still sing in tune.

I too am altering;
fatness and falling hair,
grey at the temples;
wartlike excrescences

appear on my back,
on my arms and legs;
grave-marks on hands.
I'm more like an old frog

131

than I ever used to be,
twinged by arthritis,
gout warnings in toes.
I have more in common

with our vintage cat
than with the children.
All this is not amazing
in a life where old poets

retire into envy
and drink themselves to death
among their admirers
in out-of-the-way places.

Ageing is a faintness
like a line in Shakespeare:
old, old, old, old.
Say it over and over.

Prep School Days

*The ivy clusters thickly round the old grey stones. The
King is on his throne and the pound is worth a pound.
Over in Europe the comic foreigners are jabbering and
gesticulating, but the grim grey battleships of the British
Fleet are steaming up the Channel and at the outposts of the
Empire the monocled Englishmen are holding the niggers at
bay.*

– George Orwell, 'Boys' Weeklies'

Old Boyce was telling us about Lord Curzon,
how he stood 6ft 3in in his socks
and was Viceroy of India.
In winter the visiting mothers had furs on
when Half Term interrupted timetables and clocks –
and the pitches were windier.

But young Mr Curran, in his suede shoes,
with his pullovers and wavy hair,
said we should be grateful for the Soviet Experiment.
He was new. From Oxford. We accepted his views.
It was the Spanish-named French Master who raged
                                        like a bear,
causing dismay and merriment.

He was small but very spruce and dapper,
dented desks with pointers, wore double-breasted
                                        waistcoats
and well-tailored suits.
We read Westerman and Henty and Sapper
and went for seaside walks by the rocks and windy
                                        boats.
In our concrete pool we naked-bathed like newts.

On the nude bottoms, beaten for various offences,
everyone pruriently wondered at the purple-red marks
(did the Art Mistress get quite riggish?) –
we knew little of the sins of the senses.
'Hath he *marks* to guide us to him?' A hymn-joke.
                                        What larks!
'Please, Sir, Henderson's being piggish!'

I had homesickness and nervous insomnia,
nightmares, afraid-of-the-dark, even infantile
                                        croup . . .
but it's the neurotics that get the books written.
In schola privata pereunt omnia . . .
There's probably a Latin tag in all that alphabet soup.
The Matron said I should read a book called *Every
                                        Inch A Briton*!

But I was good at games, with timing if not muscle,
masochist tackler, Captain of the Rugger Fifteen, not
                                        too pathetic –
the English Master gave me nothing but praise.
There were two Heads in partnership – Wetherall and
                                        Russell.

133

Russell was fatherly and very sympathetic.
I think of him with a backward love, from those prep
school days.

In the Old People's Home (1914)

This is the last anchorage. HMS *Incontinent*
is in trouble and signals of distress
come from HMS *Repetitive* and HMS *Wanderer*.
HMS *Anxiety* is getting steam up.
The harbour is full of signs of activity,
which are all ignored by HMS *Vainglorious*
as she rides at anchor in perpetual majesty.

Across the water, puffing busily,
come the officious tugs *Snapper* and *Orderly*.

Violent Passions

The mouth can be quite nasty in a bite
The lover's pinch can be malicious too
Legs kick, as well as tangle, in a bed

Words can be harsh and not console or rhyme
Fighting is also love's especial food
Hands can enlace with hands or round a neck

The tools that pierce can be unyielding steel
Attractive nails can score, like claws, the face
Fingers can spread on cheeks, harmful and strong

Hair can be pulled in war, that's stroked in peace
The fighting female differs from the male
The spitting cat attacks the barking dog

Boom Christmas

Because the people of Britain know that the end is
                                              nigh
and the Instruments of Satan are already installed on
                                              our shores,
they go mad for the Good Life, for the glass and the
                                    food and the thigh,
lusting after Consumer Goods like kerb-crawlers after
                                              whores . . .

They know this is their Last Chance, it may not come
                                              round again,
they know the sizzling turkeys may well be the Final
                                              Birds
and each one knows what's fried may possibly be his
                                              brain,
as the comforting Christmas carols ascend in their
                                    fifths and thirds . . .

And all this is traditional, in times of great Dying and
                                              Plague,
like the Fornication on Tombstones and the
                                    Drunkenness in the Streets,
it's a clear indication of a Giant Despair, it's not in
                                    any way vague –
now it means bodies in plastic bags, as once it meant
                                    winding sheets.

The Winter Hotels

Oh, think of hotels where the stars of the bars
        say 'What'll you have?'
and the barmaid's a ringer for an opera singer
        in *Pag*. or in *Cav*.!
They're sad out of season, with very good reason,
        commercials alone

keep the whole thing going, the whisky flowing.
    They lower the tone –
but that bosomy beauty must do her duty
in season and out,
like a loyal Boy Scout . . .

When the men get flirty and jokes are dirty
    as children's knees
(though the family fun is over and done
    and the winter seas
bash the pier about, no one ventures out,
    and the winds are gales)
that's the time when Rosy can feel quite cosy
    with her ring of males,
from richest to poorest (not one is a tourist),
a hub of desire
like a glowing gas-fire . . .

For the mums and dads and the likely lads
    are away and gone –
how could they stay? And that holiday
    has now moved on,
it's there perhaps in the album snaps,
    as the seaweed dries
(that they took from here as a souvenir)
    and the summer flies
that annoyed the drinkers, the laughing winkers,
have buzzed and are dead
by the windowpane's lead . . .

Nobody talks about undercliff walks
    and the lounge's gloom
is deep and dreary, where boozed and beery
    in that roistering room,
with their sexy singing, the boys were bringing
    the place to life –
a tolerant smile, at least for a while,
    on the lips of a wife,
condoned the offence and the pounds and pence,
as the money was spent,
flickered and went . . .

The short winter's day brings blight and decay,
     a pub's like a church
where the evening dims without any hymns –
     and the salesmen lurch
into sweet liqueurs and the brash 'What's yours?'
     like a loud response
echoes in night and the ailing light
     makes bar-sinks fonts.
Though there's nothing wrong with this evensong,
what's worshipped here
is just brass and beer . . .

Gods and Heroes

And then, like doves or long-winged thrushes caught in a
net across the thicket where they come to roost, and meeting
death where they had only looked for sleep, the women held
their heads out in a row, and a noose was cast round each
one's neck to dispatch them in the most miserable way. For
a little while their feet kicked out, but not for very long.
    Next Melanthius was dragged out across the court and
through the gate. There with a sharp knife they sliced his nose
and ears off; they ripped away his privy parts as raw meat for
the dogs, and in their fury they lopped off his hands and feet.

    – Homer, *The Odyssey* (translation by E.V. Rieu)

Odysseus himself didn't do this – but he ordered it.
He didn't mind being covered in blood and shit.
Victorian Hellenists showered him with love,
equally with Gentle Jesus and the Holy Dove,
they taught the young gentlemen to adore the Greeks
in long school terms that lasted weeks and weeks.
Perhaps as English animal-lovers they found
sentimental satisfaction when the old hound
recognizes him – Odysseus drops a tear –
at his homecoming after the umpteenth year
of fairy story adventures and active fun
(Pallas Athene kept putting blanks in the gun

so that *he* always survived, *he* wasn't shot;
his comrades were expendable – Odysseus not.
Not Wanted On Voyage, one could almost say,
as they met sticky ends in every possible way).
Perhaps, too, Victorian eyes grew dim
when his Old Nanny recognizes him.
This also, for her, is a tearful scene.
Though Odysseus, naturally, isn't so keen
to have it known universally that he's back.
He seizes her by the throat and says 'One more crack
out of you and I'll see you meet your death
on the day that all the Suitors run out of breath!'

Odysseus is quite like Hitler – or like Goebbels –
he comes through cruel and sly as·Homer burbles
on and on in his primitive masterpiece,
laying the foundation of The Glory That Was Greece;
he couldn't really be much trickier or slyer –
you could call him The Trickster, or even The Liar.

The modern counterpart to fix on
might be, conceivably, Richard Nixon.
Cooling, the earth and planets move –
our politics don't much improve.
We grumble about rates and taxes,
what falls in Africa is axes,
chopping up unwise opponents
into their separate components.

We're civic bees (a liberal hive),
while they skin Russians (and alive)
in not-so-far Afghanistan –
Stalin was much like Genghis Khan
(more devious though) in some respects.
No need to strain your intellects
to see that we've not grown much better
since someone carved that first stone letter.
The ghastly blinkered mad religions
kill unbelievers like rock pigeons.
All Faith, they say, is like a jewel –
but why is it so bloody cruel?

The Bob Hope Classic Show (ITV) and 'Shelley Among The Ruins', Lecture by Professor Timothy Webb – both Saturday evening, 26.9.81

1   Here's the Bob Hope Classic Show,
    devoted to the status quo!
    All the seasoned showbiz comics
    love their leaders, their Atomics
    lost in pools where chicks plunge in
    and the wide-brimmed Texas grin
    isn't black or dispossessed,
    likes big money, girls undressed,
    rides hell for leather, clippity-cloppity,
    at anything that smells of property.

    Money is the Cleopatra
    that seduces Frank Sinatra –
    fat and ugly women too,
    all Republicans, all who
    (lookalikes of old Liz Taylor)
    never dug mad Norman Mailer.
    They have money, and the gumption,
    with conspicuous consumption
    to flaunt how wonderful they are –
    that note they hit will always jar
    while poverty is still around
    and every day is gaining ground.
    A country shared out by the Mafia!
    To call it great – what could be daffier!

    They tie one on, they go on benders, on
    us falls the blight of Dickie Henderson!

2   Eng. Lit. goes hand in hand with Architecture,
    with a small audience, quiet in Keats House
    on that same evening, at a lantern lecture –

the contrast of the mountain and the mouse
you well might think, the caring and the callous,
    the brash unthinking and the ones with nous.

A slide of Shelley (the Baths called Caracalla's),
    he sits there reading with an open collar –
nothing could be more different from Dallas

    and thought that's ruled by the Almighty Dollar –
he liked composing in the free fresh air.
    In that bright landscape he's the bright corolla,

a troubleshooter, like oil's Red Adair,
a man who thought Society should be fair.

Professor Webb tells us that ruins, for *him*,
    weren't simply beautiful or picturesque
(such thoughts were decadent, effete and dim)

    but like a lesson taught from History's desk
that showed how in the end the bad régimes
    were just traced patterns like an arabesque

figuring the desert, scarcely remembered dreams,
    and tyrants ended strictly for the birds
who lived for grandeur and the victim's screams,

    like Ozymandias. The wealth, the herds
of stricken slaves, all vanished in thin air,
    gone like the breath of long-since-spoken words:

Look on my works, ye Mighty, and despair!
Yes, Shelley thought Society should be fair.

And so from ruins what *he* drew was hope –
    unjust societies could lie down and die –
they made his heart leap like an antelope,

140

he thought that one day there might well be pie
in equal portions shared to one and all
    and not reserved (and doubtful) in the sky.

His optimism, we think, wasn't small.
    Ruins didn't make him sad, quite the reverse,
failure was shadow from a hope so tall

    it spread its radiance into all his verse;
although injustice got into his hair,
    he thought the better would succeed the worse

and never gave in limply to despair –
a man who thought Society should be fair.

Cruel and Unusual Punishments

How a masochist must long for the electric chair!
The wonderful bondage of his/her hands and feet,
the claustrophobic hood fitting over the face,
the metal cap so snug on the shaven cranium,
the plate on the shin and best of all
o best of all
the gagging effect of the mouthpiece –
so leather and lovely
that Spinkelink, asked for his last statement,
could only say 'I can't speak!'
which the Governor elected to take for his last
                                    statement.

Surely one could find volunteers to be electrocuted!
Just as people who agitate to bring back hanging
are always writing in for the job of hangman
or, it may even be, of hangwoman;
they are the sadists, the positives to that negative.

Towards the End of a Novel of 1910: A Passionate Outburst

For nearly a full year
these were the words I dearly longed to hear!
I love you – when you said them in the conservatory,
with the clashing billiard balls just audible
and later the doomful and ominous gong
as it were spreading the news, for from that little
                                    statement
grows a great volume of sound,
church choirs, responses, vows, vows and vows!

I waited so very long
for those few stuttering notes to burst into song!
I love you – from the prominent bosom and the
                            narrow-waisted gown
that constricted your softness, I accepted it,
the sigh from your head on my shoulder,
like a waft of cigar scent on some dark summer
                                    terrace
it flavoured the warmth of the night,
giving rise to events, a smoke message,
                        important . . .

I had faith and belief,
like a beleaguered town that daily expects relief!
I love you – I knew I should hear it from the
                            finger-traced lips
and I revolved it in my mind like the
dark brown brandy in the glass,
a pleasure to come, a delight to be savoured,
a future enclosed in a phrase,
so we could go forward like trains at signals greening!

In Memoriam Sir John Betjeman
(1906–84)

So the last date slides into the bracket
that will appear in all future anthologies –
and in quiet Cornwall and in London's ghastly racket
we are now Betjemanless.
Your verse was very fetching
and, as Byron might have written,
there are many poetic personalities around
that would fetch a man less!

Some of your admirers were verging on the stupid,
you were envied by poets (more highbrow, more
                                        inventive?);
at twenty you had the bow-shaped lips of a Cupid
(a scuffle with Auden too).
But long before your Oxford
and the visiting of churches
you went topographical – on the Underground
(Metroland and Morden too)!

The Dragon School – but Marlborough a real dragon,
with real bullying, followed the bear of childhood,
a kind of gentlemanly cross to crucify a fag on.
We don't repent at leisure,
you were good, and very British.
Serious, considered 'funny',
in your best poems, strong but sad, we found
a most terrific pleasure.

Christmas Holidays

The Imperial War Museum was once quite small,
housed in part of a building in Whitehall.
I went there in the Christmas Holidays when I was
                                        ten –

standards, pistols, carbines; red squares, charging men
in that partly romantic art that cannot be said to lie
but still doesn't adequately express how woefully men
                                             die.
Uniforms worn by Troopers and Generals, no doubt,
models of guns perhaps – but one thing stood out. . .

'The skull of a man shot from a gun,' it said.
And there was this unremarkable bony head.

It didn't say who he was, or what he had done.
I realized this was a punishment and not horeseplay or
                                            fun.
I didn't even know for certain if he was killed.
I'd seen a man shot from a gun, and I'd been thrilled.
He landed in a net the other side of the arena,
stood up and took a bow – with a pleased and
                              untroubled demeanour.
Bertram Mills' Circus, a holiday treat, at Olympia.
But here the evidence that he came through was very
                                much skimpier –
nonexistent in fact. I imagined him pushed down the
                                    barrel,
then flying through the air like a Christmas carol.
Would he land on his feet, would he be all right?
I pondered these things quite a lot of the night.

I hoped he survived. But the skull? That was a puzzle.
There's a sadistic drawing of a man tied to a gun's
                                muzzle
in Gilbert's *Bab Ballads*; his eyes pop out of his head,
the gunner holds the fire. It's clear he'll soon be dead,
exploded over everything. The best execution to choose
(thought the British in India) because it upset Hindus.

I found out all this, bit by bit, and the more I was
                                enlightened
the more I became aware of evil, and frightened.
Guilt, Sin, Retribution: tracks in the brain,
                        deep-grooved.

When I next went there, that exhibit had been
                                        removed.

NOTE   *I have been told that the collection I saw was not in
fact part of the Imperial War Museum, but of a similar
institution.*

In Favour of the Greek

Like old men who long for their cocks to
leap up and run like an agoraphobe in the
marketplace to that desirable denseness,

that female festivity where all the
most holy odours dwell, so pleasing to
men and gods, and Zeus in particular,

where the rites are the rites of Aphrodite and
every couch or bed is blessed like a
temple by the glorifying goddess –

like these, at the end of our life, at the
end of a long run in the sand, or a
wrestling or the throwing of a javelin,

we know the Games move to a close for
the other sands run in the hourglasses, also
time is proclaimed by the wet clepsydra

as well as the clepsammia; these are the
stolen hours the poets often take into
their melodious and mythomanic cognizance,

and the Games too are only a figure and
our dying eyes can just see the wood nymphs that
are gathering round in a forest of metaphors.

The Black Mass

(See A.E.W. Mason, *The Prisoner in the Opal*)

Who are these people in the room to watch us? They
                                         are the initiates –
the ones in cloaks, the ones in masks, the ones
                                          shrouded,
the woman of pleasure, the criminal woman, the
                                seeker black with ingratitude,
the bogus intellectual, the Judge with ambitions, the
                                      fat aristocrat,
they are in love with malice and wishing for evil.

She is nude as a chicken neck, she lies crosswise,
arms stretched, feet together, she is the altar, a living
                                       woman.
The worshippers are muttering and whispering with
                                  the hum of bees,
there are wraps, white shoulders, she lies on a black
                                     coffin-pall,
her eyes are closed, her breasts rise and fall with
                                  tumultuous breathing.

A great lamp in the ceiling throws down light, golden
                                  and dazzling.
The celebrant prostrates himself. From silence he
                                begins the service
with the true Mass, the Mass meant to deceive, the
                                Latin prayers,
spoken to entice the True God into the bread and
                                  wine,
so that the mockery and the wickedness can begin.

I am wearing the black velvet tunic, the incense hurts
                                  my eyes,
the scarlet velvet cassock, the lace-edged surplice, the
                                mask with purple lips,
crowned with the red hair, the Judas colour.
I am a woman like her. In the church I've studied
the wayward swaying of the acolyte.

146

Nobody recognizes me. Although I'm afraid of him
he's self-absorbed, he licks his lips in triumph,
he hardly notices me. I know the occult backwards,
I worked in a library once from M to O,
I know how Christ hangs upside down on his cross.

They are all masked except him. She wears a black
                                        silk mask,
she too is deep in an aura of triumph, her eyes shine
                                        bright,
he has the priest's cassock, the alb and stole. He is
                                        dreaming,
as I swing the gold censer by its linked gold chains,
remembering history's brilliant followers of Lucifer.

The light falls downwards on the cold clear picture –
she crosses herself upwards, not downwards, with her
                                        thumb –
she only is important and Adonis is important,
there will be a sty of animals met in a battle of lust,
but still the fine young god dispenses only the cold.

I look beyond my long-curled-delicate-eyelashed mask
and see the picture. Adonis the Sterile, Satan –
The Grimoire of Honorius advocates murder –
the two big golden six-branched candelabra,
with tall black candles stinking with sulphur and pitch.

On one panel naked figures dancing back to back,
white fat human faces, pain, rewards and tortures
and Satan's blue eyes that burn unbearably bright,
unutterable sadness, a youth, slender, erect,
white as a girl, the face too delicate.

And now the spoiled priest calms the blasphemies
and leads them to his purpose. As at the sacred climax
a great trembling takes her body and limbs, cries
                                        uttered low
like the whimperings of an animal, I see that still
my bracelet haunts her wrist, good evil omen.

He holds the chalice high above his head,
places it down between her breasts, three times.
The third time, and the cries become one long-drawn
                                          wail,
a strong convulsion shakes from head to foot,
her arms relax, a rattle scours her throat.

The knife comes down, the hidden knife comes
                                          down,
the blood runs into the cup, a broken, conjuror's
                                          rhythm,
I am the magician's girl who does not flinch:
'Now, if ever, greet your worshippers!
You have a sacrifice worthy of you! Come, oh come!'

The knife hilt upright, shafted in her flesh.
Above her heart one breast is striped with blood.
I am exhausted, frozen, I know I still must run –
until the cloak is thrown over my head,
the hand over my mouth. I do faint then.

Innocence

*'I love these little people; and it is not a slight thing when
they, who are so fresh from God, love us.'*

> – Narrator in *The Old Curiosity Shop* by
> Charles Dickens

No, not so.
Babies love only themselves
and think the whole world is there for them.
Children are selfish
and learn only slowly not to grasp and grab.
Even the cutest kid
is far less Ego than Id.

In 1940,
a hundred years after
Dickens went so overboard for Little Nell,
that Adolf Hitler
was plastering England with jealous bombs
in a childish rage
only enemy blood could assuage.

Yet they *have*
an innocence, they're honest,
the one thing they can't do is pretend,
infants speak true,
what they feel they certainly show.
They're not divine –
but they're not hypocritical swine.

Robert Graves

When Robert Graves got involved
with a wildly unsuitable woman
his problems were *not* solved –

though he, later, did get married
to a much more suitable woman.
But he was considerably harried

by an arrogant arid virago –
a madly unsuitable woman.
If he'd sailed off in an Argo

like Jason, and left them all screaming
(each clearly unsuitable woman),
it might have been better – but dreaming

of Goddesses (White) and of Muses
(the *younger* unsuitable woman)
is what the male masochist chooses!

O Governesses and O Nurses!
From the strains of Unsuitable Women
came the excellence of his verses!

Are You Married or Do You Live in Kenya?

(A Young Man Projects Himself into a High Life Fantasy)

I'm there in the Aberdare Highlands
with Diana and Joss – and all the others –
where all the little drinkipoos
can make us fairly stinkipoos
and you can't identify the fathers,
though you know the mothers
(oh yes, you very definitely know the mothers).

I'm there in the twenties and thirties,
drinking in Tart's Hotel and the Gin Palace,
voyeurs bore holes in bedrooms
and what's done in the said rooms
is known to all the decadent de-lovelies
who admire the Phallus
(it really is White Worship of the Phallus).

So many names with 'de' as prefix!
Lord de Robinson will be *my* handle –
half-seas-over, floating seawards,
Idina blows the feather mewards . . .
it's sixty-nine perhaps, with a new partner,
or putting out the candle
(old dirty talk said 'putting out the candle').

Zebras, leopards, herds of eland,
a lovely landscape makes us all light-headed
as much as sexy joys do
(hard work is what the boys do),
wives are in common here and so are husbands,
no woman goes unbedded
(the Old Etonians see they're not unbedded!).

NOTE *See* White Mischief *by James Fox, concerning the murder of Lord Erroll by a fellow-Etonian.*

150

Places

Some poets love a county like a person –
and that could certainly be said of Gurney,
who made a Mecca almost out of Gloster,
bright as a star in childhood's Christmas stocking.
Imaginary but real, like thoughts of Heaven,
these local habitations have them bending,
Powys with Glastonbury, Housman's Shropshire,
Hardy with Dorset and his Cornwall doggy,
and Norman Nicholson alone in Millom,
all mixed in admiration, blended figgy
pudding and waits and dancing, Nine Men's Morris
and everything old and sanctified with honour.
The fiddlers play, and all the world goes round.

But I could never think like that of London,
London is good and bad, a teasing monkey
(remembered from a kids' book with a moral),
and not for worship in such all-out postures.
You know it, you can't love it, it's all changing,
it's not like Wenlock Edge or any fable,
the fine white buildings are its best of beauty,
it isn't sweet or quaint or bathed in cuteness,
it isn't Rome, New York, or French like Paris –
part stately, scruffy, treeful, never ranting
or boastful (though so praised by Dr Johnson),
it's not a dove, a sparrow, or a condor.
The thinkings that *I* feel don't make a sound.

I.M. Anthony Blunt

ob. 26 March 1983
Portsea Hall, Paddington

They took your body, in its coffin, to a battered
                                        whitish van,
    quite plain,
from the flat that held the Poussin. Only classic
                                        Poussin can,

151

unstirred,
remain
quite so classically unaltered by the fate of mortal
                                        man –
    no word
    of pain

ever shakes the dancing shepherds or the clear blue
                                        summer sky.
    It's sad
you were shaken by a maverick clever buccaneer like
                                        Guy.
    You had,
in one sense, a lot of genuine pressing thirties
                                    reason-why.
    Good, bad,

who should say, who saw the Fascists creeping up the
                                        'Europe' map?
    Dead? Red?
Both together not unusual! Hitler was the kind of
                                        chap,
    some said,
who stopped commies. Race against time! And the
                                    last important lap!
    He *led*!

Pressmen, who would sell their mothers for a
                        front-page story's sake,
        howled loud,
threw your fox-name (it was easy, just a piece of Fleet
                                        Street cake)
        to the vast
        hound-crowd.
I remember charm and knowledge, wit too – *that* was
                                        never fake –
        time past
        allowed.

152

Parnassian Conversations

I should be very mean indeed
if I ever criticized you for not being 'literary'
or not liking conversations that are Parnassian,

though this is the stuff on which some wives feed
and go for at parties, who make merry
in front of the Pashas and gyrate like Circassian

slave-girls at the Court of a Bard!
I don't want in any way to bend your nature –
after all, I can't sing in tune, I'm not numerate.

People are people, it would be very hard
if there were some piece of Lit. Law or legislature
that said everyone had to have the same sense of
                                        humour! It

would be cruel and useless to say 'Love Hardy, or
                                        else . . ..'
not everyone is sensitive to nuances that are verbal,
even God is in the end a matter of personal opinion –

I can't jump on you like policemen with big boots,
                                ski jumpers at Hels-
inki, for not skipping through Ashbery like a gerbil!
Your love is far more important than Yeats or
                                Laurence Binyon!

Only a Few Thousand Can Play

Poetry is a very ancient indoor game
like chess and draughts and knucklebones;
it can arouse emotion, it can be fun,
but you must always remember the galaxies
where the writ of T.S. Eliot does not run,

and the streets that are full of don't-knows
with other ways of using spare time;
verse-writing is a hobby, or a craft,
pursued by the uncommitted singleton
who into a great sea launches his raft,

not knowing quite where he will land or how,
if the rough rhymes will hold the logs in place
or the dovetailing stand the tall waves.
It's only then that the artificer
sees how, in rough weather, it behaves.

Can a Woman Be a Shit?

Can a woman be a shit?
The short answer, I'm afraid, is Yes –
though you would never guess
when a lesbian feminist bursts into song,
saying how no woman can ever do wrong, or be
                                        wrong!

It's an insult just for men,
everybody has always said and thought;
they say good manners ought
to stop us using it when ladies are concerned,
but to tell the truth (not just female truth) it's often
                                        earned.

How could Evil have a sex?
It certainly doesn't have an age,
though on a Victorian page
you will find the innocent purity of the child.
But don't believe it! Evil's a card that's always wild.

Mysterious Africa

Sonnet Parnassien

Our ships around her coasts make daily nibblings
And touch her inlets and her deeper bays;
Mostly they unload and sail in a few days.
She is alone, a country without siblings.

Her dark interior, how sinister or happy?
Larger, at least, than any sailor knows.
We know giraffe, elephant, water buffaloes
(Tales of gorillas, cannibals, okapi) . . .

Zebra, lion, antelope are like small change –
But her exotic miles hold more than these,
Legends that we can misapply and bungle,

Beyond our limited nineteenth-century range,
Pygmies, they say – or giants tall as trees?
She keeps her secrets in her solid jungle.

What's in a Marriage?

Nobody knows what goes on in a marriage.

–Stewart Scott

Outsiders never see the inside –
what happens behind closed doors
they guess from the raised or succulent voices,
the dark cries of 'You bastard!'
or an ecstatic 'Oh, darling!'
(the things that don't get into Poetry Book Society
                                    Choices)

if they ever get so near the inside!
Mostly, at a party, a slip
or a metaphorical hem is showing,
there's a mood hinted at,
a two-way exchange of feeling,
an atmosphere of Before-the-Storm, or After (the
                                    thunder going).

There are lots of bullies on the inside,
weeping blackmails fill a room,
and quarrels stem from slight, or from very lost,
                                    causes.
Outsiders don't hear that
hidden passionate music –
they see the violins and trumpets poised only, during
                                    pauses . . .

155

Deathbeds

In the old days when people died
the whole family gathered round the bed
standing or kneeling (patriarchal or matriarchal)
and the last frail blessings and goodbyes were
                                        said . . .

and people also said things like 'His race is nearly run'
and 'Fear no more the heat o' the sun',

and the old cock had fallen into desuetude
and the womb no longer wept its blood –
yet the children stood there (filial and familial)
by the upright grandfather clock's sad ticking thud,
and everybody's tears made it an occasion not to be
                                        missed
as the last dutiful kisses were kissed . . .

but now they are spirited away, behind curtains,
hidden in hospitals, wrapped warm in drugs,
they don't see the kids for whom (paternal or
                                        maternal)
they had the love; and solitary, slower than slugs,
the unconscious hours move past them. Nobody
                                        wants to know
or cares exactly when they go . . .

The Man in the Opera Sings to His Loved One

You're like the jolliest picnic in a children's book,
like the bright sun in the morning is the way you
                                        look,
you're just the most beautiful dish that any cook
                                        could cook!

I simply adore kissing your ears and your toes,
it's all the course of true love – that's the way it
                                        goes –
you're wonderful enough to cancel out a whole
                            weekful of woes!

I feel terribly happy that I'm the one you like,
my desires all run away with me like a racing bike,
I am amplified like the song that goes into the mike!

And all I can think about is: What did I ever do
to deserve the First Prize of a marvellous person like
                                        you?
Hooray! that Fate singled me out to be the head of the
                                    queue!

Some Say

Some say
life is cheerless,
as when the son realizes
that the dead mother
has gone for ever
and all the variously-loved-ones
gone for ever . . .

Some say
there is a Heaven
where we meet again
those we want to meet –
but suppose some others
don't want to meet them
now or ever?

Some say
all you can hope for
is to practise an art,
do well with your work,
love a few people;
failures, successes
don't last for ever . . .

Into History

Marched eighty miles in five days; crossed a river.
We were going to cross, they said, another river – but
the nearest crossing was blocked by their 6000.
For five days, and hungry, we marched the river
                                        bank,
the enemy keeping pace on the northern side.
On the sixth, a forced march across a plain,
we got ahead; two damaged causeways, hasty
                                        sappering,
and we were over.

Two hundred miles or more in twelve starved days.

October 20. Scarcely a day's scarce rest.
October 21. Marched eighteen miles;
the next three days, another fifty-three.
Three marches more, they said, and we'd be safe –
the port, and home.

October 24, late in the day, the scouts came back.
Enemy ahead, they said, deploying for battle.

That night round a little village, clustering in,
ate skimpy rations, confessed sins, heard Mass,
and armed for battle.

At first light, knights and archers out.
A thousand yards ahead, across the field,
we saw the enemy, between the eachside woods,
stand or sit idle, breakfasting, with jokes,
some getting fighting-drunk (*our* wine was small!) –
such confidence in numbers, vast superiority.
The archers dug in stakes for cavalry.

Three or four hours of waiting, worst of all.
Cold muddy ploughland, sown with winter wheat.
So short of food nine days, nuts and berries
the archers' feeding. Rainwet and cold,

stood in our ranks, many with diarrhoea
but anchored there, mail leggings laced to plate
                                              armour,
foul with discomfort.

The order to advance. We stumbled slow and cold
over ploughed ridges. And into History . . .

NOTE *See the account of the battle of Agincourt (1415) in*
The Face of Battle *by John Keegan.*

Father Love

To see you standing there, a great big beautiful son,
twenty-three years old and back from two months in
                                              America,
gave me a pang; it was love, it was seeing a vision,
it was what Margo your mother was obviously
                                    feeling, with kisses;
for women, in spite of the Sisters, can have sons and
                                          love them.
But men kissing and holding aren't really part of our
                                          culture.
It's the slap on the back, something more than a
                                        handshake
yet not as emotional as the arms-round embrace.
I stood there. I was happy – but I never touched you.
I was pleased, I was proud as a parent, I said 'Hello,
                                          fruitcake!'
or some other greeting, banal from the Marx Brothers
                                        thirties . . .

That's the way it takes us, but it wasn't always so.
There were days of no stiff upper lip and no biting
                                        back tears.

America, some say, is a big crooked country
and has been since the Volstead Act and Jesus Saves
got it organized for crime (with what good
                                    intentions!) –
but you weren't coming back from the dead or some
                                    Ultima Thule,
although I suppose you could have been shot by a
                                    lunatic.

So perhaps emotion wasn't in place; but, once, men
                                    wept openly
and threw their arms about, hugging the prodigals
and squeezing the loved ones, both breathless and
                                    tearful.
I think the Greeks did, and even the Romans
who thought fairly highly, their books say, of
                                    hardness
and all the republican virtues. They did, yes, I think
                                    they did.

We are so used to the thought that nothing is perfect.
A novelist invents a most attractive girl with a nose
                                    like a ski jump
and we know for certain that (as with the moon)
                                    there's always a dark side.
But this was unlooked for and happy, pure gold on
                                    the stream bed
or a delicious chocolate coming random from the
                                    box.

St Syphilis and All Devils

As I sit eating a Heinz Big Soup
I can hear the choir of St Syphilis and All Devils:
they are singing for me in a little chapel-of-ease,
part of the ruins of St Erysipelas-the-Less.
Big Nasties in their robes conduct the service.

The motorways are chill, and cold the concrete,
there is no nourishment in a spaghetti junction,
the foods and wines are trapped in cold tin
as everywhere the sleety rain comes down
and all the cars whizz past like lions and demons.

Unemployed boys are freezing in disaster,
the frizzy-haired girls are cold as Eskimos,
everything is packaged, disaster is packaged,
human contacts are the taunts and stabbing,
dead boredom at home, outside the hellpacks . . .

And now they unwrap the little packaged wars
lodged in their tinsel at the foot of the Christmas tree,
there are little bangs and crackers; but the big presents
remain to the last. Who will get what? All the
                                    choristers
rise and explode in a giant crescendo . . .

Rusted iron in broken concrete and thin dead trees.
Clear on all the transistors that demonic choir
is singing enthusiastically of human breakdown,
fat fiends in surplices, St Syphilis and All Devils:
working for a profit, putting *us* in the collection.

'If'

If you can keep your head when all about you
   Are losing theirs and blaming it on you;
If you can trust yourself when all men doubt you,
   But make allowance for their doubting too:
                                    etc., etc.

My mother had it at home, framed on a wall.
Now, much less seriously, it's in the loo
(Kipling's Commandments) but still advice that you,
if you're wise, wouldn't deride at all.

161

The first two lines seem made for family rows
(it has a sort of floral, mistletoe, border);
'It's asking a lot!' my daughter says. Tall order
most certainly, fuller of whats than hows!

What feminist would want to be 'a man'?
Protestant work-ethic, stern and stoic;
might make a prig – but not a political cat –
yet it's consoling for the also-ran,
though we can mock, more humble than heroic,
we still can see what he was getting at.

Grandfatherism

If they want to make me a grandfather,
my children will have to hurry up –
I'm rapidly approaching that point of no return
where animated bust (or storied urn)
or mute verbosity of paper verse
are all that can go further than the hearse . . .

so, although the heart warms for children
(it's narcissism but universal),
no one may ever say 'Don't wake up Grumpy!
He's very tired!', 'Don't shout, it makes him jumpy!'
and the versatility of the genes
(that adds up to more than a row of beans)

may never be made manifest in my case.
I might be liverish and bad-tempered
and, if so, I apologize, well in advance –
I shall be past my best. And if, by any chance,
the little voices fall on my deafening ears,
they may have come too late – by a matter of twenty
years.

Conversation with a Friend in Cambridge

I seriously thought of writing this poem in the style
of Henry Newbolt, in the style of 1906, because at the
moment I have his *Selected Poems* to review, because
he (like my father) went to school at Clifton, because
my father was up at Christ's in 1906; there were
many complicated and sentimental reasons. Also,
more obscurely, because my father was thirty when I
was born and I first met you when I was an
undergraduate at Christ's in 1936 – thirty years after
he was there in 1906. O numerology!

So it's a long time, and forty-one years I should
guess since I saw you last.

So the conversation had to be about who was still
alive (the first consideration), about what they were
doing now. The obvious usual under such
circumstances. But also about that vanished
Cambridge before Petty Cury was a pedestrian
precinct, before the War, even. *Le monde
d'avant-guerre*, as the French might say. As Henry
Newbolt would certainly say: about Youth.

About who was in love with who (a grammarian
would say 'with whom'), who liked, who more than
liked; and in that not completely unchanged
Cambridge summer I tasted again the bitterness and
the sweetness of that time. The hardness of growing
up, the shyness that was painful. You told how
somebody who was thirty (a great age to people of
eighteen) explained to you how the good thing about
growing older was that you became less shy.

But we move on, everybody moves on. Youth has its
joys and its great unhappinesses. Nostalgia, longing to
go back? That's the last journey I would want to
make. No sensible person would ever want to be
young again. If we die in a time of peace we shall lie
cooling in a hospital, the orifices plugged with cotton
wool or wearing a sort of nappy (second childhood
indeed!) before they put us into the freezer to await
cremation or burial. But the people one likes are still
the people one likes . . .

163

Fair Women

When I was young
I used to see the
photographs in the paper
of the women for whom men
had seen fit to do murder:
big battleaxes or only half-pretty,
hauled into some court in some city.

They didn't seem
at all attractive –
photographs show most women
(at least the snapshotty ones)
not much apt to coax semen;
and in those prison-van circumstances
their charms didn't have the best of chances.

They weren't like stars
that gleamed on screens (like
shining-haired Joan Bennett);
with their supporting police
they were more like Mack Sennet,
bulging old bags, the targets for crowd hisses –
I couldn't imagine covering them with kisses.

But now I know
two people only,
always, are involved there –
and this is more of a mystery
than Holmes ever solved. There
is no place for cameras or other outsiders –
the only third person is Love, with her blazing
                                    outriders.

As each stood,
her V of hair dark,
so clearly, perfectly naked,
she seemed a goddess perhaps,
the man was proud to make it,

that love – the V between her legs a Y and furry,
her face in close-up (as photographed later) blurry . . .

On top of them
the men lay hard, and
sucked their pinksoft nipples
(they might have been terrible hags
or sluts – that view's other people's)
until long hatreds built up, or short quarrels,
to Death – nothing to do with photography or morals.

Three Weeks to Argentina

Shall I wave my little
Union Jack?
Shall I go all out for
a big attack?
Shall I sing: 'My country
right or wrong!'?
Shall I rattle out a
sabre song?

Or shall I write of
sailor boys
deep in the sea, that can
make no noise?
Or of feckless, careless
young marines
missed by the girls
and the wet canteens?

It's hard for an old man,
who's seen wars,
to welcome that devil
and his claws.

They reach from the ocean,
clash in the sky,
make the earth into
a shepherd's pie.

Professionals love it,
the admirals all,
a chance to show that they're
on the ball.
Newsmen like it,
because it's news –
but fathers and mothers
have different views.

17 April 1982

Did You See the Ace of Spades?

Tilly told me lots of bitchy stories about Adele Astaire . . .
'She saw me with Friedrich and with Prince Obolensky;
she is very jealous of these two tall, handsome men; she is
so hot to get a man and is so unable to. She has quickies
with the stage-hands. She calls them into her dressing-room
and they have her on the floor.'
    . . . I became rather cold towards Adele. She was rather
wild. I remember once in New York, she got out of my
Rolls-Royce on my side, by lifting her legs over the gear
lever, and deliberately showing everything in so doing. She
saw the expression on my face and said, 'Oh, hello! Did
you see the ace of spades?'

    – Edward James on Tilly Losch and Adele Astaire,
                                    The Observer, 18 July 1982

Fred and Adele Astaire!
Like Mickey Mouse and Minnie Mouse,
the simple innocent dancers!
Lady, Be Good! was there,
written in lights, the Empire, Leicester Square –

the songs, but not the show
(1928 and I was twelve)
because of the gramophone records
I did indeed know!
They still carry a strong nostalgic glow.

And, later, *Funny Face*,
this one I certainly saw,
puberty's edge, or just after –
but the blood didn't race
in heart, pulse or that forfended place.

She simply seemed quite cute,
comic and with no hint,
as she tap-danced with her brother,
of old forbidden fruit,
diamonds, spades or any other suit . . .

It's nice to know, with age,
that she was human too
(though who trusts feminine gossip?),
sexy, out of the cage,
and lived where lionsize desires rage . . .

After those five decades,
and I'd never seen it then,
(she aristocratically married),
though all desire fades,
I know a lot more about the ace of spades.

The Mischievous Boy

Love jumped on us before we knew his name,
twisted our arms at prep schools,
hid up our mothers' skirts,
oh! we were bent
by knitted bosoms
and that ladylike scent!

Love was a tyrant in his belted shorts,
was good at games and comely
just as the Bible said,
behind the scrum
a hardworked angel –
no wicked words like bum.

Love came, not physical in any way;
demanding friendship only,
the simple name of friend
was all we sought –
but his refusal,
what hellish pain *that* brought!

The Town Mouse and the Country Mouse

The country poets – Thomas, Gurney, Clare –
loving the landscapes, treescapes, cloudscapes,
seem far removed (as Hodge from Fred Astaire)
from all the sly sophisticated Byrons
who delight only in a town's environs.
The Mount of Venus is the hill *they* see,
where every hair in close-up is a tree.

For city-dwellers fields are cold and wet –
and full of dimwits, rustics, clodhoppers,
though land means money (no Lord can forget).
In overlordship they were unforgiving
and Clare, we know, could barely scrape a living.
The prosperous farmer never saw much harm
in the forced labour of his prosperous farm.

Patrons and peasants both, they could agree
that land's not landscape, treescape, cloudscape.
Crops from the soil and apples from the tree,
all of it business, warlike, they were waging –
there was a price on what looked so engaging.
Romantic barren land was not much good;
except as timber, who could love a wood?

The Puritans

The generally held view is that it's the ascetics
who think sexual intercourse so appalling,
and what in pop songs used to be called falling
in love; they use words like 'lusting'
and think it's all disgusting.

But in fact it's the homosexuals, male or female,
who really go off course and scream, and shudder
like a ship blown onto the rocks without a rudder,
at the idea of men and women copulating
and the warm wet of mating.

The attitude to the parents, perhaps? or are they
                                                jealous,
knowing they won't succeed in restraining
these heretics in marriage beds who're staining
the sheets with that tribute all must render,
as love's made flesh, and tender.

The Falklands, 1982

This must have been more like the Boer War
than anything seen in our lifetime,
with the troopships and the cheering,
the happy homecoming, the sweetheart-and-wifetime,
everything looking over and solved,
and no civilians involved –

except a few stewardesses, Chinese in the galleys
almost by accident taken
willy-nilly on The Great Adventure,
where the Argentine fusing of the shells was often
                                                mistaken –
lucky for each floating sitting duck.
Oh yes, we had luck!

Luck that the slaughtered World War I soldiers
who died on the Somme and at Arras
would have welcomed, in their dismal trenches –
though that's not to belittle the victory of the Paras,
who lost, all in all, very few dead,
good men, well led.

At home, indeed, it was terribly like the World Cup,
though far less bright, commentated, stagey,
security making the war news nil, mostly,
but good value when they finally stopped being
                                    cagey.
Was the *General Belgrano* really offside?
A few hundred died.

And the outstanding achievements of the great Press,
particularly that section called 'yellow',
that wrote 'Up yours!' on missiles, went berserk
and shouted 'GOTCHA!' in a giant coward's bellow –
and circulation rises, like *The Sun*.
But was it well done?

Kipling's 'Recessional' told us to beware of Hubris,
and not give way to flag-waving
(they don't in the Lebanon, or Northern Ireland) –
if men's lives are worth giving, they're also worth
                                    saving.
Who let them start the bloody thing?
That's the question, there's the sting.

Part Two *The So-Called Sonnets*

Sonnet: Pepys in 1660

Everybody is openly drinking the King's health!
The King is about to be back! There are bonefires
                                    everywhere!
Stable government, King and Parliament, not
                        Cromwell's wobbly son!
Yet Pepys, at sixteen, saw with satisfaction the King's
                                    beheading.
'There's a Divinity doth hedge a King,
rough-hew him how we will!' – Samuel Butler's joke.
Charles II promises a free pardon,
proceedings only against those named by Parliament.

As you read, you can see what is coming.
Exhumation and gibbeting of regicides –
hanging, drawing and quartering for those still living.
We are still in the century when Shakespeare died,
where the racks and the fires were not thought
                                    barbaric . . .
with Pepys, his music, his ideas of order, a civilized
                                    man.

NOTE   *20 October 1660 'I saw the limbs of some of our
new Traytors set upon Aldersgate, which was a sad sight to
see; and a bloody week this and the last have been, there
being ten hanged, drawn, and Quartered.'*

– Samuel Pepys, Diary

Sonnet: Equality of the Sexes

I'm sure if I were a woman I should hate
being regarded as someone designed by Nature
to answer the telephone, make sandwiches, make tea;
or be fucked, look after a family, wash, cook, sew.
I would want to be an engineer, I would want to be
                                                    regarded
as a person whose sex, though inescapable, was
                                                    accidental
and not of the first importance. Though we don't
                                                    deny
there *are* maternal feelings – and traces of
                                        masochism . . .

still, though men are in the rat race, and the American
                                                    Satan
with not much help from others could burn us all up,
even so – if men are devils – we mustn't think all
                                                    women
are perfect, downtrodden angels. There are nasty
                                        people about
of both sexes – surely you know some? Equally nasty
(or equally nice?) – that's one 'equality of the sexes'.

Sonnet: Your Turn in the Barrel

There's an old dirty story that goes like this:
There were seven men in an isolated mining
                                        community.
One, lately joined, asks 'What do you do about sex?'
'Well, you see,' they say, 'we have this barrel.
There's a special hole in it, very conveniently placed.
Every day one of us, naked, gets into the barrel. He's
                                        there all day.
Joe on Monday, Ike on Tuesday, Bruce on
                            Wednesday – and so on . . .'
'But what about Sunday?' 'That's your turn in the
                                        barrel.'

172

Surely this is a very potent parable.
Writers can always bear the criticism of others.
Criticism of *them*? They don't much like it.
Also, it applies to the deaths of other people –
most of us face them with some equanimity.
It's only when it's our turn that we seem much
                                        moved.

Sonnet: Snobs' Corner

When my daughter Jane went to the Holland Park
                          Comprehensive
she sat with two friends who had been at her Primary
                          School –
because they were bourgeois (one of them even an
                          aristocrat)
they all three spoke the BBC's standard Southern
                          English,
without a trace of the surrounding glottal Cockney.
At once they were mimicked, called toffee-nosed and
                          snobs.
The slurrers and h-droppers christened them Snobs'
                          Corner
(and indeed they weren't Cockneys, Irish or West
                          Indian).

This was all – in a roundabout way – good for them,
to meet unprivileged, poor people on equal terms.
But what I ask is, wouldn't it be better
if instead of the Two Nations, the Posh and Dustbin
                          education,
free or fee-paying, some effort was made to spread it
                          all equally?
To get the rulers and the ruled on the same side of the
                          fence?

Sonnet: Supernatural Beings

You can't ever imagine the Virgin Mary having
                                    vulvitis or thrush –
she's not a real woman, she's a supernatural being,
not like the real women who are snoring and farting.
Aldous Huxley in an essay said that the angels
painted so often in Italian pictures
would need huge pectoral muscles if they were ever
                                                to fly . . .
But angels, like the Virgin, are supernatural beings.
It's all done by magic. If you can, you believe it.

And not so much *if you can*, more *if you want to* –
if you want to imagine something a bit kinder than
                                            people,
full of love and bursting with benevolence,
you go for these smiling supernatural do-gooders
that look a little patronizing to an ordinary man
and still can't prevent you getting cancer or a cold.

Sonnet: Going to 'Guys and Dolls'

Of course, as soon as you add music, the whole thing
                                            changes.
Music can make even misery into beauty.
The small-time crooks, the tricksters, murderers, of
                                            the thirties
become somehow charming eccentric characters –
like the eighteenth-century highwaymen in *The
                                    Beggar's Opera*
who can all sing in tune and seem romantic,
or the starving students in the jollity of *La Bohème*.
The music gives everything an extra dimension.

Does it falsify? It's bound to falsify.
All music is always a great cheerer-upper.
Even the rough sound of the populist screaming
is mild compared to the hangovers and bad trips,

the sad teenagers, with unemployment hanging round
their necks.
You can transmute it, through a trumpet or a
saxophone.

Sonnet: Playing for Time

This was the telefilm of women in Auschwitz,
written by Arthur Miller, with Vanessa Redgrave
as the lean head-shaven French nightclub singer
in the camp orchestra – a great performance.
One critic called it Daughter of Holocaust
(a critic must have his little joke)
but it's only right we should be reminded
how racism persists right into the gas ovens (Jews
and Poles)

though humanity, common to all, should bridge the
gap.
And how all these things did actually happen.
From stress and malnutrition they stopped
menstruating,
their shaved heads too made them look sexless –
they could have been men. All you could say was
(and this was perhaps the point) they all looked
human.

Sonnet: The Power of Sex

While you're doing it, the love is genuine.
The animal tenderness wrapped in soft skin!
An impulse of real love, you're filled to bursting,
the caresses are their own love declaration,
however transitory it is, quick or commercial.
No Great Romance could do better,
speeches and attitudes and sensibility
much less Things In Common and Standard
Marriage . . .

175

But if you look in the eyes of a dog that's fucking,
he has an unaware, abstracted look.
He looks as though he isn't enjoying it much,
a question of physical jerks, exercise not pleasure.
The power of sex in us is very different.
Tenderness, gentleness, they're both built-in.

Sonnet: The Last Days

'Why have you put me here, underneath the earth?'
'You are still with us.'
'That cannot be. Beethoven is not here.'

      – Schubert in delirium, during his last illness

When you lie in a hospital, in an old folks' home, in
                     your final illness,
all your defences are down. The brothers and sisters
                    you didn't get on with
can visit you at will. Sly women who expect legacies
can come and knit by your bedside, buttering you up.
Boring women with tactless talk of the deaths of
                    relatives –
the kind of friends you could do without – they all
                    swarm round you.
Even looking at them makes you tired, let alone
                    talking,
and you are scarcely protected by bossy nurses or
                    matrons.

If you are one of the distressed gentlefolk who live
                    into their nineties
in a fee-paying establishment, you'll find they take
                    furniture,
pinching a chair, a small cupboard (if you have such
                    things of your own),
a dishonest night-nurse will take any trinket of silver,
even the silver-framed small photo of a wife or a
                    husband.
Life must go on, they agree. If you can no longer see
                them, what good are they to *you*?

Part Three

A Pilgrimage

W.H. Auden (1907–73)

Wystan Hugh Auden, poet, was born in this house on
the 21st February 1907 – *inscription on 54 Bootham, York*

*Max: By the way, I forgot to tell you. There's one possible
      I saw yesterday, Mrs Stagg – the wife of the
      under-manager at Windyacre Mine. We might do
      worse. Vegery gegoegod bust.*
Ceslaus: Tegight cegunt?
*Max: I should think so. Her mouth's small enough,
      anyway.*

> – Fragment from *The Enemies of a Bishop*,
>   unpublished play by Auden and Isherwood

Before you know quite where you are
you're standing there by Bootham Bar,
with handsome houses,
a now degraded road that feeds
traffic to Harrogate and Leeds,
a school that rouses

memories of one Cambridge friend*.
A.'s beginning is my end.
He started here,
Constance Rosalie gave out
a poet who was like a shout
and far and near

we clustered round to hear the Word
as clergymen ancestors deferred
to his new genius.
He put the thirties in their place,
Life hardly dared to show its face,
while like gardenias

---

* Frank Thistlethwaite, once at Bootham's School. The Auden
house is now one of the school buildings.

the lovely images were strown
in careless verses, quite full-blown,
bright in what's darker,
yet doomed, though serious and select,
to feel the Dracula Effect,
like Minna Harker.

The trouble of those old decades
before the telly and Teasmades!
He told of madness
deep in the body politic
(so right, though he himself was sick)
and all our sadness

whiffled down through those sensuous lines
where Western Decadence declines –
though, to speak truly,
much D.H. Lawrence nonsense too
was there to urge both me and you
to be unruly,

obey a Leader and take vows
while lovely women, those poor cows,
stayed strict at home.
(He made a U-turn of a sort
and finally came into port
not far from Rome.)

He was engaged once, married too,
and had a girlfriend he could screw,
but all his joys
lay in the arms of flaunting Chester
(a most notorious butch-molester)
and various boys.

Osborne and Carpenter declare
such doings as would raise the hair
on heads of Mormons –
if any lad has a wet dream
they beat him, naked, pray and scream –
what a performance!

He certainly gulped sex like food,
quite the reverse of any prude,
and, wholly greedy,
he wolfed huge helpings that he carved –
his cock was never stinted, starved,
or poor and needy.

That limestone landscape and those holes,
the lead mines that could save our souls –
a feminine body
and Mother's too, it seems to me.
There's not much else that it could be.
And, cute as Noddy,

he loved them and was never irked
although those mines were now not worked –
Dad's lust, I think,
was over, there was Mum, serene
and *his*; as though Dad hadn't been!
and with the ink

he poured such symbols, partly known,
into the poems. We should clone
not Dons or Wardens
but such eccentric bards as these
and make our bookish bread and cheese
from Wystan Audens.

The Peter Porter Poem of '82

This is going to be an ordinary friendly poem,
                              nothing very spectacular,
as it lollops along in the domain of what has been
                        called the republic of the vernacular.

Thirty years ago I first met you at a small party given
                              by Charles Rycroft –
but it wasn't until later that our paths became
                    brothers, like Sherlock and Mycroft.

At that time I had been more or less 'silent' for almost
                              a quarter of a century
(as they say of poets) and the likely lads, in Faber
                        fable, tough and adventury,

were Gunn and Hughes with their loonies in leather,
                        rampageous pigs, cats, hawks,
all ready to murder you quickly; from lad- and
                Nature-lovers there were few protesting squawks.

You on the other hand were into the serious satirical
                              Colonial-in-London bit,
lighting Latimer candles to Culture – and a good
                              many candles were lit

by the best poems in that first book (*Once Bitten,*
                              Twice Bitten),
which one could certainly call a very fine first book (if
                        not the best book ever written).

So we were into satire. Our London was brash,
                              immoral, surprising –
'What a city to sack!' – it was sacked by advertising.

We met in pubs halfway between your civilized
                        agency and (much less so) mine.
Oh, there was literary laughter, and bottles and
                              bottles of wine!

Later we both worked at Notley's – where no
                        highbrow had to grovel –
and I remember Trevor (with feminine help) xeroxing
                              a whole novel.

'I see you're both working late', the Managing
                              Director said
as he went off to his routine gins and tonics and
                              dinner and bed.

'A nest of singing birds', Ewart, Porter and
                                     Lucie-Smith;
Oliver Bernard had gone before, creating a substantial
                                     Bohemian myth.

That satire rings truer now, in the money-mad world
                                     of a Thatcher,
and in the rye, alas, we're left without any catcher;

but writers, wrote Wystan (to Christopher?), are
                                     ironic points of light.
And I think you've certainly been one, before you go,
     and I go, and we all go into that not-so-good night.

A Little Musique in 1661

(See Samuel Pepys, *Diary*)

When twenties gramophones were tinny
and girls were shaking it in mini
immodest skirts
with bathroom gin, bootleggers, mobsters . . .
who knew that you *did eat two lobsters*
or cared? It hurts

to think how history behaves so flightily –
my head, you noted, *akeing mightily*
from *pints of wine*,
The Pillers of Hercules, *The Goate*
keeping your Navy men afloat –
where they could dine

on *chine of beef* and *leg of mutton*,
burnt-wine and *sack*, that every glutton
supped like a whale,
new-come-to-town North Country bugger
nine-pinned by *Rhenish wine and sugar*
or cups of ale!

They also gave some frightful wallops
to platters full of *eggs and collops*,
to eat an *udder*
was commonplace, although the thought
does not entice us as it ought,
but makes us shudder.

One friend did tell, and made *much sport*,
describing *his amours at Port-*
smouth to one
of Mrs Boates daughters; a kitten,
a pretty girl play of the Gitterne,
to hear – what fun!

In clover cloven hoof, hot pig!
So thinking there to *eat a wigg*
you late came home –
a dish of Anchoves gave you thirst,
fuddled perhaps, you never burst,
each chromosome

was *very merry with the ladies*,
though sermons gonged of Hell and Hades,
your *morning draught*
was standard, *barrels* too *of oysters*,
as *pickled* as old monks in cloisters,
both fore and aft,

kept you shipshape and in good case.
Your *flagelette* (and you sang bass)
was womanlike
in giving you and others pleasure;
good time, good tunes, proportions, measure,
no marlinspike

could separate melodic strands
(like piano pieces for eight hands)
when *ayres* were woven;
brave echo banged a bastinado,
opiniastrement, rhodomontado,
and pre–Beethoven!

Music was food – and you had cause
to love the art that Henry Lawes
practised divinely;
not reckoned by the frivolous, you
worked hard at what you had to do,
and did it finely.

NOTE   Sack *is sherry*, burnt-wine *brandy*, collops *are pieces of fried bacon, a* wigg *is a cake or bun. In the old days people did actually burst from overeating. A gitterne is a kind of guitar, a* flagelette *(flageolet) is an instrument of the recorder family,* ayres *are tunes.* Opiniastrement *is stubbornly (French),* rhodomontado *means a boast (examples of Pepys' use of 'fashionable' words). Pepys was very conscientious in his work for the Navy Office as well as loving pretty women and music.*

Royal Hunt and Storm in Streatham *

When a girl is on the bed
something's warm and wet and red.

Such inviting sights are seen
as delight the Paphian Queen.

One night-watchman never knew
until the age of sixty-two.

In those mystic Cyprian caves
the Mistress rules her willing slaves.

Vast the members and erect
she can with her rod correct.

* Those to whom this poem seems obscure are advised to read *An English Madam, The Life and Work of Cynthia Payne*, by Paul Bailey (Jonathan Cape).

A Lesbic Thespian display
is the order of the day.

Exhibited, the cock will crow
in a slowly sensuous show.

Kinky letters in a host
rustle in by every post.

Some in cupboards grow more fond
of the strict restraining bond.

Dainty, feminine, soft lips
titillate the turgid tips.

Signor Dildo strictly stands,
urged by liver-spotted hands.

Nymph and Satyr change their dress
in venereal excess.

Leather vestments can excite,
and the flesh that Love may bite.

She is Queen, our Royal Madam,
Eve to fallen sons of Adam.

Rugger Song: The Balls of the Beaver

(Tune: 'Caviare Comes from the Virgin Sturgeon')

Castorium helpyth ayenst many Syknesses.

– Trevisa (1398)

The valuable drug Castoreum *is taken from the inguinal glands of these animals. The antients had a notion it was lodged in the testicles, and that the animal, when hard pressed, would bite them off, and leave them to its pursuers, as if conscious of what they wanted to destroy him for.*

– Pennant *History of Quadrupeds* (1781)

Castoreum comes from the balls of the Beaver –
Balls of the Beaver – very fine stuff!
A Beaver is truly a gay deceiver –
And often found in a lady's muff!

Beleaguered Beavers will bite their balls off –
In that confusion they escape –
Huntsman checks his hunting – calls off
All that rowdiness and rape!

Now, I'm quite glad I'm not a Beaver –
Virile value's bad, you see!
It's my girlfriend – I can't leave her –
If I did a Beaver – she'd leave me!

The Pope and I

(Tune: 'The Sun Whose Rays' – *The Mikado*)

The Pope, whose face,
with robes and lace,
   brings such joy to the Faithful,
could never be
charisma-free
   or horrid, hard or scatheful!
Or hide his light
by day or night
   under a bush or bushel –
it will shine high
and reach the sky,
   proud as the Hindu Kush'll!

I mean to be *The* Bard
   before I die –
we really work quite hard,
   the Pope and I!

I've been on stage★
and on the page,
    and he has written plays too –
infallible
with every Bull,
    he's had his share of praise too!
No, we don't shrink
from printer's ink
    we're, each of us, a writer –
we share that crown
on field and town
    shines brighter than a mitre!

We're intellectual,
    we're no small fry,
we're truly on the ball,
    the Pope and I!

★ A one-act opera *Tobermory* (1979) with music by John Gardner.

It's the Songs

A Thirties Foxtrot

I'm a member of the Retrospect Collectors Society
and I collect old records as an act of piety –
I was playing a long-player of Rudy Vallee
(Twenty Suave Tracks By Yale's Golden Haired
                                        Crooner),
as bland and potent as a big sherry in a schooner,
he was the famous college boy bandleader of his day,
the *first* crooner (before Bing) if you don't count
                                        Melville Gideon,
and he sang in the style that the old Greeks called the
                                        Lydian . . .
I was sitting, typing to the music, when up came a
                                                track
that really took me back . . .

186

I was sixteen
at a summer East Coast cottage,
mooning to the soupy tune
from a very supportable
portable gramophone,
full of undistributed sex and quite alone . . .

It's the songs
from the days when you could dance
that remind you of romance,
how love was thought to be the righter of all
                                      wrongs –
it's the songs!

It's the songs
that stir in you like yeast,
like a mystery from the East,
with the powerful unknown magic of Hawaiis and
                                  Hong Kongs –
it's the songs!

Of course we'd heard of love –
was it beneath our notice or above?
Some wouldn't touch it (it was radioactive),
some moped and were romantic, some attractive
and very active . . .
there's nothing more confused, I'll wager,
than the average teenager!

It's the songs
remind you of an instinct
and the feelings that were sex-linked
as they beat in you like bonking tribal gongs –
it's the songs!

It's the songs
that infect you like the plague,
make you vaguer than a Haig –
once burned, you still don't handle them with tongs –
it's the songs!

It's the songs,
with their four beats to the bar,
no matter where you are,
that grip you firmly, as Fay Wray King Kongs –
it's the songs!

What innocence! we think,
what oceans still of neutral printer's ink,
typewriter fingers worn with calluses,
what years and further years spent in analysis
in Denvers, Dallases . . .
and love, from far unknown prehistory,
is still a magic and a mystery.

It's the songs –
how they still communicate
that highly charged emotive state,
mesmeric messages in Morse's shorts and longs!
It's the songs!

NOTE   *The track referred to was 'The One in the World',
recorded 29 April 1929.*

De Quincey's Three Opium Dream Sonnets on the Wordsworth Family

1 Mrs Wordsworth

O Thou, so tall, so thin, with bean pole height –
Considerable obliquity of vision
Thou also hast, a squinting that Derision
Might too well claim would make a Left of Right!
Thine intellect not of an active order,
Thy only words, some say, a mere 'God bless you!'
For of thy Thoughts thou art a silent hoarder
And grave Philosophy would but distress you!
Thou art a Perfect Woman, nobly plann'd,
And few have seen so little of the World –
That once saw *Morecambe Bay's* extended sand –
In sweet confusion by a stranger hurl'd
Thou canst not speak, nay, colloquy would hurt you,
Dim burns thy Lamp of modest Female Virtue!

188

2 Dorothy Wordsworth

O rarely have I seen, among Eve's brood
Of English birth, a more determinate
And gipsy tan! Sweet, swarthy pigmy! Rude
Thou art not, and, though celibate
'Tis not from lack of courtship that thou holdest
A firm Companion to thy awesome Brother,
Thy babbling speech might well deter the boldest!
Thou cleav'st to Him, though woo'd by many
                                             another,
O'ercome entirely by thy winsome stammer!
Thy Suitors know thou art content to be
In ignorance of many things, to yammer
Or cry aloud in aid of Literacy
Not thine! Thy knowledge of the sacred cup
Was never systematically built up!

3 William Wordsworth

Great Wordsworth! Object of sublime devotion!
Thou walkest like a cade, an insect that
Obliquely wanders in its forward motion!
Thy legs are pointedly condemned – dog, cat
Walk better, cry the female connoisseurs!
Wry, twisted walking, and by slow degrees
Thou edgest off companions to the burrs
And gorse that hedge the high road's symmetries!
The worst part of thy person is thy Bust,
All from the shoulders narrowness and droop,
That give effects of Meanness! Ah, too just
The sculptor's disapproval of thy stoop!
Dorothy walks behind thy crablike crooks:
'Can that be William? How very mean he looks!'

NOTE *These sonnets are based on De Quincey's writings on Wordsworth and the Lake Poets. A 'cade' is a dialect name for a kind of insect that cannot walk straight.*

189

Edward and I

We guard the pillow on your bed,
                    Edward and I,
and keep it ready for your head,
                    Edward and I.
The nightdress hangs there on the door,
the fur-trimmed slippers on the floor
expect those feet that we adore,
                    Edward and I!

While I in thought and he in fact,
                    Edward and I,
are guardians, we have made a pact,
                    Edward and I,

to stay there always, each a sentry,
and (though we die!) deny all entry
to the lewd lords, degenerate gentry –
                    Edward and I!

The bed by day, the chair's long nights,
                    Edward and I
share with bedspreads, panties, tights.
                    Edward and I,
jumbled with stockings, slips and bras,
reflect on drinkers flushed from bars.
We know the dangers of fast cars,
                    Edward and I!

Like medicine men who point the bone,
                    Edward and I
can hex admirers, we alone
                    (Edward and I)
remind you not to swing a breast
or lift a leg for any guest –
we are the loved ones, not the rest,
                    Edward and I!

Combined, we keep you from such harm,
                    Edward and I,
I – spirit! He – the secular arm!
                    Edward and I
are dedicated to your worship,
and death to dirty dogs and curship;
we sing this hymn to your sweet Hership,
                    Edward and I!

NOTE   *Edward is a small Edward Gorey cat, stuffed with*
beads.

A Word to the Wise

. . . one of Britain's naughtiest and most popular poets.
                              – The Good Book Guide

A good many poets are haughty,
despising the unlettered mass,
but *we* know it pays to be *naughty*
(the way of a lad with a lass

is always attractive to readers) –
that's where popularity lies,
with the old fast reaction sex breeders
and the explicit bosoms and thighs!

No poet can be a best seller
unless he's an expert on hair,
like a forkbending straight Uri Geller –
getting rich as his writing gets rare;

and everything raw, wet and steamy
makes readers in thousands enthuse,
Mack, Mick, and Matilda and Mimi
are moaning aloud at his Muse!

Oh, the critics may say 'contrapuntal'
and write of his verbal technique
but unless it is all fully frontal
it's as dull as a very wet week!

Verse may be symbolic or Sapphic,
and written with wonderful words
but unless it makes love photographic
it's strictly, *we* know, for the birds!

You may boast of your spondees and trochees,
your rhyme royal and your villanelle –
it's the love dances, hot hokey-cokeys,
stop it getting as boring as hell!

And that's why each sly sexy oldie
is so keen to flash and to spank –
though at heart he is mean, mild and mouldy,
it's all money (you bet!) in the bank!

Beryl's Poem

In the old days when Abraham was sacrificing Thing
not many of the Jews could have a little jump out.
All the concubines belonged to the patriarchs.

Many claimed God had given them permission.
Women taken in adultery were stoned
with real stones, not whisky on the rocks.

It was a rough ride. No cart ever had a spring.
The Lion of Judah could bite quite a big lump out.
Couples were rare, as rare as Noah's arks.

Onan was punished for his lonely emission.
Desire reached a very sharp point – well honed.
But only the Holy Men had hens to match their cocks.

'Came Away with Betjeman to Pull Him Along Through Wulfstan Until Dinner Time'

–C.S. Lewis' Diary (1927)

Come away, Betjeman! Pull for the shore!
Pull on through Wulfstan and anglo that sax!
This is the tune that entices us more
Than vernal Vaughan Williams or beautiful Bax!
We can be happy, so happy, we twain,
With liege-lord and serf and intransigent thane!

Come away, Betjeman! Mince down the High,
Think not of Wystan or sorbets or sex!
Drink not the wine, of the neatherd's young thigh
All the enchantment can only perplex!
Plain living, high thinking – of such there's a dearth,
We'll raise it and praise it on our Middle Earth!

NOTE   *At Oxford University in 1927 C.S. Lewis was John Betjeman's Tutor. Lewis regarded him as a hopeless young aesthete, and his attempts to interest him in Anglo-Saxon seem to have ended in failure.*

Lincoln Kirstein: Rhymes of a PFC

In an Art Nouveau pizzeria
I thought about Lincoln's book
and restaurants called *Da Zia*
from when I took my first look
at Italy, wilder and freer
than any Tour with Cook –

for we came in at Gragnano,
Christmas 1943,
and worked our way up to the Arno
and right to the top of the tree,
mens sana in corpore sano,
La Spezia! Fiddle-de-dee,

we weren't those combat fighters!
Just air defence of ports
and airfields! But detritus
we weren't, or out of sorts,
and we were quite as bright as
those young heroic sports

who bought it at Anzio, easily
the worst FU of the war –
we turned up there later, queasily
surveying the tragic spoor
of the great hot beast. Oh, weasely
we slid in under the door!

Not terribly efficient,
I was an officer then –
but I started to get proficient
among the enlisted men –
the drill was more than sufficient,
not to mention the Bren!

You think you know about stripping –
just try stripping a gun!
The Bren and the Bofors are ripping
and furious fast-thinking fun.
In summer the sweat starts dripping,
in winter your hands are numb . . .

Let me entreat your cold ear!
I was a Private too,
a blinking bob-a-day soldier
(that's twenty cents to you)
but still an immortal soul, dear,
if Padres tell us true –

conscripted, the old East Surreys,
with NCOs from the Raj
who put us in several hurries
and knew their butter from marge –
the cookhouse even served curries!
Our ignorance was large,

the square was there for the bashing
and France was folding up,
June 1940. For mashing,
some swedes* were holding up
the whole effing issue, not dashing
but slow as a loving-cup,

they were the bleeding Dorsets,
all hating it, farmer's boys
old-fashioned as grandma's corsets,
and drill wasn't one of their joys –
a Sergeant, a practical whore, sets
high standards for virgins and coys . . .

At least I can say sincerely
(like thousands) that I was there,
more clever than brave and more nearly
the tortoise than any young hare –
but I loved my life quite dearly
(a thing that isn't so rare).

The US Army Air Force! Boy,
I was attached to them once!
Don't signal it out in old Morse, boy,
or foul it all up like a dunce –
that breakfast! a true assault course, boy,
(such hunter comes back to, who hunts)!

Pup tents and ice cream and chow lines
and movies and combat boots –
I knew them. Each war book that now lines
my shelves – I'm right there at the roots,
in the mud. War, like a sacred cow, lines
us up for these deadly pursuits!

So it's gone, and we go, but a witness
to what they suffered is fit
and Kirstein's verse has a fitness,
to humour the horror with wit,
to pinpoint its actual itness –
the glory, the shame, the shit.

* Cockney slang for rustics.

Love in a Valley★

Valkyrie's Valspeak in Awesome Valhalla

I used to think Wotan was vicious
in all that gear, a real soc, a mega hunk.

We flew high, a bitchen sesh,
it was radical!

Those pointy things on his helmet
were truly gnarly, the Heinies were
tubular.
And the Lowies.

Totally!

The bud was caj
we scarfed out. It was hot.
He maxed OK

OK!
How come he get so gross?
such a zod, so nerdy?
a shanky spaz?

OK!
Now I wanta say:

Gag me with a spoon!
What a geek!
You were mondo cool
but now you're grody
you make me barf
you're not buf any more . . .

★ Spoken, as it were, by a Valley Girl in Los Angeles, living in or
near the San Fernando Valley.

Oh my God!
Kiss my tuna!
What a nerd!
Get away!
Your fat butt disgusts me!

MS Found in a Victorian Church★

Golly! Let's debag old Kingers!
What a brilliant thought!
One of our most King Size singers!
Praise him as we ought –
That would be extremely hard!
But still we'll jolly well teach him
To be a Bard!

Though we love him daily, nightly,
Calling people shags
Is the fault that very rightly
Makes him lose his bags!
To respect his fellow men –
That idea may some day reach him
And his pen!

Flying tackles are in order,
Grab him round the waist,
Hold him hard South of the Border,
Give him quite a taste
Of the fate of sods and pseuds
When they bow down and beseech him
In their feuds!

Let him know the harsh unzipping,
The outcome of the knees!
Violence is simply ripping –
Down his Y-fronts, please!
Gosh! We've got him! Chewing gum out!
In unmentionable places bleach him,
Scream and shout!

★ Thought to be a poem by Sir John Betjeman about Kingsley
Amis, but the presence of another hand has been suspected.

A Soft Spot for Him – and Her

(A Night Club Song)

Once Bach wrote an Air on the G String
before it was used by the dancers –
who hid pubic hair with a G-string,
as was known in Las Vegas and Kansas;
then the thirties invented the G-Man, a new kind of
man,
and in Britain they'd furniture once that was labelled
G-Plan.

But now, red-hot and sparkling new,
the G-spot comes to you!

O the G-spot
is a wee spot
penny-size but more than / penny-wise
on the front wall of the vagina
and active from Chichester to China!

O the G-spot
is a free spot,
not ashamed before your / very eyes
to glory in ejaculation
and stand erect – with proper titillation!

O very bitter is
the lot of the clitoris,
quite in disgrace
it hides its face –
outdistanced by this famous female spasm
that gives to girls their final
vaginal orgasm!

O the G-spot
is a she-spot,
it's so great that it could / win a prize
and it's truly hidden treasure,
and glad to be there for one purpose – pleasure!

The Heel Has Come Full Circle

Old Mugg has come home,
he's truly done roamin',
he's homed in to Rome,
old Mugg has come home
to where he was homin',

St Peter's great dome
has changed his religion –
sanctimonious gnome
(what a gnome, what a dome!)
and religion's his pigeon,

like Venus from foam
he appears, that great actor,
like a sage with a tome,
full of faith, froth and foam
and a sick-making factor!

A McGonagall-type Triolet on the Full Revoltingness of Commercial Fast Food

A great double-deck of pure beef with melting cheese,
                     pickle, ketchup and mustard!
Complete your meal with our crisp French Fries and a
                     cool thick Shake!
Enjoy too the fried jumbo-size jumbo-tough
                     breadcrumbed macho legs of the Bustard,
a great double-deck of pure beef with melting cheese,
                     pickle, ketchup and mustard,
with a few lightly boiled rats' foetuses on the side, all
                     masked in creamy custard!
Wash it down with a warm Guinness, topped up with
engine oil – and dunk in it our supermale Elephant Cake,

a great double-deck of pure beef with melting cheese,
                    pickle, ketchup and mustard!
Complete your meal with our crisp French Fries and a
                            cool thick Shake!

NOTE   *The first two lines of this poem are genuine food
advertising of March 1984 in a London take-away/eat-in
restaurant.*

The Dugong

(Lewis Carroll Watches Television)

That dugong looked so deadly sweet,
    it lay there and it looked
like something very good to eat,
    just waiting to be cooked.

I thought I heard its spirit speak:
    'They drown us when we're caught,
for they are strong and we are weak
    and life is very fraught!

And soon we shall be quite extinct –
    the experts say ten years.
This statement's true, although succinct.'
    It then burst into tears.

'With outboard motors and canoes
    they chase us on the reefs.
We're on the menu, though they choose
    to hold some odd beliefs.

They think echidnas are our mums
    and ancestors of old.
They roast us, with the beating drums,
    we're valuable as gold –

part of their import-export trade,
    related, too, to *man* –
this claim the priestly ones have made
    since rituals began.

200

With sympathetic magic too
  they try to hunt us down.
It makes us very bored and blue
  as any girl's blue gown!'

I heard the mild and murdered beast.
  My mouth was full of veal.
I wasn't troubled in the least –
  it looked a perfect meal!

NOTE *The natives of Papua New Guinea are engaged in
hunting the dugong or sea cow to extinction. They believe
that the things of the sea can never be exhausted. The
programme that Lewis Carroll watched was a David
Attenborough programme: 'The Kiwai – Dugong Hunters
of Daru'. A certain hardness, and even sadism, can be
found in Carroll's poetry (see 'The Mouse's Tale' in* Alice
in Wonderland).

Evil Girl Guide in Torture Horror

EVIL GIRL GUIDE IN TORTURE HORROR –
Ordeal of Mabel, 75.
You wouldn't read about it in Gomorrah
(Evil Girl Guide in Torture Horror)!
Sue (18) and her simple-minded lover – two sadist
                              Japs crying *Torah! Torah!*
Cigarette-burns salt-rubbed, clothes-pegged eyes, a
plastic carnation stuck up her nose, rat-bitten,
indecently assaulted with a toilet brush,
laxative-overdosed, robbed, regarded as an easy con,
was Mabel lucky to be alive?
EVIL GIRL GUIDE IN TORTURE HORROR –
Ordeal of Mabel, 75.

NOTE *The first two lines of this triolet are headlines from*
The Sun *of 24 March 1984; and, as in poems by Peter
Reading, the facts are true ones, as given in that paper's
account of the trial.*

201

A Wee Sang for the Tourists

Come my Lords and Lieges, let us all to dinner for the
Cock-a-Leekie is a cooling.

    – James VI of Scotland (on a Baxter's Soup Label)

Och! I long for yon Auld Reekie,
where they're drinkin' Cock-a-Leekie
                      soup,
where the lassies are sae musky,
a' the better for a whusky-
                  stoup!

Where the pipes are busy skirlin'
and the kilts are wild an' whirlin'
                 wide –
where the music's like a fountain,
Arthur's sittin' on a mountain-
               side!

Embro Toun's nae warm Devonian
an' she's no a Caledonian
               Hell –
cauld an' in nae over-hot land,
the bra pride o' Bonnie Scotland –
            swell!

Tourist Guides say she's romantic
an' they cross the great Atlantic,
             glad
tae see clear what made Burns sary
an' yon tragic Queen, Scots Mary,
          sad!

Edinburgh Rock! Identic-
ally, like the Mound, authentic
          Scots!
An' nae matter what your mood is
the Past Appeal o' Holyrood is
          lots!

John Knox, Stevenson, Sir Walter –
History wad surely falter
                                    if
names like these cam off the roster,
nane o' them is an impostor!
                              Syph

an' a' disease unmentionable
(they wadna live on tae a pensionable
                                    age)
got a hauld on th'auld Scots Lords!
Houghmagandie-lovin' sots! Lords!
                              Sage,

we forget sic things an' Mary's
Bothwell, Darnley shine like fairies
                              nou!
Fine auld Lady o' the Lake-rid,
come to Embro, Scotland's sacred
                              cou!

The Mating of Pseudoscorpions

British Pseudoscorpions. *Fertilization is effected by*
means of a spermatophore, which in pseudoscorpions consists
of a small rod bearing a globule of seminal fluid at the top.
It is deposited by the male during the course of an elaborate
nuptial dance, etc., etc.

– Information display in the British Museum (Natural
   History). Pseudoscorpions are only a few millimetres
                                    long.

Pseuds and pseudopoets mating!
Long displays worth celebrating
in the most elaborate verses!
Kids' play, Doctors and pert Nurses!
Barings of the bum and tit you all
know is true poetic ritual –
an Editor can show his sonnet,

she can nymphlike dance upon it –
not spirits only that she raises,
as caressingly she praises!
In a wine bar, dark and smoky,
he can stun her with a trochee,
initiates are into mysteries
you won't find in Natural Histories . . .

Pubs are Forests of green Arden,
where Odes To A Surrey Garden
melt hearts and parts of young aspirants
and Editors are forceful tyrants –
they're locks in which they'll make their keys stick
with Eng. Lit. love that's anapaestic!

Spermatophores are simple lyrics
where landscapes lie in panegyrics.
He will drop them. Vestals hover
above that seminal spot of bother.
Fertilization! Consummation!
Pseudopoets of the Nation,
with their magazines and readings,
pseudoscorpions' dancelike pleadings,
flicker-flames that don't light fuses,
are dear to all hearts – but the Muse's!

The Pilgrim's Progress

In the City that men called Destruction
there were riot, rebellion and ruction –
all around was depraved –
Christian longed to be saved,
and Evangelist gave him instruction:

Go ahead to that old Wicket Gate –
forget Pliable's, Obstinate's fate!
Cross the Slough of Despond
(it's a Doubt-ridden pond)
to Celestial City, old mate!

Worldly-Wiseman, and his pal Legality,
were diversions. But in that locality
Good Will helped him through.
Past the Gate, what was new
was Interpreter's pictured morality . . .

At the Cross, next, his Burden fell off.
But the Sinners were still there to scoff –
dopey Simple and Sloth,
and he passed by them both,
and Hypocrisy (big-headed toff).

Still, the Shining Ones gave him a boost,
and a Roll which he frequently used.
Difficulty (a Hill)
at first made him ill.
There were lions on chains (but not loosed).

And then Prudence, Piety, Charity
gave him discourse, without much hilarity;
they were virgins, of course,
a benevolent force.
One was dark, one was blonde, one was carrotty.

So next day he went down with elation,
to the Valley called Humiliation –
(the Delectable Mountains,
with fruit, flowers and fountains,
had been shown him, a strong inspiration).

WHAM! BAM! Up the creek with no paddle!
A foul fiend there, astride and astraddle,
my gosh and by golly! On
the path stands Apollyon
(says Salvation is all fiddle-faddle)!

Then fierce combat ensued (half a day)
till the fiend dragon's-winged on his way!
Chris had hardly drawn breath
when the Shadow of Death
stretched its Valley before him, okay?

Full of Hobgoblins, Dragons and Satyrs,
howling, yelling, and other such matters,
with clouds of Confusion
in darkening profusion,
and fiends that could tear him to tatters.

But his Sword and All-Prayer got him through,
past quags, gins, nets, traps – Pagan too
and Pope, two great Giants
both breathing defiance.
They were all there, lined up in a queue!

So he overtook Faithful quite soon,
who gave out about Wanton's sex-tune,
how he steadfastly went,
braving Pride, Discontent
and false Shame. Pilgrim songs, to the moon,

they both sang – and passed Talkative by.
Next it's Vanity Fair, my, oh, my!
All fashions, all vogues,
cheats, games, whores and rogues!
They seem simple, where others are sly . . .

So, arrested and put in a cage,
chained and beaten, with malice and rage,
they speak fair, no denial –
but they must stand trial.
Lord Hategood is Judge, that bent sage!

They are charged that they, mean and penurious,
scorned Lords Carnal Delight and Luxurious,
Lord Old Man and Lord Lechery –
to Beelzebub treachery!
So Lord Hategood gets perfectly furious.

In fact Faithful is tortured and burned,
eternal Redemption thus earned,
with angels and bliss.
Now Hopeful finds Chris.
They march on and will never be turned

by the twerps that in Fair-speech abound.
Lady Faining, Mr By-ends, are found,
Mr Smooth-man (Mr Any-Thing's
at home with too many things).
Mr Facing-bothways is around.

The Plain is called Ease; the Hill, Lucre –
it's a lot like a long game of snooker.
Rest from mayhem and slaughter,
by the stream of the Water
of Life, it's a cool Poulaphouca*!

Doubting Castle, its lord Giant Despair,
are the next things of which they're aware.
There are no surprises;
suicide, he advises,
is the way to get out of his hair!

Next he shows them the bones of the slain
and, for good luck, he beats them again.
'We're a couple of dummies!
This key that's called Promise
will relieve us' cries Chris, 'from our pain!'

So it's off to Delectable Mountains –
gardens, orchards, and vineyards and fountains –
it's Immanuel's Land,
shepherds give them a hand.
Mountains Error and Caution! Past countings

and reckonings, by-ways to Hell
are all round, with a brimstony smell.
But they climb up and peer
from a Hill that's called Clear –
there's the City, as clear as a bell!

* a waterfall in Eire.

Still Faint-heart, Mistrust and one Guilt
frighten Little-faith up to the hilt,
seven devils get Turn-away.
It's hard to discern a way,
but at last they're off, no blood is spilt –

and they're netted by Flatterer next,
a specious ungodly mar-text.
Now they're set for Mount Sion,
as bold as a lion,
though by Turn-back and Ignorance vexed.

Through the River of Death, the last thing,
and the Shining Ones' trumpets all ring!
That melodious noise
tells us all of the joys
of the Pilgrims who sing with their King!

The Inventor of Franglais?

A Comment

*Thence to Jervas's, my mind, God forgive me, running too
much after sa fille, but elle not being within, I away by
coach to the Change – and thence home to dinner; and
finding Mrs. Bagwell waiting at the office after dinner,
away elle and I to a cabaret where elle and I have été
before; and there I had her company toute l'après-diner and
had mon plein plaisir of elle – but strange, to see how a
woman, notwithstanding her greatest pretences of love à son
mari and religion, may be vaincue.*

– Samuel Pepys, *Diary (23 January 1665)*

Well, God, j'ai souvent pensé
(in clear or fractured français),
a pris the soul of femmes –
but toutefois the Devil maudit
is souverain of their body
and has his will of Dames!

He does all that he voulait
to each partridge or poulet,
we're instruments – c'est tout!
Bon Dieu, above, has thunder –
le Diable rules what's under –
très bon for me and you!

Les female protestations
qui annoncent their detestations
of all luxurieux men
sont for the record only,
le corps stays soft and lonely
et le fait again et again!

The Importance of Being Earnest

Jack Worthing is free, fit and fine –
and he knows about women and wine.
Less coarse than a sandbag,
he was found in a *handbag* –
on the Brighton, that famous old line.

Algy Moncrieff does a Bunbury
to places like Paris or Sunbury –
to see a sick friend
who is nearing his end –
but in truth he's at Joysville or Funbury!

There are two girls: Gwendolen, Cecily,
who go round full of wit, and quite dressily.
Lady Bracknell's the Aunt –
not her fault that it shan't
end in tears and in all ways quite messily!

C.'s governess, prune-faced Miss Prism,
Canon Chasuble; heresy, schism
fly away when *he's* there.
She'd be willing to share
any fate as his mate – cataclysm!

Now Jack's told one lie or another,
told Cecily he has a brother
called Ernest – who's wicked –
this isn't quite cricket
(no one knows yet who might be his mother).

So the Albany country-house lads
must endure the girls' maidenly fads –
C.'s a chick who in *her* nest
wants no one not Ernest.
Ditto Gwendolen. *Christen us cads*!

is the favour they both of them ask,
it's the Canon's canonical task.
But – one last catechism –
Lady B. questions Prism,
and the Truth is revealed, with no mask!

That (how fateful and how well-arranged!)
for a *novel* the young Jack was changed
by Miss Prism, his nurse,
and for better or worse
he's the brother of Alg., long estranged!

Even better, his true given name
will revive the young Cecily's flame!
For it's Ernest (no catch!),
so it's game, set and match
(and the winner was wit in that game)!

An Easy Lai?★

But is it very hard?
Ah! Why not ask the Bard?
    He's the one who knows.
He's wily, he's a card,
a fryer without lard,
    to whom each ill wind blows

★ This is, in fact, the hardest kind of lai (a medieval French form
of obscure origin) known as the *virelai ancien*.

some straw; invention grows,
his bricks pile up in rows –
   all of them make the grade!
Though critics stand like crows,
crying down his furbelows,
   saying spade should be a spade,

he surely has it made.
Although his talents fade,
   his lines like spikenard
smell sweet – or marmalade –
like cleverly carved jade
   they merit our regard!

A Wordsworthian Sonnet for Arnold Feinstein, who Mended My Spectacles in Yugoslavia

Feinstein, artificer of proven worth!
O Saviour of my spectacles! Thou didst know
Exactly where that tiny screw should go
And how to place it there! Of all on earth
I honour thee! Of such men there is dearth –
Great Scientists that yet will stoop so low,
To rude *Mechanics*! Our Life cannot show
A truer Nobleness, or of such pure birth!
Yet thou, by Struga, in that moving coach,
Spinoza-like didst work upon the lens
With aptitude more great than other men's,
Reintroducing it! O dread approach
Of bookish blindness! From which I was set free
When Fate ordained that thou sat'st next to me!

Happiness is Girl-Shaped

(The Copywriter Sings)

You're twice as trad as Acker Bilk,
you'd be delicious
                    crumbled into milk,
there is no other of your ilk!

You're very clearly bran-enriched,
I'd like to have you
                    hedged and ditched,
no hype for you is over-pitched!

My heart, for you, has raced like Arkle,
you've got that cute
                    refreshing sparkle,
you are my light that will not darkle!

You have that tangy lemon zest,
great things have happened
                    on your chest,
you're way out there beyond the rest!

You make life bright and dazzling new,
you are the first
                    of precious few,
I'd like to have a private view!

You set me off like fire alarms,
persuasive as
                    a salesman's charms,
I'd make down payments on your arms!

You are the rhyme that's always true,
the whitest wash
                    that's slightly blue –
let me consume my life with you!

Rush That Bear!

There's a breathless hush over Crescent and Square
   and the Gardens are sad and still
    while everybody, yes, everywhere,
    wonders: Will
Sir John go over the hill?

The agonized cry goes up: *Rush that bear*
to his grieving, tormented side!
   This is the comfort, in his despair,
   far and wide
all wish for him, tearful-eyed!

This is the single much-more-than-toy
   that can succour him in his need –
    Archibald, seventy years of joy,
    of joy indeed,
as Venerable as Bede!

So take him by taxi, by tube or by train,
   fly him so high in the air!
    Give us some hope, let us breathe again
    (oh, if we dare!)
and speedily RUSH THAT BEAR!

NOTE   *In October 1983 Sir John Betjeman suffered a heart attack and his childhood teddy bear, Archibald, was brought to his hospital bed.*

Two Kiplings

1 Sixty-seven and going West

When your hair gets thin and your tummy expands
and the frog-spots play all over your hands,
when benign skin-cancers cover your back
and warts, all over, are on the attack –
why, then you'll know (if you haven't guessed)
that you're sixty-seven and going West!

When your face gets fat with a jowly jaw
and your teeth feel like a neglected saw,
when your legs walk easily into cramp,
and your eyes grow tired in the reading lamp –
why, then you'll know (if you haven't guessed)
that you're sixty-seven and going West!

When you feel arthritis in finger-ends
and the stiffness of Death lays out your friends,
when the hand writes wobbly and memory goes
and your hearing weakens, from head to toes
you'll have the *proof* (if you haven't guessed)
that you're sixty-seven and going West!

2 John Kipling

(posted missing in 1915, aged seventeen)

Warned against women, he went off to war,
Dad's most treasured cub in the whole Wolf Pack,
Abraham's Isaac – but where was the ram?

Trained to kiss rods, to kiss and adore,
He never would blub, he was white, not black,
He had a little bread – but never any jam.

A Small Elite

(George Macbeth and I)

We can both say 'I'm a genius'
(since it all depends what you mean by genius)
though to misspellers we might be henious★
crimes –
a huge claim made by tiny, teeny us!
But still, at times,

★ or even Heaneyous

214

we have 'touch' like Gerulaitis
(with the skill of Gower or Gerulaitis) –
for those who speak of arthuritis
we
are see-through frauds like certain nighties.
A different key

is what we play in – and *hoi polloi*ing
(all the screaming screamers, *hoi polloi*ing)
masses would find us quite annoying
pseuds –
since Pop is what they're all enjoyìng,
and genteel nudes.

I thank you that you called me Scottish
(never skilled like Burns but truly Scottish),
though horrorpots are horrorpottish
it's
quite nice to know not all are sottish –
a cap that fits

we share, though we're South of the Border
(in exile both for certain, South of the Border)
where they rhyme this with Harry Lauder
and
we're hounded by each out-of-order
analysand!

A Happy Encounter at a Literary Function

(Tune: A simplified version of the song in *High Noon*)

What blazered arm lay on my shoulder?
    Say, was it Laurence, of the Cott'rell clan?
As I must die (and burn or moulder)
    I can't deny it was that very man!

And I was more than glad to see him!
    A welcome rainbow, from the sun and rain!
To toast him, wine him, or high-tea him
    Would be a pleasure keen as best champagne!

For from the Compton Fund the money
   Lay on us through his efforts truly great!
If we were crumpets, this was honey –
   And proved him, ev'ry inch, a genuine mate!

Craig Raine and I, and Dr Dannie Abse
   Were in New York then, with Patricia Beer,
Where Laurence, Fairy Queen and quite Queen
                                        Mabsy,
   Kept us in funds and truly free from fear!

Britain Salutes New York! That was the message!
   He *managed* us! The Pickwick Arms Hotel!
Like horses that step orderly in dressage
   He led us round that circus very well!

And now some *fees* are paid for readings,
   And we know well to whom our thanks are due!
To you, dear Laurence, and your pleadings!
   Only and always, from us four to you!

Life in Scotland, 1852

Neighbours are landladies
landladies are neighbours
and their speech is in the street,

wee complaints are colloquies
colloquies are wee complaints
on their steadfast Scottish feet,

miners are miseries,
miseries are miners,
but their coal provides the heat,

tempers are open fires,
open fires are tempers,
when the bold landladies meet!

216

Blue Maggie

(Red Ken's Song)

She isn't saggy, she isn't baggy,
she's quite inconceivable, her hair's unbelievable,
Blue Maggie!
Of course she cares! (if it's Stocks and Shares),
she's not quite real, as slim as an eel, and truly
genteel,
Blue Maggie!

She's full of friction, she's Science Fiction,
she's extra-terrestrial, bimetallic, bimestrial,
Blue Maggie!
She never defers to ideas not hers,
she's quite absolute, and resolute, and mad as a coot,
Blue Maggie!

A Ballad Re-Creation of a Fifties Incident at Barnes Bridge

'Tis the ghost o' Colquhoun an' the ghost o' McBride
That do balcony-lean by yon auld riverside,
An' they baith are sae fou' they can scarcely see –
For they're baith at a party (where booze is free) –

An' the Sassenachs there wi' their highbrowish
speech
Mak' a nebulous nectarine oot o' a peach.
But Colquhoun an' McBride hauld theirsels weil
aloof,
Aye drinkin' the drinks that are ower proof.

Nae word do they speak, but they lean an' glower
Wi' the pissed perfection o' painterly power –
An' as they lean there the sun gaes doun
Like a watercolour o'er London toun,

In a' the sweet tints that the calendars love,
Wi' a braw great pink flush i' the skies above.
Och! they *do* notice this, tho' their eyes are glazed,
An' baith wi' horror are sair amazed –

Colquhoun turns tae McBride wi' a fine disgust
At the sight o' that distant an' reddenin' dust.
'Mon, but it's horrible!' 'Aye, but 'twill pass!'
An' they ply, baith, the gold, unremittin' wee glass!

NOTE   *This haunting is quite a possible one, being based
on an actual incident. Colquhoun and McBride were two
painters of talent from Glasgow, well-known in the forties
and fifties.*

False Colours

Everybody's heard of the young man in London
who went round seducing American girl students
by telling them he was Ted Hughes . . .

I bet he was only *one* of them –
I bet in Northern Ireland there are pseudo-Heaneys,
imitation Betjemans active in Metroland,
false Roy Fullers stroking a lustful moustache
before the proud beauties,
in the North perhaps a deutero-Geoffrey Hill,
a Bunting wrapped in some deceptive skin.
All men of foresight and acumen, telling the tale.

There will be, too, a few rather queerer seductions
engineered by Americans posing as Thom Gunn,
scholars disguised as John Heath-Stubbs . . .
the kids in Cornwall must beware the cater-Causley.

And a good many Fleur Adcocks must be drawing
                              the young men in,
there's probably a Patricia Beer operating in Devon,
and a doubtful Maureen Duffy.

All students everywhere must be terribly careful!

A Godly Undertaking

I continually pray for the SOU-
L of the novelist Evelyn Waugh.
It seems dark and obscure, half a MO-
LE, and unfriendly and raw.

It didn't much like fellow-ME-
N, it was snobbish and cruel to the weak,
and it harmed what he wrote with his PE
N and the words it induced him to speak.

It took sides, where it could, with the STRO-
NG and all privilege led it astray.
It's in Hell, I expect (am I WRO-
NG?) – that's why I so steadfastly pray!

British Weather

It is the merry month of May,
when everything is cold and grey,
the rain is dripping from the trees
and life is like a long disease,

the storm clouds hover round like ghouls,
the birds all sing, because they're fools,
and beds of optimistic flowers
are beaten down by thunder showers,

under a weak and watery sun
nothing seems to be much fun –
exciting as a piece of string,
this is the marvellous British Spring!

Under the Staircase

(For Several Voices)

Semi-Chorus A: Under the staircase
under the stair
you won't find anything rich and
                           rare –
things more likely
that shouldn't be there,
a china pisspot brimming full,
emu's eggs in cotton wool,
things that are scary,
sad or sinister –
the strangled body
of the Prime Minister!

Semi-Chorus B: Never look
under the stair,
oh, have a care!
Hanks of hair
and bones all knobbly
lie in wait like an old nightmare –
to make you weak and wobbly!
The hacked-off head
of a grizzly bear –
don't look, don't look,
even for a dare,
under the stair!

Semi-Chorus A:	It isn't a rare case,
	it isn't rare
	to find a Something lurking there –
	to stare you out
	with its horrible stare –
	something mouldy, mad and
	moulting,
	infantile and quite revolting!
	Hedgehogs squashed
	on the highway camber,
	kittens in creosote,
	frogs in amber!
Semi-Chorus B:	Never look
	under the stair!
	Foul, not fair,
	Baudelaire
	in Vicky squalor
	lies embalmed with a poxed *au pair*,
	with ink-stink on his collar!
	Better be dead
	than stoop and peer –
	don't look, don't look,
	it's bad, it's bare
	under the stair!

The Mistress

A Betjeman Rewrite★

There's lust in the beds of London
(and he is a husband surely)
and love in the beds of London
(and she is a wife, or nearly);

★ The poem to which the reader is referred is 'Lenten Thoughts
Of A High Anglican'

there are evening beds in London
(and wives and mistresses share them)
and afternoon beds in London
(the charms, legs and arms, they bare them).

There's love and there's lust in London
(to separate them's not easy)
and The Mistress is great in London
(and the appetite isn't queasy).

And this is the way in London
(underground love – like travel),
there's knotting and play in London
(that only Time can unravel)!

Fairly High Windows

(based on an idea of Vernon Scannell's)

They fuck you up, your King and Queen.
   They may not mean to, but they do.
And things that are no way your scene
   All have to be extolled by you.

They have a strict and soppy code
   That never bends much or relents.
Each Royal Birth's a fucking Ode
   And camp as any row of tents.

The Laureate misery's handed down,
   Letters from fools too, sack by sack.
You have to wear that iron crown.
   You're not allowed to give it back.

NOTE *Written in expectation of Philip Larkin achieving the Laureateship, June 1984.*

End of Term, 23 July

I offer you the salmon trout of kindness
and Edward from his bed approves the gift;
in this I serve, like Milton in his blindness,
this is the gold that daily diggers sift,

the cloud-based and proverbial silver lining
that hangs around our ordinary life,
the precious metal some say needs refining,
the help of husbands to a working wife.

The loganberries will appear, quite *glacé*,
enrobed in mystical, pure, Single Cream,
the fridge-freed wine will be a *Royal Crustacé*,
a *blanc de blancs*, a draught that's like a dream.

The chocolates come from *Charbonnel et Walker*,
each catalogued as any champion cat.
Marrow and new potatoes! No trick talker
could better this, or make a meal like that!

Lexicography

(A Trough of Low Pleasure)

Like a lepidopterist with a fine new specimen
Carried carefully home from a successful sortie,
What did I do with this marvellous trophy?
    Spread it out and put it under the microscope!

This, the OED in its Compact Edition,
Carried a reading glass, a standard extra.
What did I search for? Just like anyone,
    Looked up CUNT, to see it under the reading glass

(The same would have been done by the magazine
                                        editors
And by all the publishers, including Virago,
It's an important word and basic in folklore,
   Known about and spoken, over the hemispheres),

Keat's friends drank to it as Mater Omnium,
It's full of sexual overtones and sensual undertones,
It has a kind of inwardness that some call mystical.
   So I crept, so slowly, over the printed mass,

Not wanting to disturb it as it basked in the sunshine,
Tiptoeing in to net it. I reached CUNCTATION,
Which means delay, delaying, or tardy action;
   Turned the page, to CUNNING, under the reading
                                        glass.

I was sure I should see it, what a triumph! Quietly
I moved on to CUNSTER, a conner once in
                              Scotland . . .
And then, in upper and lower case, I saw it:
   Cunt –: see CONT. Injustice! Under-represented!

When COCK is there in glory with words like
                     CLAPPERDUDGEON
(Meaning a man who was born and bred a beggar).
So I turned to CONT, in a mood of disappointment.
   It's 'To punt (a boat, or barge)' over inland
                              waterways!

PUNT for CUNT! That dictionary was joking!
Surely some scholar was laughing his head off!
I passed on, to the Supplement (CHIP–SPARROW,
                              CLEAVAGE).
   Still not there! What sadness, under the microscope

No wonderful butterfly opening wings and closing
Or even frozen timelessly in grave lexicography –
Absent without leave, as they said in my Army days!
   Shut the book and put it back, with the reading
                                        glass.

The Song of the Old Soldier

Across the miles and miles of burning plain
the Army's marching, marching, and marching yet
again.
Oh, yes, the fucking Army
is the terror of the land
and where the sea is wavy
you can see the sodding Navy –
but miles and miles above us,
where they can't raise a stand,
is the airy fairy Air Force with its joystick in its hand!

Across the miles and miles of frozen kelp
the Army's marching, marching, and marching
without help.
Oh, yes, the fucking Army
is the terror of the girls –
there are fewer girls than gravy
for the poor old sodding Navy,
and miles and miles above us,
like the swine above the pearls,
is the airy fairy Air Force with its profile and its curls!

Across the miles and miles of mountain range
the Army's marching, marching, and marching
without change.
The fearless fucking Army
leaves the babies in its wake,
while young Dan is doing Davy
in the silly sodding Navy –
but miles and miles above us,
drifting on without a brake,
is the airy fairy Air Force like a fancy piece of cake!

Drinker to Lover, Drunkard to Lecher

A glass of wine
won't say *No!*
or *Don't!* or *Let me go!*
You won't be asked
by any jar:
Who do you think you are?
You'll never hear
from pints of bitter
the hard words of a baby-sitter . . .

No double gin
answers back –
it hasn't got the knack –
it can't look pert,
annoyed or coy –
You're not my kind of boy
is something it
will never answer –
or yet *You're not much of a dancer!*

A vodka's smooth,
can be neat,
and vermouths can be very sweet –
they don't avoid
encroaching lips
or smack your fingertips.
They know their place,
won't fail to meet you,
and know exactly how to treat you!

Mr Ewart

Mr Ewart won't answer letters,
Mr Ewart is old and tired,
he is fed up with his betters
and his worses aren't admired.

Mr Ewart would like to founder
like an ancient worn-out ship
where the fathoms all sleep sounder
than the flake-outs on a trip.

Mr Ewart would like to vanish
with a minimum of fuss
either womanish or mannish,
or be run down by a bus.

Mr Ewart won't speak to people,
he is deaf, his eyes aren't good,
his response is now so feeble
you know he hasn't understood.

Mr Ewart is antisocial
and is quite opposed to fun,
all he knows is that much woe shall
come upon us – one by one.

Mr Ewart is sick of living,
he'd like quietly to lie down,
return the gifts that God is giving –
and get to Hell out of this town!

The Joys of Surgery

(dedicated to Richard Selzer, author of *Mortal Lessons*)

There's the riot and the rut –
when you make that first clean cut!
As the scarifying scalpel
makes you higher than an Alp'll –
blood appears in pretty beads,
that thin line directly leads
to the laid-bare opal fat,
you feel randy as a rat
and you don't lose much momentum
when you see the gauze omentum!

What's more horny than a heart
heaving with the surgeon's art?
and the clicking of the clips
is a series of short trips,
you're turned on, lit up, elationed –
quite as knocked out as the patient!
The abdomen's Aladdin's Cave
makes you want to rant and rave,
intestines, serpents of Old Nile,
curve and coil – you have to smile –
and you give a tender shiver
at the dark joy of the liver,
while the pink peritoneum,
lovely as an Art Museum,
strikes you with desire and dumb
till you very nearly come . . .

God made this delightful chasm
for your own intense orgasm!

A Putney Art Dealer is Censured by a Local Inhabitant for Displaying Detailed Female Nudes

Many people don't like pubic hair.
They say, quite simply: *It shouldn't be there!*
It's far too brash and bushy and animal.
In Art, it's often absent, minimal
or covered discreetly with swirls of drapery –
like pig's blood dropped on spotless napery,
reminds of the nature of the beast,
and sits like a ghost at the frolicsome feast.

Victorians thought it was coarse and crude,
although their painters quite loved the nude –
with 'Roman Baths' and 'The Wives of Hannibal',
enough plump flesh to entice a cannibal –

when it was safely in antiquity
it didn't smell of moral obliquity.
Puritans still, with our prudish fears,
we haven't changed much in a hundred years!

'The Sun' Also Rises

Oh, isn't it exciting!
There's going to be a war!!!
We hope there's lots of fighting –
we missed the one before!

Already men are drowning!
We're brave, we have no fear,
as patriots we're downing
our fearless pints of beer!

Two Harriers, one cruiser?
Our lads will put it right,
while we stay in the boozer
and carry on the fight . . .

Though we have high expenses
we shoot our mouths off quick,
large gins and their defences
are sure to do the trick!

At Death we're shouting 'Gotcha!',
we're perfect shining knights –
no diplomatic botcher
has any bleeding rights . . .

How grand for circulation
and for the Tories too,
a floor show for the Nation,
and free for me and you!

How grand for Mrs Thatcher –
she's almost out of sight!
Now Foot can never catch her,
though running day and night!

It's lovely on the telly,
home strategists agree,
when the Fascist underbelly
gets hit in time for tea!

We're full of warlike features –
and every word is priced –
despising spineless creatures
like peaceful Jesus Christ!

We know there's news in 'traitors' . . .
and as the hot war nears
like stripshow fornicators
we roar it on with cheers . . .
we hope it lasts for years!

20 May 1982

An English Don Wants to Go

Do I want to go to
that big crooked country
where the girls say
You don't know shit –
but you're kinda cute!
Do I want to go?

Yes, I want to go to
that amazing oil-rich country,
where the kids play
with bum and tit
and they're gonna shoot –
yes, I want to go!

230

Where my clipt, affected
English utterance
goes with the big stiff
old upper lip –
and I'm kinda mute,
with my English utterance!

Where entry's effected
by high-class utterance,
high as a cliff,
with a horsey clip –
and the campus will salute
my most English utterance!

The Retirement from Rugby Football of Bill Beaumont

Oh, what a wonderful winsome match-winning
                              walrus
        has left our part of the sea!
Even in Scotland (where they thrive on broken play)
        and in Wales (where they fancy themselves)
        all the Rugger fans agree!

Captain of England in twenty-one mind-bending
                              matches,
        and that includes a Grand Slam!
Leader of Lions (what a pride!) where tourists roar,
        he quite steadily pushed on ahead –
        without razzamatazz, POW or WHAM!

He started at Fylde, but before that (and clumsy) at
                              Ellesmere
        at school he was a full-back.
He led by example (he *grew* into the captaincy,
        say the journalists); humour, hard work,
        they were his form of attack!

He never put the boot in or (nearly) squeezed
                              somebody's balls off,
                his play was remarkably clean.
He had the ability to win the ball when
                it really mattered – what more could you want?
                He was magnificent, but not mean.

Andy Irvine, Ollie Campbell (those great ones) have
                              both paid tribute
                to the best Captain they've known.
He wasn't commercial, he just loved Rugby,
                so solid, lumbering, rollerlike, steaming,
                wholesome, well-loved and home-grown!

But now a new computerized axial tomography scan
                has shown damage to the occiput.
From a fair kick on the head. And it's curtains
                (the Press says sadly) for ever and ever
                for his England boot and its foot!

Literary Bios

Was she a bitch? Was he a swine?
Oh, which was which? Both yours and mine,
before it's cut, the thread's a tangle.
It all depends on the different angle.

Was she an angel? and was he *good*?
Something strange'll be understood –
some behaved well, some behaved badly,
the happiest ones could end so sadly.

Louis MacNice? Louis MacNasty?
Pearl without price – or pretty ghastly?
He or she, the shot-silk colour
has a two-way shine that gets no duller.

Wystan, Dylan, doubtful smile,
Duke of Milan, or egophile –
the bountiful bios all come running
to say how stupid! how simply stunning!

The Owl Writes a Detective Story

A stately home where doves, in dovecotes, coo –
fields where calm cattle stand and gently moo,
trim lawns where croquet is the thing to do.
This is the ship, the house party's the crew:
Lord Feudal, hunter of the lion and gnu,
whose walls display the heads of not a few,
Her Ladyship, once Ida Fortescue,
who, like his Lordship very highborn too
surveys the world with a disdainful moue.
Their son – most active with a billiard cue –
Lord Lazy (stays in bed till half past two).
A Balkan Count called Popolesceru
(an ex-Dictator waiting for a coup).
Ann Fenn, most English, modest, straight and true,
a very pretty girl without a sou.
Adrian Finkelstein, a clever Jew.
Tempest Bellairs, a beauty such as you
would only find in books like this (she'd sue
if I displayed her to the public view –
enough to say men stick to her like glue).
John Huntingdon, who's only there to woo
(a fact, except for her, the whole house knew)
Ann Fenn. And, last, the witty Cambridge Blue,
the Honourable Algy Playfair, who
shines in detection. His clear 'View halloo!'
puts murderers into a frightful stew.

But now the plot unfolds! What *déjà vu*!
There! In the snow! – The clear print of a shoe!
Tempest is late for her next rendez-vous,
Lord Feudal's blood spreads wide – red, sticky goo

on stiff white shirtfront – Lazy's billet-doux
has missed Ann Fenn, and Popolesceru
has left – without a whisper of adieu
or saying goodbye, typical *mauvais gout*!
Adrian Finkelstein, give him his due,
behaves quite well. Excitement is taboo
in this emotionless landowner's zoo.
Algy, with calm that one could misconstrue
(handling with nonchalance bits of vertu)
knows who the murderer is. He has a clue.

But who? But who? Who, who, who, who, who, who?

NOTE   *This poem was written to be read aloud, and the
'oo' sounds at the ends of the lines should be intoned like the
call of an owl.*

THE COMPLETE LITTLE ONES (1986)

Part One *All My Little Ones*

Hail and Farewell

The sick Get Well Card simply says DROP DEAD!

Double Haiku: Britain and Surrealism

Since we live in a
country where shops sell German
Juice and Big Choosy

Cat Food, where they say
'She laughed like a drain!', we just,
really, don't need it.

Folk-Hero

The one the foreign students call Ted Huge.

Variation on a Pompeian Brothel Graffito

I like a girl with a big black mat
(worth a serenade, a song, or a sonnet)
between her legs – but in addition to that
it's got to have WELCOME written on it.

Negative

A landlady is not a countrywoman

A *mariage blanc* is not a white wedding

A planchette is not a ghost writer

A sperm whale is not a Don Juan

An *oeil de boeuf* is not a bullseye

A mons veneris is not the Venusberg

A peccary is not a serious sin

Simulation/Stimulation

A sex film that doesn't show a male erection
is really cheating;
it's like showing gourmets at a banquet
and not showing what they're eating.

Creation Myth Haiku

After the First Night
the Sun kissed the Moon: 'Darling,
you were wonderful!'

Haiku: The Season of Celebrity

With summer comes the
bluebottle; with pleasant fame
comes the journalist.

Edwardian Haiku: Scrubbers

Women scrubbing floors –
high ladies in this posture
admitted lovers.

The Surrealist Landscape

A huge can of soup is walking the pavement

The evening oleanders are softly barking

All over the world the sea turns orange

A fish-headed man makes loves to a woman

The cats all, suddenly, have six legs

The roses, of course, are smelling of seaweed

A giant hand in the sky makes the thumbs-down
sign

These were the names of the novels

A Wine Called Albert

The Witty Young Friends

The Sex-Benders

Nobody Wants Me

Mrs Gentry And The Basilisk

The Perfumed Sinner

Come And Get It!

The Rhyming Slang of the Postcards

If she sends you a duck
she wants a fuck

If she sends you a hearse
she's got the curse

If she sends you a ship
she's taking a trip

If she sends you a bed
she means 'Drop dead!'

The Alliterative Lament

Those who laughed have been laid low

Those who kissed have been killed

Those who sang have been slaughtered

Those who danced have been done away with

238

Those who loved have been liquidated

Those who smiled have been smitten

Those who exulted have been exterminated

The Characters that made the plays so marvellous

Old Doghope in *The Thriving Wives of Swivedom*

Red Knob in *Lust*!

Lord Catchpenny in *The Devil To Pay*

Lady Mantrap in *The Provoking Misunderstanding*

The Graf von Tippfehlern in *Die Ausstreicherin*

Miss Petticoat in *The Great Value of Underwear*

Alice B. Agony in *It All Begins at Sunset*

Seasonal Double Haikus: The Mating Season

1 The young man, naked,
lies with the girl impaled on
his cock. She's smoking.

They move, very slow,
it's like something under the
sea, so beautiful.

2 The girl says 'How do
you want me? On my hands and
knees?' He arranges

her. This is what the
Victorians always called
'unnatural vice'.

3 The little Jewish
girls have small wet cunts that taste
of gefilte fisch,

they wriggle so, so
happily, under lovers'
probing, tickling tongues.

Form

If
I
wrote
it
all
out
like
this
(the
way
the
amateurs
do
and
the
conceited
zeros)
I
should
kill
myself
with
boredom
!

The Beginning of an Augustan Ode to Masturbation, Written at the Request of Several Ladies and Gentlemen of Quality

Oh, Masturbation! Lord of Kings and Queens,
That from our Cradle bring'st us such Delight,
               By Day and by Night
That hold'st this Realm in Thrall,
And hast so many Modes and untold Means!

The 1930s Sex Novel

She undid his uniqueness
and tickled his twosome.

Double Haiku: The Lost Compositions

Haydn's 'Hen', yes. But
we've lost his 'Caterpillar',
his 'Sheep' and his 'Goat',

and, of Beethoven's,
his 'Mosquito Symphony',
his noble 'Frog March'.

A Daisychain for the Queen's Jubilee (1952–77)

Unique queendom! Mother! Renew
wives, sons, sad daughters!
So only yesterday you, undaunted,
dedicated, dominating, gave
easily your royal love endlessly,
yes, set the ethnic crown nobly
yet tremulously yours!
Simple earned devotion now will
lessen newly your real, lived,
dumb burden. Now we elevate
emotional loud delighting
garish high hymns solemnly!
Yours soundly! Yours serenely!

Note
The Daisychain was invented by my wife in the
spring of 1977, when she suggested that I should
write a poem where each word began with the last
letter of the word before. Perhaps 'unique queendom'
is stretching this rule a bit, but the principle is there.

Haiku: Hell's Grannies

Och! Women Old Age
Pensioners, clogging Post Off-
ices! (I'm eighteen).

Early Tribes

Primitive prickmen
lustfully levering
the weight of women
fucking the fatness

242

Winter Haiku (Expanded)

Filling hot water bottles
with a plastic funnel, I think of
Mme de Brinvilliers' water torture.

A Short History of Renaissance Rome

Popes full of sex and simony

The Poor Rich

They're eating crippled strawberries, wounded beef.
Why, everything they eat is dead!
The vegetables die as they are pulled,
they give up their roots like ghosts,
beheaded cabbages, desperate potatoes
longing to propagate, the blood of those tomatoes
is acid for them! All fish is fish-veal,
blood-emptied, colourless.

Pigs bleed to death – they eat the rending scream.

Women's Work

The moony womby poems that taste of blood.

Patronage

With a wry smile they wheeled out the inflatables
to inspire a community sense in the dogshit streets.

Invasion

Is it not passing brave to be a king
and charge in arabhood through Selfridges?

The National Games

The main event was Throwing The Jelly Baby

Sideshows included Runes and Tongue-twisters

One bardic exercise was Travelogue in Trochees

There was a Competitive Dash to the National Dish

Strange music was made on a one-stringed
                              instrument

Racial Dancing got combined with Rounders

They drank till dawn from The Cup of Hatred

The Critics and the Golden Age

'the life-giving importance'

'a master of hyperbole'

'the mystery embodied over against them'

Like ash and volcanic mud

on Pompeii and Herculaneum

time and death fall

on Putney and Hurlingham

Rugby Special Clerihew

Damaroids
help tired old men with haemorrhoids –
but, in sober truth,
the best aphrodisiac is Youth.

T. Sturge Moore

When I was young
I found T. Sturge Moore
a very boring poet –
but now that I am old
I find him even more boring still.

Penal

The clanking and wanking of Her Majesty's prisons.

John Reginald Halliday Christie

'The same stone which the builders refused: is
become the head-stone in the corner.'—PSALM CXVIII

So the man who was once called
'Can't Do It Christie'
and 'Reggie-No-Dick'
by disappointed girls in Halifax,
rose to be the greatest sex-maniac
of his generation.

Life-Style

The farmyard squeals in the breakfast bacon

The sun is shining in the noble vintage

The eggs are clucking in the honourable omelette

The wheat is windswept in the loaves we love so

In the beefburgers the bulls are bellowing

The peat-clean water wobbles through the whisky

The calmness of cows murmurs in the milk

On the 'A' Level Syllabus

Running-Dogs of Power by C. P. Smog

Selected Short Tories by W. D. & H. O. Wills
(includes Lord Piglet)

Cock Rise to Candlewick
(old-time wife-swapping in Outer Suburbia)

The Duchess of Murphy by Sean O'Webster
(impact of the Troubles on a Ducal household)

Rory O'Lanus by Patrick MacShakespeare
(the stirring drama of Celtic and Rangers)

Selected Perms by W. Money

The Little Pictures

A refined old lady cries 'Oh, crosswords!' when she
    drops a stitch

A madman tries to cut his throat with an electric
    razor

A man in tweeds and a cap says 'The summer is still
    with us!'

A girl in a sweetshop is vacant. 'Cruncher? I've never
    heard of Cruncher!'

An impresario describes a new kind of cricket, played
    on bicycles

Secret Service memoirs: 'The prettiest thing I ever set
    spies on!'

Kneeling Poet Laureate presents an *Ode To Sex* to the
    Queen

Impacted

There was a young lady of Penge
who was killed when a stone at Stonehenge
with great force and no sound
drilled her into the ground.
So sad a death none can avenge!

The Difference

The difference between churches and factories
everyone understands –
it's the difference between the laying on
and the laying off of hands.

Haiku: After the Orgies

All the Maenads had
terrible hangovers and
unwanted babies.

Two Nonsense Limericks

NONSENSE LIMERICK I

Eggwood limestone filbert horse
prayerbird angel trefoil gorse
tabard tunic
writing runic
semaphore semaphore morse!

NONSENSE LIMERICK II

Cathedral, amphetamine, string,
annuity, edelweiss, ling,
indemnity, cheese,
alabaster, demise,
ululate, underestimate, sing!

Thought About the Human Race

We are just a passing smile on the face of Venus.

Downfall

the
ass
   yri
   anc
      ame
      dow
        nli
        kea
          wol
          fon
            the
            fol
              d.

Serious Song

Elitist people
are the sweetest people
that one could ever know,
they're really choosy,
quite sincerely choosy,
they prefer Shakespeare to any
two-a-penny, jumped-up, bumped-up
illiterate so-and-so!

The Old-Fashioned Epigram

Her face was old and drawn –
and then it was carefully painted.

A Great Poem

This is a great poem.

How I suffer!
How I suffer!
How I suffer!

This is a great poem.
Full of true emotion.

Ordinary

Ordinary poems for ordinary people
is an ordinary poet's dream.
This sounds like a moderate wish – but always
the ordinariness is extreme!

Odd Men Out, Stateside

Micky, Dicky, Ricky and Licky
played Randy Roulette with Bernadette, Colette
and Nanette

Rocky, Jocky, Pocky and Cocky
played Come Clean! with Arlene, Marlene
and Josephine

Wacky, Lacky, Tacky and Macky
played Upside Down Cake with Adina, Marina
and Robertina

Military History

When they sent in the Old 69th ('The Muffdivers')
they defeated the Amazons in a few short skirmishes.

To Be Sniffed At

If young men are sniffing
at the thought of women,
this is like a stallion
pawing lustful ground.
The sniffs you hear from old men
are far more disbelieving,
it's a disillusioned
non–admiring sound.

The Defeated Husband

For breakfast I had

                  an egg and bad temper

For lunch I had

                a herring and bad temper

For tea I had

                    tea and bad temper

For dinner I had

                chicken and bad temper

The Anti-Cerebral Gut-Reaction Poem

Eh?
       Um?
Ah!
Oh!
Oo!
       Ugh!
       Yuk!
Pow!
Wam!
Zonk!
       Aaaargh!

Eve and the Apple

A young girl whose life-style the malicious
described, loosely, as too meretricious,
said 'When the boys peel me
and delightfully feel me,
I just feel like a Golden Delicious!'

Autumn

Life is sad and so slow and so cold
as the leaves that were green turn to gold,
as the lonely lake fills
and there's ice in the hills
and the long loathly winter takes hold . . .

Night Scene

There's a slow tolling bell in the dark
as the keepers are closing the park.
Like a desert, it's bare;
and each tree and each chair
is a blurred indeterminate mark.

The Father of English Poetry

Spade-bearded Geoffrey Chaucer
only rhymes with saucer –
a word that wasn't around
when everybody went for (and *everybody* went for)
        that marvellous Chaucer sound.

The Not Exactly Haikus

1 SOPHISTICATION

In the highly select brothels of the East
they are putting rouge on the lips of the vulva
to please the oil millionaires from the West.

2 SPECTRUM

On the bookshelf, as well as the *Collected Shorter
Poems of W. H. Auden*, we also find
The Sillier Poems of Sebastian Hairnet.

3 MIRACLE

As the preacher speaks loud against lust
the hard erect penis of God storms out of a cloud
and beats him into the earth.

4 TUDOR

Then Margery Mylkeducke
her kyrtle shee didde uptucke,
looking forwarde to a fucke.

5 SUCCESS

A lunatic who thinks he's living in the Nineties
writes a book of Stevensonian essays:
In Pudendis Muliebribus. Everyone is ravished.

6 HAIKUS

Anything sufficiently short and solemn
or portentously trivial
will be much admired by many.

Power Politics

When it's only a girl on a bicycle
we cross even though the lights are against us.
If she were a bus or a horde of cars
our feet would falter.

The Sexual Sigh

The small buttocks of men, that excite the
women . . .
but ah! the beautiful feminine broadness!

What the Rich Children Imagine

It's a bad life
for the poor children.
They're eating tabby cats
with kitten sauce.

Haiku: The Time of East/West Comparison

Madame Butterfly
marvelled at Pinkerton's big
cock (why she loved him).

On the Ambivalence of Male Contact Sports

Among men who play Rugger
you seldom find a bugger –
nobody strokes a bum
in the scrum.
Nevertheless . . .

A Remarkable Thing

A remarkable thing about wine,
which we drunkards and lechers all bless so,
is the way it makes girls look more fine –
but ourselves, on the contrary, less so.

The Edge On Us

At the Chelsea wedding
the accents are so high, sharp and bright
you could cut the cake with them!

Consequences

When Dr Feelingverse
met Miss Woodright
at the Literal Centre,
he said to her
'Your feet are uneven';
she said to him
'Keep your dactyls to yourself!'
and the result was
a litter of blind poems.

A Dull Morning Enlivened

On a dull morning
a student brings me a poem
comparing her husband's cock to an aubergine.
I think: this is more like it!

Americans

Americans have very small vocabularies.
They don't understand words like 'constabularies'.
If you went up to a cop in New York and said
'I perceive you are indigenous!' he would hit you on
    the head.

Transformation

It's sad when girlfriends turn into wives,
and wives turn into housewives – lust
flies out of the window. It isn't 'Bite me again!'
but 'Don't sit in *that* chair – it causes dust!'

An Emblem of Government
(Elizabethan)

All your bookshop assistants
are notable stealers of books.

Education
(Lord Leatherhead's Song)

Nobody ever can call me a fool,
because I once went to that Eton School.
No one can say that I'm backward at knowledge,
because I once went to the old Eton College.

Haiku: The Sex War

Foreskin-flensing Jews,
clitoricidal Arabs,
are locked in conflict.

Found in V. S. Pritchett

How, Rachel asked, did the raw young man come to
        be
married to Sonia, an actress at the top of the tree,
fifteen years older than he?
'The old girl knew her,' he said; 'she
was his mother's friend.'

                                    – *Did You Invite Me?*

Black Clerihew

President Amin
demanded sex with the Queen
as the price for releasing the British
(he was feeling remarkably skittish).

Ink

The ink of the love letters is dry,

and that's as much as to say
that the sperm that flows between the lovers
is also dry.

History, like the bones of the dinosaurs,
is always dry.

L. O. V. E.

A sadist sent a masochist a letter.
It said: 'Slave, I demand your presence! Quick!'
On the envelope was S.W.A.L.K.
(Sealed With A Loving Kick).

A Pronounced Difference

The simple villagers on the Meuse
in their ignorance speak of a *masseuse*.
Bellowing confident, like a moose,
the Americans call her a massoose.

The Short Blake-Style Gnomic Epigram

A voice was heard from a bottle of hock,
saying:
I am the ghost of W. H. Auden's cock!

After Death

They say Death's perfect Peace and Rest. That's
    interesting.
But if we don't have consciousness, how shall we
    know we're resting?

Dark Consolation

Even the little battered baby,
as it lies dying in its cot,
has known moments of happiness.

Julia Wood

If Julia Wood, if only Julia Wood!
I know, by instinct, it would be so good!
If only, only, Julia, Julia Wood!

Ah, but Wood Julia? I think Julia Wood
if I approached her gently – as I cood –
for Julia's not a babe in any Wood;

yes, I believe that Julia truly Wood,
she's not fictitious like Red Riding Hood.
Julia Wood like to! I'm sure Julia Wood!

Natural Enemies

The last people to be sentimental about cats will be
the mice.
The last people to honour the memory of Churchill
will be the miners.

Image

A girl is
idly
flicking a
lighter
making it
come

A Memory of 1953

I swear by all the rules of evidence, the
timekeepers and the clocks,
that at a Boat Race Party I heard a girl
seriously say:
'You can always tell the Oxford crew, they're the
ones with the dark blue cox.'

The Fullers

And among those masterly poems, some are
schoolmasterly too.

The Indian Love Lyric

Her rose is open.
It flowers with love.

Her black hair binds me.

If that rose closes
part of me will die.

Card Play

(folk poem)

Lay the King of Cads
on the Queen of Whores,
set the Five of Dogs
on the Knave of Thieves,
place the Two of Hands
on the Two of Tits
and the Four of Legs
on the Ace of Beds.

Put the Three of Dreams
by the Queen of Love,
take the Ten of Toes
from the King of Knives,
from the Eight of Fingers
move the Two of Thumbs
be ready for Good Luck
when it comes.

Haiku of Female Old Age

Many old women
are like empty paper bags,
with that crumpled look.

The Basic Desires

I want to drill a hole in your chicken

pull your rabbits to pieces

manipulate your guinea-pigs

destroy your pets for ever

Le Petit Poème Français

Hélas pour ces froids *gentlemen* anglais
(avec leurs femmes laides),
dont tous les membres (sauf que le membre viril)
sont absolument raides!

Insults To The Brain

In 1948 somebody told me
about Dylan Thomas's behaviour in The Gargoyle,
how he would go round the room on all fours
begging at the tables, like a dog, for a drink.

'Little Dylan wants a little drinkie!'

Good for a laugh – from the unsympathetic
or the envious other poets
or the professional disrupters, who think it's funny
to ring strangers on a Sunday morning
screaming 'Quarter to seven! Time to get up!'

But what (besides alcohol – the direct cause)
made him do it?
That is very far from a laughing matter.

Part Two *More Little Ones*

To Margo

In life's rough-and-tumble
you're the crumble on my apple crumble
and the fairy on my Christmas tree!
In life's death-and-duty
you've the beauty of the Beast's own Beauty –
I feel humble as a bumble-bee!

In life's darkening duel
I'm the lighter, you're the lighter fuel –
and the tide that sways my inland sea!
In life's meet-and-muster
you've the lustre of a diamond cluster –
a blockbuster – just a duster, me!

Clearing the Desk

Just a minute while I throw this badger
out through the window, squash a few squirrels,
blow up a pig, shoot some bloody hawks,
eliminate the bats and tortoises,
crucify all crows,
pulverise a pike, make the owls into omelettes,
dig a grave for the ground-hog!

Now I am ready to write.

A Possible Line of William Empson

A tie, in dining cars, commands respect

A Possible Line of Alfred, Lord Tennyson

The rhododendrons at the end of June

A Possible Line of John Clare

The little tittlemouse goes twiddling by

Seasonal Triple Haiku: The Tourist Season

From Santa Croce,
into the warm piazza,
they pour. A blonde asks:

'Where's the bathroom?' She
bugs the Italian guide.
He remains charming.

Another woman
says: 'They sure were a power–
ful bunch of artists!'

An Exeter Riddle

Sitters on the mead-bench,   quaffing among
                            questions,
I saw a thing –   tell me its totality.
A boy sped by,   his feet did not grind gravel,
high was his head,   incautious in the company
of the might of mountains   and a rock-rent liquid.
His hands moved little,   his legs seemed listless,
yet he woke the wind   and exacerbated echoes,
wending not to war   in a charging chariot,
unhelped by horses,   whirling like the wind.
Test-tube technology   covered him completely.

264

Seen for a second,   he was gone ghostly
as though he had never been.   Vouchsafe me
this vision!

The Death of a Mother

So pitiful and small, such skin-and-bone!

Religions of the Absurd

What people believe
is often unbelievable.
That a virgin could conceive
is inconceivable!

Haiku: Locomotor Ataxia

Four steps. A long halt.
The old man has a poet's
bad creative block.

The Atheist Typographer in
Theatreland

Outside *Jesus Christ Superstar*
it says how it's so long-running
and there's a quote from *The Times*
that calls it 'mind stunning' –
but that's a literal, it seems to me,
the second *n* should be a *t*.

Lines on the Death of Pope Paul VI
By E. J. Thribb (17)

So. Farewell then
Pope Paul VI.
My friend Keith
is learning Italian.
He says VI stands for
Veterano Intrepido.

But at least
you weren't called
Sixtus the Fifth.
In the old days
Popes were confusing.

Keith's Mum
says you were holy.
She says holy men
are very good and make
pronouncements
about things of importance
to women, e.g. birth control.

Some said you
were infallible.

Personally
I find it hard to say
what I feel about you.
Keith says
750 million Catholics
can't be wrong.

The Mississippi

I am Old Man Mississippi,
full of Time and Mud –
you all must be pretty nippy
if I ever flood!
Swim in me? You would be dippy!
Foolish flesh and blood
would end woeful, dead and drippy!
Keep your distance, bud!

Seamus Heaney

He's very popular among his mates.
I think I'm Auden. He thinks he's Yeats.

The Criminal Code

Just one God, right? For me and you
it's God next door, the mate of Stew.
Football we know, we've been to Craven
Cottage – but what's an 'image' and
                    what's 'graven'?
We swear all right, in court and out –
there'd be no fucking life without.
Church? What a hole, like in the head!
All *we* want from a church is lead.
Honouring parents? Likely lads
think nothing's squarer than their Dads.
Don't kill on jobs – unless it's plain
they'd recognise your lot again.
You're joking, surely? Thought you knew,
kids can commit adultery too.
Write it on walls: THOU SHALT NOT SQUEAL
(for us there's no such word as 'steal')
but if free pardons come your way,
then perjure, shop your mates, O.K.?

Don't know what 'covet' is. A man
must grab as much loot as he can.

North Love

I never sycamores so sweet
as to behold the walls of York
and to patrol her dimpled feet
as lazy of the minster talk

so happy of the hard-won stone
her weight inevitable bears
a pinkness that is mine alone
and worshipping her tender ears

the lightness of a summer dress
I love some colour of her eyes
the more of me and she no less
whose beauty comes as no surprise

exacerbate the fingered hand
unspeakable the quiet hips
of love such charm as contraband
and not compared the shapely lips.

Mock Christmas Carol

Jesus Christ was born today!
Hooray, hooray, hooray, hooray!
Whatever any of you may say
He was born to cancel our terrible sins
And save us all from loony bins!
Hooray, hooray, hooray!

Jesus Christ was born today!
Hooray, hooray, hooray, hooray!
This is no time to watch and pray,
Let's all get drunk and drink a toast
To the Virgin Mary and the Holy Ghost!
Hooray, hooray, hooray!

Jesus Christ was born today!
Hooray, hooray, hooray, hooray!
Over-eating's a lovely way
To do Him honour; each Yuletide gift
Gives Him a God Almighty lift!
Hooray, hooray, hooray!

Haiku: The Wit and Wisdom of Cyril Connolly

Connolly called the
British 'sheep with a nasty
side'. How very true!

A Titled Lady

At once a picture comes into my mind of a stately
beauty, topless perhaps, being manoeuvred into a
                                          ballroom
by a burly footman. He walks slowly backwards,
                                          firmly
grasping one of her excited nipples in each white-
                              gloved hand.

History

Ensuing events impede the backward view.

Cricket, Lovely Cricket!

It's an experimental congruence!
It's a probationary similarity!
It's a proving lucifer!
It's an investigatory rapport!
It's a probing likeness!
It's a dry-run flamethrower!
It's a try-out igniter!
It's a fact-finding similitude!
It's a researchful correspondence!
It's a trial contest!
It's a Test Match!

Variation on a Theme of William Blake: Ambitions of Young Women

Some girls long to influence men's hearts
but others concentrate on other
equally private parts.

On Reading the Poems of Matthew Prior to an Audience of One at the Poetry Society

It was one of a series called *Celebrations*.
One Scotsman, a teetotaller, turned up.

I felt sorry for Prior, an admired poet in his day,
and in my opinion as good as Dryden
                                    (much funnier).

I read for an hour, sipping whisky and water.
Afterwards I took the audience to a pub, he
                                    drank lemonade.
Was this a reflection on my reading or the Philistines
                                    of London?
I prefer to think Prior was far too good for them.

270

Daisy Ashford

(born 1881. *The Young Visiters* written 1890, published
1919)

Lords worshipped like the Deity
by the laity!
They must have thought Rothermere
was rather mere.
They had such innocence!
The inner sense
of nine-year-old simplicity
had authenticity,
each well-got-up dainty feeder knew
what Ouida knew:
you only looked quite the thing
if a Duke gave you a ring.

Haiku: Women in Wartime

Every small arms
instructor knew they had a
cut-away portion.

Robert Graves

A remarkable poet is Graves –
he throws out far more than he saves!
Each time he's Collected
huge chunks are rejected!
Yes, it's true – that's the way *he* behaves!

Self-Adulation

There's a foul smell, like pilchards left untinned,
where Rowse, the Cornish Shakespeare, breaks
his wind.

In a London Bookshop

There's a Scots poet called Dunbar –
they looked at me as from afar –
he wrote love poems, and divine,
a master of the lovely line–
they looked askance, they looked as though
they didn't really want to know –
he knew the Court, the field, the meadow,
'Twa Mariit Wemen and the Wedo',
satires and dirges, never loth,
he used his genius on them both –
they pursed their lips in noble scorn –
among the finest ever born,
he was far superior to
the poets sold in stacks by you –
they spoke as proud as pigs in bran:
We've never 'eard of such a man.

In the Land of Vowel-Reversed Rhyming

Now strippers everywhere flaunt their white loins
in King's Arms, Dukes and Bulls and the
     White Lions –
full in the face, to Puritans, vitriol
but welcome to the tillers of the soil
(Scots granite to the Western clay, lias),
who love to watch them wriggle on the dais.
From mountain crofts and flat alluvial plains,
the Dais and Hodges, Micks and Joes and Ians,
combine with Rams, Aquarians and Leos
to worship birds and bushes, tits and toes.

Mozart

Mozart
had all the skill that denotes Art –
his scores totalled milliards
when he was playing billiards.

Not Wavell But Browning

Nobody read him, the poor sod,
He was always moaning:
I am much more way out than you think
And not Wavell but Browning.

Poor chap, he always loved Larkin
And now he's dead,
The critics were too cold for him, his art gave way
They said.

Oh, no no no, they were too cold always
(He still never stopped moaning)
I was obscene and avant-garde and obscure
And not Wavell but Browning.

NOTE   Wavell was the British general of the Second
World War who edited a conservative anthology of
English verse called *Other Men's Flowers*. To the
Victorians, Browning was the last word in newness and
incomprehensibility.

A Victorian Question

How could those crinolined ladies
flounce down on pisspots?

North American Haiku

Hail, tribes of Outer
Alcoholia – the Rednose
and Goutfoot Indians!

Broken-Rhythm Haiku

Our cat
is the greatest thing on four legs
since Fred Astaire and Ginger Rogers.

Australian Note

It's not well known in leafy Pymble
that Malory called Pontremoli Point Tremble.

Resurrection

On the Last Day the wrecks will surface all over
                                        the sea.

At the Villa Rose

The black shit of Hélène Vauquier.

Free For All

In a Competition poem I read:
'If I am not a poet
why does my heart bleed?'
And I think to myself 'Quite!
Nobody ever seems to imagine
that a poet's a person who can actually *write*.'

Orgasms of the Lower Classes

And when they come they shout out loud
        'O Didcot!' and 'O Stroud!'
Or even cry 'O Mum!' 'O Dad!'
        'Wowee!' or 'What a lad!'
But ladies murmur 'What a pleasure!
I'm truly grateful, beyond measure!'

A Possible Line of Mary Wilson in Early 1979

Oh, dear old Betjeman, please do not die!

Musical Echoes

Who could make, out of musical notes floating
like sunbeams and motes, art?

                                        Mozart.

Which composer of the British nation was
most unlikely to call a station *el gare*?

                                        Elgar.

Who, if a girl in the gardens of Spain said
Play that again! might defy her?

                                        De Falla.

Who wrote a *Bolero* with a theme that a fool
in a dream could unravel?

                                        Ravel.

Whose huge family tree (what a lark!) was
all musical, branch, twig and bark?

                                        Bach.

Who sometimes woke in the night with a scream,
it would seem, crying: *Marguerite is NOT all sticky
with sentimentality and covered in goo! No!*

Gounod.

A Possible Line of Kipling, Concerning George Macbeth

He's a gentleman of Scotland, living South

Ambition

I tell you frankly
I want to write a poem that is so moving
that it leaves all other poems standing.

I want the readers
to be queueing up like mourners when a Pope dies,
crying their eyes out, loving their emotion,

I want the actors
to dramatise it all over the BBC,
misprints and all, in love and sorrow,

I want it to be
a statutory legend in its lifetime,
built to outstare the twittering birdlike critics.

Rural Rhymes

I know that God made badgers all
And blessed each hawthorn by the way.
Each animal, however small,
Is there to teach us how to pray,
And every little hedgerow flower
Bears silent witness to His power.

276

There is a blessing in the rain,
As it descends on me and you,
And in the ripening of the grain
We all can see God's purpose too –
Ah! no escape! We flee, we run,
But He shines o'er us like the sun!

Part of a Legend

Sir Launchalot sails his small pinnace on the Lake of
    Love.

Children's Books

When you read a line like:
They all took a Day Return to Pigglepopkin
you know you're reading a children's book. .
Without funny names children's books could not
exist.

'13 Die as Copter Ditches in the Sea'

13 die as copter ditches in the sea –
    and all the rhythm's broken.
This is the death of our technology –
13 die as copter ditches in the sea,
the printing presses whirr a threnody,
    technical details. No last word was spoken.
13 die as copter ditches in the sea,
    and all the rhythm's broken.

Martial Arts

1. *Good*

Avidus, greedy for praise, is a good fellow,
he's good at drinking with the reviewers –
no wonder they call his poetry good too!

2. *A Name*

That nobody Shaxberd, whose name nobody seemed
    able to spell
and who lived almost unknown in his lifetime,
has done an infinite amount of harm.

By giving hope to so many thousands of bad
    neglected poets.

3. *Virago*

Agrippinilla lives in California.
She's well into Cunt Positive
and proud of her bullet-shaped clitoris.

Triolet: Buying Records in July

I've purchased *The Ring*,
I shall play it this winter,

a long-drawn-out thing,
I've purchased *The Ring*

where for hours they all sing,
it's not cryptic like Pinter.

I've purchased *The Ring*.
I shall play it this winter.

Billy Budd

The sailorboys all gave a cheer
for their Captain, that old 'Starry' Vere –
he was the bugger
in charge of the lugger
and incontrovertibly queer.

Triolet: Wine in Old Age

The old men ballet round the loo
and rise, in turn, from drinking wine.

This is a thing they have to do.
The old men ballet round the loo.

It's like a dance, it's like a queue.
Though bladders weaken, they feel fine.

The old men ballet round the loo
and rise, in turn, from drinking wine.

Alcohol

Oh, so slowly the brain starts to go
as the cells are burned out, row by row,
and they're never replaced –
so we're certainly faced
with oblivion – the last thing we know!

Tourist Traffic

If you're in the market for fucks or
a girl or a boy who just sucks or
desire an Egyptian
of any description –
get going on a slow boat to Luxor.

D.T.

Dylan Thomas was rotund
and orotund
with the voice of a portwine parson.

Chorus of a Kipling-style Poem about Teenage Violence to Parents

So it's
　　a strong straight left for the Mum you love
and a hefty kick for her arthritic hip!
　　It's the iron hand in the iron glove
and some knives of different sizes to give Dad some
　　nice surprises
and the black eye and the swollen lip!

Der Hölle Rache Kocht in Meinem Herzen!

(Hell's revenge is cooking in my heart!)
　　　　　　　　– *Die Zauberflöte* (Schikaneder/Mozart)

The Grigsons are a team. They do very well.
Jane does the cooking. Geoffrey gives us hell.

The Highbrow Hangover

Today I am feeling subfusc
and as brittle and brusque as a rusk,
most frighteningly friable –
no action is viable –
not a man nor a mouse but a husk!

Food For Thought

Munchester! Stockpot!
In a train you can eat England!

Ancient Wisdom

The Myths are there for micky-taking.
The High Streets are there for money-making.

The Wars are there for killing people,
Old Age to make the strong ones feeble.

Sex is there to bring on babies
and give gay dogs the barking rabies.

Life is there to irritate us
and make us feel our lack of status.

Double Haiku: Sexism

All the tall thin gay
solicitors tell their boy
friends how women are,

without exception,
about three feet tall at most,
with big smelly cunts.

A Very Wise Remark Made By Harry Collier At Cambridge University in 1935

Why does a publican have a large belly
and his wife an enormous bust?
There's a reason, my acute friend said.
They fit like jigsaw pieces in that *mêlée*
occasioned by conjugal lust,
when they're locked together in bed!

Sauce For The Goose

To hate being a sex object? All very well and good –
and perhaps some men's desires are a bit mean and
        shoddy.
But when has anyone been thrown out of the
        sisterhood
for lusting after another woman's body?

Who Is Circe?

Who is Circe? what is she,
That all these swine commend her?
Sexy, bald, and drunk is she;
The Devil such force did lend her.
Underneath the Upas Tree
All the fiends attend her.

Weltanschauung

If you look at the world, it looks bad!
And this can make some people sad.
The slightly demented
are fairly contented,
the happiest ones are quite mad.

The Young Poet in the Literary World

The big insensitive faces / come up to you at parties
and you are wondering
who that terrible-looking fat tart is,

and she turns out to be a / greatly revered novelist
and that old purple man
a Prize-Winning Poet – unless you're pissed.

The words may have been winning / but the flesh is
     weak;
like everyone's, it ages.
A profile like that of an Ancient Greek

is foxed so much more quickly / than the humble
     paper
that holds a masterpiece –
grave marks stain hands, all that kind of caper.

You think they should look noble? / but no, it doesn't
     follow.
Each is just the mould that
once formed the statue; and, like all moulds, they're
     hollow.

Divorced Women in Dormitory Towns

The lives they travel in are like comfortable cars –
but they bore them. Oh, nothing happens!
With enough money and custody of the children,
do they sometimes regret the drunken husbands?

Lovers are hard to come by. Romance
in the brash shapes of feminine longing
left them twenty years ago. All that equipment
simply languishes unused in houses with gardens.

They are most like the day-trippers who drive
into safari parks. They're afraid to go out
into the world of lions. Claustrophobes,
they watch their sweet bodies shrivel like grapes.

Martial and Domitian
('The Book Of The Games')

In those days it wasn't keeping up with the Joneses –
it was keeping in with the Emperors.

If he held Games, you had to praise them.
After all, look what he provided!
The amphitheatre filled with water, for a real sea
                                        battle,
women killing lions on the dry sand,
a condemned criminal crucified *and* eaten by
                                        animals,
tigresses fighting lions, bears elephants,
a rhinoceros goring a bull like an old leather ball –
a genuine banquet of assorted cruelties.

How could anyone fail to praise an Emperor like
                                        that?

A Line That Might Be A Stumbling Block To The Puritan Faithful

The patriarchs, with all their concubines

Haiku: Mrs X

An old police dog
sniffs my knickers. I charge him
£8,000. Wow!

Haiku: Thirty Years Ago

I climbed up her white
redbushed body. She had big
green eyes like a cat's.

Haiku: Foreplay

Undressing, she laugh-
ingly hung her panties on
his hard hatrack cock.

Reputations

Poets are very touchy. They have to be the greatest.
Or (if not quite *that*) at least the latest.

A Hair of the Doggerel

It's so unfair that alcohol makes you fat
and feel, next day, like a half-dead bat.
The Devil's at the bottom of this, it's understood, for
    you
would expect something so nice
to be terribly good for you.

The Sad Widow

Candy-floss Blackpool, wet and windy, with the
    sadness
of the sad sad widow
Pier and ballroom, hotel bar window, with the
    sadness
of the sad sad candy
Flossy sea-spray, wrought iron, whelk-smell, with
    the sadness
of the sad sad Blackpool
Popping brown seaweed, chip shops, windy, with the
    sadness
of the sad sad widow

Blackpool, rock pool, boarders, sandworms, with the
    sadness
of the sad sad widow
Thin landladies, thin-sliced bacon, with the sadness
of the sad sad wetness
Sea wind, raincoats, crab claws, windblown, with
    the sadness
of the sad sad floss-stick
Ballroom, bar-room, bright lights, rainstorms, with
    the sadness
of the sad sad widow

NOTE   This was written on a course at the Arvon Foundation,
Totleigh Barton, as a poem-game. Two or three students,
improvising, act a short piece on a theme dictated by another

student. Spurred or inspired by this, all present then have 12
minutes in which to write a poem on some aspect of what has
been performed.

In Austria

When you drink a *Qualitätswein*
you will never be a loser –
this just means the wine is fine
for the fairly choosy boozer.

When the *Bestattungsunternehmer*
takes the butcher and the baker
he is not a loud proclaimer
but a quiet undertaker.

Brandteigschokoladencremekrapfen –
pronounce it, you will make mistakes!
But nothing terrible will hapfen,
these are simply chocolate cakes!

Spring Song

Lovers are rolling over like cats in the sunshine,
allowing their tummies to be tickled,
licking one another,

full of the excitement of finding a new person,
happy in the warm emotion.
The questions come later.

Soon they will discover there are two different people
involved in these affairs; quite simply,
spring is never summer.

Haiku: Culture

Ah, wee-wee! The great
French writers: Rubberlegs and
Ballsache and Racing!

Pantoum: Worship

So much I deify your glorious globes
(and kiss your round re-entrants and your cleft –
the Oriental earrings in your lobes
are all you wear) I touch both right and left

and kiss. Your round re-entrants and your cleft!
On your white skin the blacks of body hair
are all you wear (I touch). Both right and left
I see a Heaven feminine and fair,

on your white skin the blacks of body hair,
where both shine with a single, sexual light.
I see a Heaven feminine and fair
that overwhelms me now – it is so bright

where both shine with a single, sexual light,
the two, the privileged, that make the love!
That overwhelms me. Now, it is so bright –
yet comforting, the finger in the glove,

the two, the privileged, that make the love
(the Oriental earrings in your lobes),
yet comforting (the finger in the glove).
So much I deify your glorious globes!

September

It's warm and it's wet in September
as the summer burns down to an ember –
but the cold weather comes,
freezing toes, tits and bums,
in the two months that follow December.

In Memoriam

Like grim death, we say. A grinning death
gets painted on black leather.

Not for these. Three tourist motorbikes
with right of way on unknown French roads.

One looks back. He wavers
into oncoming traffic.

Notifying. Taking the body home.
Telling the parents.

Not work for twenty-year-olds.
Or seeing it.

Hardest of all, accepting it.
Accepting it.

Mushroom-Shaped Haiku: In a Season of Despair

We think, as we look
at our children: is this the
last generation?

Triple Haiku: Measure For Measure

Measure for Measure
has three creepy characters –
Angelo, the Duke,

Isabella. Why
does he abdicate? Simply
to test Angelo?

And why does she *not*
scream *Vows*! *Virginity*! when
he offers marriage?

Belgrade

The two big rivers neighbour in the North

The early morning trams are suffering elephants

The sliding doors cremate the airport baggage

The tourist blouse can cost a whole week's pay

The spice is hidden, deeply, in the meat

The plums are resurrected in hard juice

The alphabet rejoices, two-in-one

Chastity in Bloomsbury

Virginia was right in a way
to keep Leonard Woolf so at bay –
though she lifted her vest
for her V. Sackville-West,
that was only in amorous play!

A Person

She's mean and full of minge-water.

Competition Piece

There was a young lady of Leicester
whose boyfriends all fondly caressed her.
They squeezed both her boobs
like toothpaste in tubes
and then went ahead and undressed her.

A Possible Line of Dr Samuel Johnson

The Pious Reasoner his Tear withholds.

Part Three *Extra Little Ones*

Found Haiku: Waterloo Station Gents

I want to whip the
bare bottom of a pretty
girl tied up for it.

England At Christmas, 1982

O silly little, proud and silly, country
so good at ceremonial, limited wars,
football (occasionally)! Snob Billy Buntery
gives all the rich, rich presents – Santa Claus
has handed out the land. He hates the serfs,
the common people, so uncommonly low;
loves dogs, cats, hunting, cricket, the green turfs
that make a stately-homely postcard show –
quite beautiful, memorials to old greed,
when what there was to take, to steal, to pinch
went to the bastard Baron on his steed
or landowners, enclosing each square inch,

or City men, who raise a joyous anthem
for a fake-lady bossyboots from Grantham.

Denis

The perfect marriage, it must seem!
This is an advertising dream.

Where he is, he doesn't know.
Saatchi & Saatchi made him go!

To countries sad, or gay, or sinister.
He has to sit with the Prime Minister.

Dazed and dining, day and night,
he's not allowed out of her sight.

At all banquets there's a place
for his long square tortoise face.

Saatchi & Saatchi! We adore!
But they've a lot to answer for.

Dogs in Polite Society

Dogs always go for the loins of a guest
and sniff them with zest –
this embarrasses the rest.

The Leipzig Gewandhaus Orchestra Gives Peter Porter a Standing Ovation

H ail, hail, Antipodean Promoter of Bach,
E xcellent verisimilitudinous versifier!
I n truth His Fugues are never too *einfach* –
L ate homage, though, they rightly must inspire!

P oet, preserve your civilising mission!
E xhalt High Art (the paint, the note, the word),
T hat may all end with our next nuclear fission –
E asy indeed to think such tasks absurd!
R anged against you, the forces of the market

P ropagate Pop, Free Verse, the slack, the sillies –
O that huge Juggernaut, tell them to park it
R ight up the Snowy River! Tell hillbillies
T hat His Chorales are rousing as hard liquor!
E xhort those high-born twits in Jags to nark it!
R evive the flame that's now a fitful flicker!

Haiku: A Self-Deceiver

He's been in the same
room with Eliot, Pound, Yeats. *So*
he's a great poet!

Cinquain

Cinquains
are just silly
little pointless poems –
invented by Adelaide M.
Crapsey!

(Syllables in each line: 2/4/6/8/2)

Sextet

The sextet is more of
a whimper than a
bang – it's designed
to have a
dying
fall.

(Invented by Gavin Ewart. Syllables: 6/5/4/3/2/1)

Rural Life
(Rough Cider)

Down in Barton Sunshade
They don't drink lemonade
And the lads have hairy great enormous balls –
Every rip-roaring bugger
Is first-class at rugger,
As they come in the rucks and the mauls!

Down in Causley Betjers
The lasses love the lechers –
The pride of pricks that make their pussies pout –
They don't think it's a sin
When partners put it in,
The sin, for them, is when they pull it out!

A Well-Known Leader of the Women's Movement Goes Mad and Writes a Hymn to the Penis

O Penis, glorious Penis,
I love to see Thee rise,
to peer up to Thy pink-tipped top,
it seems to reach the skies!
I lie and worship vainly
or fall upon my knees,
Thy testicles make Three-in-One,
blest Trinity of threes!

Double Haiku: S. C. U. M. *

Our society
doesn't need one for Cutting
Up Women. It does

that already in
several ways, and very
efficiently too.

* Society for Cutting Up Men (an American feminist organisation)

Haiku: Rugger

The fly-half jinks through
like a Cabbage White zigging
clear past cabbages.

The Eclectic Chair

He's sitting in the Death Seat in *The George*
and Lethe clogs his brain with silt and sedge.

If anything now rises, it's his gorge;
his mind was once a bright and Blakean forge –

now drained as animals the butchers porge –
sees little, hears as much. He's on the edge,

he's sitting in the Death Seat in The George
and Lethe clogs his brain with silt and sedge.

NOTE   The 'Death Seat' in the BBC pub, The George, is by the
door, on the left as you go in. This is where the oldest BBC men
sit before they die. Lethe is of course the river of forgetfulness
that encircles the classical underworld. To 'porge' is to render an
animal ritually clean according to the Jewish faith.

Kiplingesque: Going West

When you see things hazy or not at all,
    Not even the oculist's card,
When at every step you're afraid you'll fall
And you have to hold on to a stick (or a wall)
    And reading is far too hard;
When the traffic slides by with a noise like mice
And everything must be repeated twice
And your friends all die and you feel depressed,
Why, then you will know (if you haven't guessed)
You're very quickly going West!

297

Variation on Two Lines of W. B. Yeats

Love is staying for a bit
in the place of piss and shit.

A True Story of a Young Woman in the Fifties

She lay on a towel sunbathing
on a genteel English beach.

A small brown dachshund rushed up to her
and began to make enthusiastic love to her arm.

She could do nothing about it. She was a lady.
In that world of ladies such things were not
        acknowledged.

She couldn't even shout (which would have been
        appropriate):
Fuck off!

When he had finished
she tripped down to the sea and washed the guilt off.

The Old Couples
(For Edward and Edwina⋆)

Of course they realise
there isn't much time left –
one old partner will soon be bereaved and bereft –

⋆ Edward and Edwina are two Edward Gorey toy cats,
purchased from the Gotham Book Mart, that sleep on our
double bed.

298

one day a sun will rise
that finds only one in the bed –
because the other one has been taken away, dead.

Proverbs and old saws
bear witness a thousand times
to this – so do all clocks and church chimes,

it's one of Nature's Laws,
but as it happens to me and you
it's always going to strike us as something new.

Gather ye rosebuds
or *Live well* say the bores
who are always sermonising the drunks and whores,

and some days *have* been duds . . .
with Death and Time on the brain,
we should make the most of the ones that remain.

What a Surprise!

How amazing – there are Communists in the
Unions!
How unbelievable – there are Fascists in the
        Boardrooms!

Ogden Nash in Naples

The favours of the girls of Naples
are not to be purchased with small items of office
                equipment, such as paperclips or staples.
Oh, no! They're much dearer.
They cost several thousand lire.

A Jewish Beauty To Her Admirers

If you would earn my true respect,
kill any old Arab, of any old sect!

Haiku: A Noted Dinosaur

Rhamphorhynchus has
a name like a character
found in *Aida*.

Drinking Song

Elated by the Great Depressant,
I was feeling fine.
Bottle, glass and lip – incessant
was the flow of wine!
Why on earth should people stop?
Drink it down to the last drop!

Ah, but wines have lees and dregs too,
they can turn the brain,
easily knock you off your legs too,
drive you quite insane,
there's an end to all the jokes
in the heart attacks and strokes!

Part of a Born-Again Triolet Comes Through the Post

I am writing to tell you about the Good News of God's
    Kingdom.
We are all looking forward with the hope of a happier
    future.
I once saw a book about India, it was called 'The
    Land Of The Lingam'.

I am writing to tell you about the Good News of God's
    Kingdom,
and everyone in Woodborough Road and Australia
    thinks it will be fair dinkum –
though the World is falling apart, the Great Surgeon
    will perform a suture.
I am writing to tell you about the Good News of God's
    Kingdom.
We are all looking forward with the hope of a happier
    future.

Note
The first two lines are the beginning of a letter received by the
author on 24 April 1984, from an address in Woodborough
Road, Putney.

The Jewel in the Crown

The best character is Mildred –
always drinking gin and getting fucked
and being nasty to everybody . . .
very proper reactions
to the Imperial situation!

Shouted Out By The Choir At The Wedding

She's a willing wife,
a cuddlecomekin!
Her contours are convenient!

He's a penile pillar
of wildfire by night,
a masculine mainstay!

Drawbacks Of Being A Woman

All girls can walk through a lavatory door –
but it's harder for them to pee on the floor!

Note
'Lavatory' = 'toilet' in the vernacular, and 'bathroom' in
America.

Bridging Apartheid With Rugger Fiends

If the Devil himself
came up from Hell,
with fourteen other devils,
and said:
'I'm a red-hot practising bugger –
but I'm willing to play Rugger!'
they'd play Rugger!

Double Haiku: De Groot

(Son of a musician and fellow-conscript, East
    Surreys, 1940)

In the latrines, some-
one had written: DE GROOT IS
A CUNT. Next to this

somebody else had
written (more harshly): DE GROOT
IS A DOUBLE CUNT.

A Never-Never Slogan

Get stoned – with Stone's Ginger Wine!

From 'The Atheist's Handbook'

I'd sooner put my trust in a drunken dentist than in
     God.

Breaking Out

So many little neatly tied lyrics!
Can you blame us if we go
for the poems that are mad, bad and dangerous to
     know!

Out Of The Mouths Of Babes And Fucklings

In a train from Southampton to Waterloo:
two young men, two young women, two babies –
one in arms, one in a carrycot.
Laughter, and 'fucking' the most popular adjective –
one of the men even called his girl a 'cunt' . . .
surely those babies will inherit a sophisticated
     vocabulary!

Nature In The Raw

The squeak of a hostess
as she sees, over your shoulder,
a more important guest arriving . . .

The squeak of the caterpillar
of the Death's Head Hawk Moth . . .

Celtic Twilights

Dublin and Edinburgh are just the same –
and whisk(e)y-drinking's the only game!

A Pseudo-Laureate Gets Started

(Notes on the Queen, etc.)

The Queen is tiny
but her crown is shiny –
the Duke's not so bad,
he's a bit of a lad,
and so is Andy,
he's really randy,
like Christine Keeler
and Rice-Davies (Mandy).

17 July 1984

An Underground Movement

The Hooded Clitoris
sits in an arbour
with her friends
Urethra and Labia,
planning and plotting
the feminist books to be
published by Fabia & Fabia.

Willis And Botham: A Prep School Poem By Bill Frindall ('The Bearded Wonder')

Willibags and Bottibogs are two strong men,
They played for England again and again.
They did well against Ozzies, Pakis and Hindis★ –
But they seldom succeeded against the West Indies!

★ Hindi is a language but occasionally, according to the *OED*,
    can be a person too.

• Haiku: A Japanese Dried Flower At A Poetry Reading •

Take a poet. Drop
him in alcohol. He'll ex-
pand in full colour!

The Deaths Of Horrible People: A Partial Consolation

When all is done and all is said,
the horrible people at last lie dead.
Reagan and Thatcher go into the blue
along with Hitler – but so do you!

2/Lt. John Hepburn, R. A.

You sat in the arse of the aircraft, watching the flak.
You were lucky that, like a boomerang, you came
    back.
You came back with a gong, hero of night attack,
To your earthbound comrades in Air Defence, in
    Light Ack-Ack!

NOTE   John Hepburn (one of the sons of Anna Wickham) was attached to an RAF Bomber Group from the 47th LAA Regiment for a month or so in 1942. He flew as a tail-gunner in a Wellington, to observe the effectiveness of German anti-aircraft gunnery – for which he was awarded a DFC. John was by no means a standard Army officer; riding a motorbike in Service Dress and black boots was about the form. His first Battery Commander was called Major Cheese. One day he was summoned to the Battery Office for a reprimand.

Major Cheese: Mr Hepburn! When you left the Mess last night I
             saw you *stagger*!
2/Lt Hepburn: Of course I staggered, Sir. I was bloody drunk!

T. S. Eliot and Ezra Pound

Eliot loved the music halls
(and he probably loved pantos).
Pound took the rubbish out of *The Waste Land*
and put it all into the *Cantos*.

The Beginning of a Victorian Novel

'Hot fuck!' cried Louisa disdainfully. 'Git outa here,
    you scumbag!'
Florence, Harriet and Octavia maintained silence,
    hidden as they were behind the door of the
    conservatory.

Not Peace But A Sword

Mosque or temple, church or steeple,
religions are keenest
on killing people!

Found Poem In A Robert Graves Letter (To Karl Gay) 14 April 1965

My life at Deya was beginning to stink.
I had to get out and think.

Haiku: G. M. Hopkins

'I got a sudden revelation when I looked at the *facsimile*
poem in Desmond Flower's *English Poetic Autographs*: I
exclaimed, aghast at the handwriting, "That man bites his
nails." "Yes," said Grete (our tame-but-wild graphologist)
"and has other comfort habits!"' Robert Graves, letter to
James and Mary Reeves

G. M. Hopkins? Could
it be Genital Massage?
It seems quite likely!

A Martian Haiku

Departure Boards at
Waterloo flick their packs like
impatient gamblers.

Ruperta Bear's Feminist Poem

We live in a society that's phallocratic
but we're beginning to make literature cunnicentric.
Already many women can only read books by
        women –
if they accidentally read something written by a
MAN
at once a horrible feeling comes over them,
the words grip them like the hands of a rapist,
with a scream they throw the book from them!

Christopher Hogwood

Christopher Hogwood
plays the harpsichord better than a dog would.
You've probably heard
him worrying away at Byrd.

Exiles From The Sun (Blake-Style)

Even in the streets of cold, wet Britain
the little West Indians can dance and sing!

Two Found Poems In Siegfried Sassoon's Diary (1923–1925) p. 197 and p. 203

1. A weakness of mine
   is for sparkling red wine.

2. Drank half a bottle of Moselle
   and feel well.

Variations On Pepys, 2 Sept. 1667*

Bab May and Lady Castlemaine
and all that wicked crew
are throwing their weight about again,
to fuck and buck and screw
and squirm into the King's regard
and urge him to do wrong –
who praise the hardness of his yard
and tell him it is long!

* 'and he is great with Bab May, my Lady Castlemaine, and
  that wicked crew'. Baptist May was the courtier who devoted
  himself to the pleasures of the King. Lady Castlemaine was the
  Senior Mistress, very given to political intrigue.

A Betjeman Variation
(Tune: 'Red Sails in the Sunset')

As hot as a hornet,
As warm as a wasp,
They're dying like flies in
The old Cottage Hosp!

1914

Rupert Brooke's young swimmers into cleanness
        leaping
landed in the mud and blood of the Western Front.

Triolet: Unsisterly Behaviour

It's the women are great willy-gigglers,
they will giggle at every mention!
Remembering beds! They were wrigglers!
It's the women are great willy-gigglers!
It's the comics sell jokes – they are higglers
and the willy-response their intention!
It's the women are great willy-gigglers,
they will giggle at every mention!

NOTE   'Higglers' are pedlars, travelling salesmen

Brief Encounters

All beginning conversations
are fumbling through the clothes
towards the fornications
that pleasures these and those;

are they sometimes sad or serious
or frolicsome with fun –
delightful, deleterious?
Until the whole thing's done

you can never know the answer.
Is *she* quite what she seems?
Is *he* the Bengal Lancer
of her long erotic dreams?

NOTE   This is a twelve-minute poem, written as an exercise on a
course at Marylands College, Woburn.

Reading

Paperbarks don't read paperbacks –
they're trees in Australia.
And to read a glossy magazine
you don't need glossolalia.

All Marriages Are Mixed

Did the Greeks have a word for it
(marital boredom)?
As every day they gazed at the same old face
from Samothrace?

• Ordering Whiskey In Ireland •

It's embarrassing to have to say
to a blonde-haired dyed barmaid:
Have you got a Black Bush?

310

Celtic

The Irish are great talkers,
persuasive and disarming.
You can say lots and lots
against the Scots –
but at least they're never charming!

Decline And Fall
(Evelyn Waugh)

For some lads it's always bad weather.
You could say that of Paul Pennyfeather.
Toffs, from Drinking Club rags,
Ran away with his bags –
He was sent down from Ox, hell for leather.

Then he taught in an awful Welsh school –
Prendy, Philbrick, cad Grimes (he's no fool).
Next it's prison – White Slaving
(Margot's face was worth saving??).
Ah, for her he was only a tool!

But he got back to Ox in the end
to drink cocoa with Stubbs, his old friend.

NOTE   This poem was written for a *New Statesman* Competition
– fourteen lines of verse, or less, to tell the story of a famous
novel.

A Shakespearean Song

All around the distant tracks
motorbikes are farting,
whores are lying on their backs,
lovers' legs are parting.
Yo ho! Yo ho!
and all we know:
Ending is not starting.

In their glassy shining tanks
terrapins are twiddling,
buttoned bosoms on green banks
feel foul fingers fiddling.
Yo ho! Yo ho!
and all we know:
Life is fair to middling.

Dying

When the horrors of old age
gather round,
the most sensible thing you can do
is to die –
you may even get
Pie in the Sky.

And the preachers
are often heard
confidently to say
that Born Again Christians,
if there's a Holocaust,
will be swept up to Heaven
by angels
straightaway!

Death And The Child

Why dat man
poo poo?
Why dat man
bum bum?
Boy, dat man
dyin!

Why dat man
wee wee?
Why dat man
pee pee?
Boy, dat man
dyin!

Why dat man
come come?
Why dat man
toss toss?
Why, dat man
hanged, son!

The World of Gerald Hamilton

They're standing proud, those male parade-ground
    guardsmen,
so like toy soldiers, stiff, erect and red.
And so they'll be – for money magics guardsmen –
in any silken, scented Knightsbridge bed.

Oral Love Song

In days when I was barking up your canyon
    the echoes coming back were soft and sweet –
not like Chicago's North Side and O'Banion
    in 1924 – and I repeat
in days when I was barking up your canyon
    the echoes coming back were very sweet!

In days when I was occupied with rimming
    you seemed responsive to that near caress,
your joy quite overflowed, and I was swimming
    in oceans of your female happiness –
oh, yes! When I was occupied with rimming
    you seemed responsive to that near caress!

You were being served, and I was doing the plating,
    a waiter running to present each dish,
to bring you true delight, not keep you waiting,
    and pander to each taste and whim and wish –
oh, surely you were served, as I was plating,
    a waiter eager to present each dish!

The Life And The Work

All my life I've worked hard
(or fairly hard)
writing silly advertisements
or writing silly poems
by the yard,

making the new sows' ears from
a silk purse;
and all you have in the end is
a lot of old-style ads,
outdated verse.

Don't ever make the future
a sacred cow!
Believe me, all that really matters
is the problematical joy
of the here and now.

My Stoicism

I can stand anything except pain –
and you can say that again!
When they start drilling my teeth
I know it's time for my friends
to send a wreath.

If, in the night, I ever get cramp
not even The Lady With The Lamp
could soothe that agony to an end
or cancel my thought that I'm going
right round the bend!

I'm also afraid that I'm going mad
(the critics would say *How sad*!)
but of course looniness might help
to stifle the terminal yelling,
the deathbed yelp!

LATE PICKINGS
(1987)

Part One

The Sadness of Cricket

(many facts from *The Golden Age of Cricket 1890–
1914* by David Frith)

The happy summer game, where fun
lies like a playful cat in golden sun –
true innocence in every ball and every run –

where all is for the best, they say,
nostalgia only when it goes away –
romantic memories that haunt the close of play –

is like that poem, 'Dover Beach',
like Arnold's lovely world it's out of reach,
and there are other lessons it might also teach.

How golden lads of Housman's sort
lose all that beauty and can end up caught –
by portliness – and far too fond of gin and port.

And how the agile cover point
slows with arthritis in each stiffened joint –
his briskest fielding now would only disappoint.

Those godlike carefree flashing blades
don't flash for ever in that field of shades
and time can trump a Trumper like an ace of spades.

All right for private incomes, turn
to them they could, money they had to burn,
the amateurs, the Gentlemen! But Players earn

their living in a young man's game –
when they retire it's never quite the same.
If they despaired, would they be very much to blame?

Coaches and pros at public schools,
they taught the rudiments to flannelled fools;
like swimmers striking out in private
                                    swimming pools,

the young were trained in all the strokes.
But did *they* feel like victims of a hoax?
Famous fast bowlers, run to fat, now schoolboy jokes?

We'd one at Wellington, that A. E. Relf,
who'd bowled for England – long since on the shelf –
in 1937 stalled and shot himself.

Remembered bowling in the nets,
a little irritable (I thought – but one forgets),
doling out stumps to junior games, like doubtful debts,

from the Pavilion's mean back door.
He had this job, I wouldn't think him poor,
but losing it might put him firmly on the floor.

Professionals lose jobs? They could.
Respectful, yes, you had to be – and 'good'.
Some amateurs cut loose, but it was understood

that there was really no appeal
(although it seems to me a dodgy deal)
when Players misbehaved; witness the case of Peel,

a Yorkshire bowler, too content
to stay in the beer tent, his favourite tent.
A Test Match bowler too, but did
                    Lord Hawke relent?

Peed on the pitch! A County game
was scene of his unheard-of drunken shame.
Hawke threw him out; and Peel's a
                              long-forgotten name.

Pro with a County? Umpire? Then
that was 'retirement' for such humble men.
Cricket Schools? Sports goods? These were rare
                              in 1910.

Though Gunn made bats. The 'Autograph'
by Gunn & Moore, his sporting epitaph.
Used once by me. My batting, though, would make
                              you laugh.

Strength, talent gone – then what to do?
Great Albert Trott, like Relf, was gunned down too
by his own hand in Willesden – very sad but true.

'His powers waned in 1904'
the record says – and just £4, no more,
was found, his wardrobe left to landlady. The score

of that fine bowler/batsman: small.
'He liked a pint'; but dropsy took it all.
In 1914 – thousands more about to fall –

Harry Graham and Johnny Briggs
died in asylums – and among the prigs
who wouldn't fancy Burns (corn rigs and barley rigs)

you might count batsman A. E. Knight,
'mental' perhaps, at least not over-bright,
who prayed while batting – an extraordinary sight!

And Arthur Shrewsbury, tipped by Grace
as runner-up in the Great Batsman Race –
he was a suicide. He couldn't stand the pace;

thousands of runs that he amassed
made Grace a generous enthusiast
but didn't help. And Aubrey Faulkner, too,
                              was gassed

in London, 1930, by
his own sad hand. It makes you want to cry –
but all they wanted was some peace, simply to die.

And Arthur Woodcock also went,
in 1910, by his own poison sent
to that far bourne. Each cricket season was lent

to Leicestershire. He coached the lads
at an American College; and their Dads
remembered him as fast as Kortright. Oiks and cads

such may have been. At 44
he thought it time to leave and shut the door . . .
The Gentlemen had deaths as well, but in the War.

Poor Stoddart was another case,
who shared great opening partnerships with Grace –
but shot himself at 52. Life's hard to face!

The blazer and the ribboned coat?
The most pathetic soul for Charon's boat
was Percy Frederick Hardy – he just cut his throat

at King's Cross Station; old and mean,
the Fates attacked him, March 1916.
Ten years for Somerset, a useful pro, he'd been

scared of the Front, the shells, the mud.
A public lavatory received his blood.
The County of London Yeomanry found him a dud.

The Captains toss. It's Heads or Tails;
but Time and Death at last remove the bails,
though you weep buckets of the Bard's
                              prophetic pails.

You can work gents into the mix.
George Lohmann died (T.B.) at 36,
and Alfred Lyttelton was himself hit for six –

an abscess from a cricket ball,
a Cabinet Minister when toffs walked tall.
A famous Foster was most interesting of all.

A tart was murdered, and police
knew that he knew her. Questions didn't cease,
frequent as cigarette burns on a mantelpiece.

He took her home (200 fags,
a bottle of Scotch whisky bought – old bags
like this) but she was young and not the kind that
   nags.

At 20 Nora Upchurch had
gone loose in London – also to the bad.
Strangled in Shaftesbury Avenue (that's also trad).

An empty house. A man called Field
confessed to Press, and all was then 'revealed'
that for two years had been quite well concealed.

'Not guilty' at Old Bailey (he
retracted all he'd said), in '33
he walked away, he was released, completely free.

But later tried the same trick twice.
This time the jury turned out not so nice.
You win some, lose some, it's the shaking of the
   dice.

Nobody gets away with much.
Even late cuts, the Ranjitsinhji touch,
leg glances, don't impress the Fates and gods
                        and such.

A Gorgon married C. B. Fry.
Call no man lucky till he's come to die;
So said the Greeks, and they had ancient
                        reasons why.

NOTES 1 *Victor Trumper (1877–1915)* One of the
greatest Australian batsmen. Like Grace and Hobbs,
he could make high scores on very difficult wickets.
He died at the age of 35.

2 *Bobby Peel* Yorkshire bowler (Yorkshire won the
County Championship nine times between 1893 and
1912). He took 102 Test wickets against Australia;
once winning a Test by ten runs (taking 8 for 67) but
had to be sobered up in a cold shower beforehand by
his Captain.

3 *William Gunn* A great Nottinghamshire and
England batsman (George Gunn was his only slightly
less famous brother). In 1896 he went on strike,
refusing to play in a Test team unless he was paid
£20, instead of the usual £10. He died a wealthy man
–because of his partnership in Gunn & Moore.

4 *Albert Trott* An Australian bowler with several
styles, and a tremendous hitter. He took 8 for 43 in
his first Test against England. When the selectors
ignored him, he played as a pro for Middlesex (4
wickets in 4 balls and later a hat-trick against
Somerset, in his benefit match in 1907). In 1899 and
1900 made over 1,000 runs, took 200 wickets in each
season. An umpire in 1910.

5 *Albert Knight* Went to Australia with P. F.
Warner's team of 1903–04. He is slandered in the
poem, since he was apparently 'thoughtful and well-
read'. Nevertheless the Lancashire fast bowler Walter
Brearley is supposed to have reported him to the
M.C.C. for praying during an innings.

6 *Arthur Shrewsbury* The greatest professional
batsman of the 1880s and 1890s. His 164 on a
dangerous pitch in the Lord's Test of 1886, against
the bowling of Spofforth, is reckoned one of the
finest innings ever played. He was an opening
batsman of extraordinary patience. He captained

England in seven Tests in Australia. Committed suicide in 1903, aged 47.

7 *Aubrey Faulkner* A South African Test cricketer, who also played for the Gentlemen. Very successful in the 1909–10 series against England. A D.S.O. in the War.

8 *Arthur Woodcock* Described as 'a magnificent specimen of Midlands manhood'. Kortright was the fastest bowler of his day, and at his best Woodcock was thought to be as fast.

9 *A. E. Stoddart* Captain of England at cricket and rugby. While leading England in the 1894–95 tour, he made 173 at Melbourne – highest score by an England captain in Australia until 1975. In his last match for Middlesex in 1900 he scored 221. His opening partnerships with W. G. Grace were legendary. He shot himself in 1915, soon after his 52nd birthday.

10 *Percy Frederick Hardy* He was a Dorset-born left-hander, but played for Somerset. Top score: 91 against Kent at Taunton in 1910.

11 *George Lohmann* One of the 'strikers' of 1896, and a principal professional bowler for Surrey. Took 100 wickets, for example, in 1892 – when Surrey were Champions for the third year running.

12 *Alfred Lyttleton* Brother-in-law of Arthur Balfour, Prime Minister. Wicket-keeper batsman for Eton, Cambridge, Middlesex, Worcestershire, the Gentlemen and England. In 1884, in a Test at the Oval, he removed his wicket-keeper's pads and took 4 for 19 with underarm lobs. In 1913, when he was 56, a blow from the ball caused an internal abscess – from which he died.

13 *The Fosters* This was F.R. Foster, who led Warwickshire to the Championship in 1911, at the age of 22, making a century in both Yorkshire matches and 200 against Surrey. He took 32 wickets that winter, in a very successful tour of Australia. But the strain showed in 1912, and he rested for a year. Nevertheless he made 305 not out against Worcestershire in 1914 (still the County record). A motorcycle accident during the War put an end to his cricketing career. He was a left arm fast bowler and a right-handed batsman. He had no connection with the seven Foster brothers who played for Worcestershire, of whom the most famous, R.E. ('Tip') Foster, captained England and died young, at 36, of diabetes. For details of the Field case, see *A Reasonable Doubt* by Julian Symons.

14 *K. S. Ranjitsinhji* The famous Indian Prince who played for Cambridge, Sussex and England. A great stylist, he was the first man to score 3,000 runs in a season.

15 *C. B. Fry* The blue-eyed boy. Scholar, athlete, footballer (Association and Rugby Union), journalist, Naval officer, schoolmaster. Played for Sussex and England. Six successive First Class centuries in 1901 (still a record). Married Beatrice Sumner, a very tough lady who (after his death) took over command of a training ship for Royal Naval cadets, forbidding all masturbation, dumb insolence and answering back.

A Murder and a Suicide in Wartime

You'd think neither was necessary,
with so many soldiers being killed –
the German, the Italian, the Russian brother –

but I came across the one
and then the other.

In 1942 the Troop was in billets,
not long before we went overseas,
Fernhurst or Fleet (I think the latter),
the memory blurs, and finally
that's no great matter . . .

There was one Welsh gunner
always being picked on by a Bombardier
for Welshness and stupidity;
this irked him like pre-thunder
pressured humidity,

so one night he took an axe
(part of the standard Fire Precautions)
as everyone lay peacefully sleeping.
Heavy strokes, blood splashing,
running and seeping,

he bashed the Lance-Bombardier's
handsome unconscious head in . . .
was he paranoid or persecuted?
At least authoritarian niggling
was more than muted.

The suicide happened in North Africa –
a big, apparently happy, gunner
shot himself with his own rifle.
What triggered that, what depression
or magnified trifle?

They said he was happily married.
Would the separation cause it?
The MO's death certificate hit one nail
on the head: in perfect health,
the body of a young male . . .

Tribes

('Here's tae us – wha's like us?')

Are tribes a good thing?
Or are they bad, and ugly –
as smugly they hug themselves
over a victory, football or cricket
or almost anything?

Irish, Welsh or Scots –
should they pride themselves so
on Kelso? do they smell so
terrifically sweet? what about their feet?
English, Irish, Welsh or Scots?

You could pride yourself
on looking like Cardinal Newman,
on being a woman or human
or deft or left-handed, or 'gentry' or 'landed'.
You *could* pride yourself.

But it's all a bit fake,
a bit bogus and silly –
a big willie, being a hillbilly,
most pride is foolish, stubborn and mulish
but in the end a bit fake!

The Brewery Tap

'Theer's no reet lass works in a pub!'
This was a Yorkshire dictum
from before the War (I did Market Research) –
and certainly landlords picked them

for blousy bosoms that charmed the lads
and real or bogus blondeness.
The regulars were bold of speech,
with a certain routine fondness,

fancying themselves as connoisseurs,
as choosers and pickers.
There were jokes about tin-openers too,
the futility of tin knickers.

Barmaids took them as compliments,
predictable and predicted.
It never went further than 'Gi'e us a kiss!'
The love-making was restricted

to what could be done in a Public Bar
without appearing shocking –
though male minds had their suspender belts
and the silkiness of a stocking.

They all equated Sex with Sin,
with naughty Eve and her apple,
and Drink was the third in that Trinity
in every Methodist Chapel.

The Brewery Tap is at the source,
where they knock one p. off the bitter,
where Satan is busy pulling the pints
and Sin bears her yelping litter

(it's all there, plain, in *Paradise Lost*) –
it's a wicked Garden of Eden,
a real-life Cockaigne where the Lord is mocked,
a sweltering sex-mad Sweden.

That was the theory. But fifty years
have made it all seem cosy;
the future of Sin in those Public Bars
isn't, now, quite so rosy.

There are fights of course, and boys and girls
can start being alcoholic –
but a glass of beer isn't filled with fear
and it isn't truly symbolic

of Wickedness and the Fall of Man.
The long slow pints of the Pensioner
are innocent things – and as for Sin,
there's not much reason to mention her.

She's out on the streets, where the pushers are,
baiting the teenage trap.
Big H, cocaine – it's a world away
from the simple Brewery Tap.

NOTE 'The Brewery Tap' is a Young's pub in Wandsworth,
part of the brewery (hence the lower price). In *Paradise Lost* Sin is
described as the mother of Death – Satan was the father.

Dying

How wonderful, how lovely, if you could just
come romping up on a charger,
in victorious armour,
with all the trumpets blowing!

How marvellous, how rewarding, if you just
broke the tape, with everyone cheering,
'What style! What daring!'
and all that triumphant shouting!

How consolatory, even, how right, how just,
the sentimental 'cellos sadly mourning
with their mellow moaning,
like TV or a sad film running!

How mistaken! For hours the just and the unjust
lie on the battlefield severely wounded
and no trumpet is sounded,
no 'cello plays for them as they lie dying!

24th March 1986

Thirty long years have passed away
since that most auspicious day –
   black and white, the photos tell
   all but the temperature and smell

(and the colour), ikons rich
in that peculiar feeling which
   makes us think – then think again.
   Stroll with me down Memory Lane

is what the simple souls pronounce
whose pound of flesh is, every ounce,
   cut from the body of the Past.
   And yet a union that can last

for so long isn't incidental
(though pleasing to the sentimental).
   Marriages fade, and slide and slip,
   but you can bet a partnership

that's lasted now for three decades
deserves poetic accolades!
   No need to be a solemn owl
   to tell us how fair winds and foul

can blow on marriages, that tack
between 'Oh, love!' and 'Take that back!'
   Romeo and Juliet too
   had their bad moments (although few).

The path of true love isn't smooth,
the ruffled feathers sex can soothe
   ruffle again – for couples never
   spend all their lives in bed together.

So, camera-caught, I'm standing there,
the March wind bullying my hair,
   with you half-serious at my side
   in the doll's clothes that mark a bride.

Would I have known, would I have thought, too,
that such 'Till Deathness' could or ought to,
   holy or not, a close communion,
   be such a feature of our union?

Nobody knows what's on its way –
we all get by, from day to day –
   but it's a marvel, plain to see,
   that you should stay so long with me!

'Love me little, love me long! –
No. Love grows different, but grows strong,
   and time can change it to its best
   by subtle compound interest.

The Old Deaths

In the Twenties, when I was ten or more,
my mother used to tell me about the deaths of
                              old people –
perhaps this was to forestall questions like:
'Why don't we go to see Aunt Annie any more?'

She would say, 'You remember old Mrs Something?
Well, she's died.' There were never any details –
as now, being grown-up, we might easily say
'It was cancer of the larynx,' or something of
                              the something.
I never asked. I wasn't very curious.
Dying, like smoking, was a thing that
                              grown-ups did.
Let them get on with it, would be roughly
                              my attitude.
I accepted it as part of life; it wasn't odd or curious.

Aunt Annie lived close, among Eastern souvenirs –
she had quite a big ivory temple or pagoda,
kept under glass. She was nice, and gave
                              me chocolates.
She was small, like Queen Victoria. Such thoughts
                              are souvenirs,

328

they are talismans and tokens; not emotional
                               rememberings.
These were the lives I scarcely touched, I brushed
                              against them.
Perhaps I was aware of an atmosphere of kindness –
an old arthritic lady, in a chair, among
                               rememberings.

NOTE   She was my mother's aunt, my great-aunt.

Lovers In Pairs

Hearing the other one breathe
is a function of all paired sleepers
   and it's coupled with the wish
   such breathing should not stop.

Young lovers lay ears to hearts
and say how it would be ghastly
   if the beating faded down
   to silence – just gone away.

They think the end of the one
would be love's end, for no other
   ever would be the same.
   Of course, they're right – and wrong,

for many will come to the beds
and twenty is different from thirty,
   as sentiment's middle age
   moves slowly and coolly on.

When old ones lie side by side
what's real at last has a look-in.
   The breathing *could*, surely, stop –
   and with it the warmth of love.

It's the penultimate bed
before the one with the gravestone.
   This is what each one thinks –
   a thought sad, loving and warm.

Taking Care of the Elderly

They leave us out on the polar bear runs
so we get frozen and/or eaten

They put us outside the villages
in the jungle where the tigers pass

They choke us to death with smoke from the fires
at which they'll roast us

They put us in high-rise buildings
where the lifts don't work

They leave us to the con-men, the yobbos,
all those who rape, murder, steal

They give us inadequate, and too late, money
                                  for heating
so we die easily and slowly, of hypothermia.

Good Times

The last ten years of a life
are often a tiny bit dodgy
for Everyman and his wife –
she ends overweight and quite podgy,

though she looks after things
she does less and less of the gardening,
arthritis under the rings,
the arteries slowly hardening;

and he's not exactly handy,
slow, heavy, and jowly and paunchy –
who once was both racy and randy,
rake-thin and raffish and raunchy!

They go into the chrysalis stage,
caterpillarish appetite
shrugged off as they move through old age,
the long snooze of the day and night.

330

Theologians say that the soul
comes out as a butterfly next.
The Bible is there to console
and soothe all our fears with a text;

but there's no doubt that old age is sad,
mad and bad are the suitable rhymes,
and the graces that both of them had
have quite vanished like all the good times.

Sons and Mothers

There's the energy
that revs like a motorbike
vroom vroom vroom,
there's the energy
that can throw a mother
half-way across a room.
Sophisticated saloon bar sexpots
advise the cat;
but nothing except violence and violence
is going to follow that.

There's the lethargy
that spreads like a blighted fog
and covers the lot,
and the lethargy
that wants the satisfaction
they know they haven't got.
When they were little, they were affectionate
and very sweet;
but now it's nothing but violence and violence
and drugs from the street.

It's not the poor ones –
as much, or more, the rich
get high, stoned, blind
(like poor ones)
and stumble hopelessly
into that teenage ditch;

it's upper-middle mums and aristos,
not just in slums
do they have to stand for violence and violence
and land on their bums.

Joe

In a dustbin class in a dustbin school
    sits Joe;
not quite a knave and not quite a fool,
    how low
can he sink? Yes, he's on the way down,
    no job
waits for him here in this dustbin town –
    to rob,
to mug; that's what all the wild boy-gangs teach
    on streets.
For the school he's already well out of reach,
    no feats
of great teacherly skill can turn him now,
    too late
for Reading or Writing or Sacred Cow –
    the State
did its best in a land of money and graft.
    But sea
swirls round Joe, with no hope of a raft –
    no swimmer he!

A Memorial Service in a South London Crematorium

Shall we go down South of the Border, right down,
    Betjeman way?
To the Cemetery in Streatham, where the mourners
    hope and pray?
Where the silent swift Cremation holds undisputed
    sway?

Down where the beefy peasants eat chips with
    everything?
There are sometimes Hymns on the telly, but none
    that they can sing –
All the worship there is vestigial, and Christ a
    forgotten King.

Everything's shortened to what the brain can
    uncomplainingly hold
And Single Syllables hold sway. The Young as well
    as the Old
Vaguely believe, in the woolliest way, in Eternal
    Cities of Gold.

Or do they? For willy-nilly this is the End of Man.
The roses on the lawn spell out their MUM, their
    DAD, their NAN,
As Sorrow hangs round the Departed, each Viv,
    each Elsie, each Stan.

It's a gesture (like a cultured pearl, the Poet's tear in
    the eye
Isn't *better* than the sob and the grunt or the naked
    animal cry)
And it recognises, in a way, that all men have to die.

Screaming Venus

If you believe the novels
(and why shouldn't you believe them?)
there are some passionate women who really let go
    and
scream and yell when they come –
it's as though a man were murdering a mad
    monkey.
And all because of continuous lubricious friction of
    the bum!

I've not met it myself
(perhaps they weren't passionate women?)
or I wasn't stimulating enough to earn this tribute.
Moans there were and some sighs –
but nothing to raise the roof or annoy neighbours,
after all the strong, sinuous
delicious locking of thighs.

One girl I loved was frigid
(but this didn't make me not love her).
Ideas about sex – if they're rigid – can often be
    wrong too.
Pleasure, yes. Orgasm, no.
That's all she had, but very much better than
    nothing.
The dance was the thing, and contiguous
ambitious quick, quick, slow.

The Deaths of Poets

('Wildlife Showcase', BBC TV)

When the old honey-gathering bees
lose their strength and can no longer fly to honey
they don't walk off into the sunset like Charlie
    Chaplin,
brave and undaunted.

They turn their backs on the hive
and crawl away from it, the dying, unflying prey
of horrible big black spiders who paralyse them
and keep them fresh for eating.

Or they fall into the deadly path
of the black ants that swarm on them and sting
    them,
gangsters dedicated to the natural murder;
not sentimental.

Agincourt (1415): A Greek Epigram

Foot-soldiers and archers that starved,
                    marched, fought.
What reward was theirs?
Pages of glory in the history books they never
                    even saw.

In Memory of Philip Arthur Larkin, CH, OBE, 1922-1985

(Westminster Abbey, Friday, 14 February 1986)

The Church has a style, and Larkin had a style –
based on the novelist's descriptive gift
for telling detail, loading every rift
with actuality; mile after narrative mile,
he buttoned up the heat of the railway carriages
with the excitement of incipient marriages,

curiously incurious, and a looker-on.
The Church isn't like that. It's keen to claim
an atheist poet who's a famous name.
He's there in Heaven, it says. For us, he's gone –
much loved, humane; that shyly gloomy humour
stays in the minds of friends, a ghost, a rumour

to those who never knew him. He looks down,
and sees at last his quite immense mistake;
Eternal Life has got him, it's no fake.
It's not a Laureate's or a Martyr's Crown,
the Order of Service says that he must suffer
this non-stop non-extinction; any duffer

must likewise live for ever. Se we kneel,
though agèd stiffness makes its pained protest –
a jazz group gets some beauty off its chest,
the choir sails on, on music's even keel.
The Lesson, with archaic memorability,
is praising 'rich men furnished with ability'.

The jazz is best. Goes straight into a vein.
No hanging about, pure feeling floods the heart
with negro sadness – lost battles, from the start,
a captive people with its captive pain.
For death, no other music holds a candle
to this – even 'Lift up your hearts' by Handel!

Singing 'Abide With Me' is always fun,
though congregations seldom keep in time
and the tune wavers. A dollar to a dime
some will be late, some beat the starting gun.
More joy (memorial) would have been afforded
if they'd used poems he himself recorded,

that stuttering unstuttered genuine voice
would have made present that elusive man,
a private person, catch-me-if-you-can
and solitary; lonely, it seems, from choice.
However good professional verse-readers,
poets are best, their own more special pleaders.

'Church Going', 'An Arundel Tomb', 'Love Songs
                                    in Age' –
sensible, conversational dying falls.
Forget the death, the death that so appals –
'a serious man on serious earth' each page
now shows him – you can cut the screams
                                    and yelling
and even organs, bidding prayers and belling –

and yet, and yet . . . an enjoyable communal act
did honour him, and certainly makes us feel
better for honouring him. A measured meal,
hieratic course by course, a sort of pact
to push the night back, belief or unbelief,
and make our death release, if not relief.

All For Love

There must be thousands of men
and in the past there must have been millions,
who have thought, 'Shall I throw it all away
and go to *her*?' Leave the wife and kids,
though friends might use the word 'infatuated'?
Many must have thought this, but many
                                more hesitated.

Something has pulled them back,
out-of-the-frying-pan-into-the-fire proverbs
or just natural caution. To make love all day
for weeks on end is a thing you can't do –
it's a diseased condition, a permanent erection.
Though love and sex are powerful (and
                                natural selection)

you still have to live through
the long shared days, the unending breakfasts,
meet the friends who gush, who hoot, who bray,
and of course she may have children too
who might easily hate you, or be resentful.
So they settle for a life that's less exciting, *un*eventful.

Miles Williamson-Noble

(*De Mortuis*)

The Colonel didn't like him (my guess).
He called him Mr Wilkinson-Noble
(there was another officer in the unit
                                called Wilkinson).
(Some people, of course, didn't like the Colonel.)

On bad days Miles looked like the dog Pluto.
He was rather affected and snobbish
(of me he said, 'I believe he was
                                a commercial traveller')
(He got married and said, '*Il faut travailler pour faire
                                l'amour!*').

337

When the unit was about to go overseas (1942)
his father pulled some strings, got him a home
                                    posting
(his father was a rich and successful surgeon)
(my father did quite well as a surgeon too – but he
                                    hadn't any strings).

When this happened the Battery subalterns
(egged on, I think, by the Battery Captain)
got drunk one night and poured cold water over him
as he lay asleep in bed (it was quite a cold winter).

We were in tents. I heard the screaming and cursing.
I hadn't been approached to assist this persecution
(he was my Troop Commander, I was Troop Leader)
(perhaps they felt there would be feelings of loyalty).

I didn't hate him, but I knew he was unpopular.
I remember another officer saying to me, 'A
                                    certain person
who's lying in bed with a scent-spray up his arse!'
(but he wasn't effeminate, just very superior).

My Battery Commander had said, 'That's the
                                    medical
profession for you!' (and he'd looked at me in a
                                    point-scoring way).
The funny thing was that after he was posted
we heard he'd been killed (was he bombed
                                    or something?).

The Lost Boys

An appeal comes through the letter box,
headed 'Missing O.Ws',
those with whom Wellington has lost contact,
those silly kittens who have lost their socks,
thinking perhaps, 'What's the use?'

or even, very possibly, dead.
Name of House or Dormitory, date.
Have they gone wild with Peter and Wendy?
Would the Padre say, 'They've gone ahead!'
Late for parade? Or, simply, 'late'.

Envelopes returned as 'Not known here'
or even, more foxily, 'Gone away'.
What of G. J. E. Penrose – Thackwell?
1918 is given as *his* year.
A.W.O.L., one might say.

Or P. Heber-Percy, 1922?
E. C. Richards, 1915?
willing or unwilling deserter,
missing or involved in a war or two –
school-shy or just a has-been?

NOTE   A.W.O.L. is the Army abbreviation for 'Absent Without
Leave'.

Advertising Elegiacs

Advertising! The men at the front are most terribly
                              turdlike!
    Backroom boys are the best; they can be human
                                    (a bit).
Clients are worst of the lot, bullies and thick as
                              a blanket,
    Presentations to *them* are true purgatorial things.
Ad-managers (if they're new) want to show you that
                              they are the masters.
    Chlorophyll once was the vogue; but the
                        Chairman's wife didn't like green!
Everything greenside was out – so campaigns went
                              out of the window.
    Thinking up replacement crap, that was the
                              terrible bore.
That's one example, of course, but examples of this
                              come in thousands.

This is what drives them to drink, and the heart
                    attack bang! at the end.
Suppose you've done it all once. Twice is not good.
                    But a third time!
Three campaigns in a row, and the brain gets a bit
                    of a twist!
Is there a moral at all? Is there, somewhere,
                    consolation?
Only that death, in the end, bonks the nasties as
                    well as the nice!

The Loved Ones

> Thou hast committed –
> Fornication: but that was in another country
> And besides, the wench is dead.
>
> *The Jew of Malta*

Men who have loved a quantity of women
go round London
from house to bar to restaurant
like Stations of the Cross,
remembering – the gain, the loss,
the once-revered addresses
of girls in summer dresses.

They run through a kind of girls' – name alphabet,
an A-Z of London,
where even the pubs remind them
of long hot love affairs . . .
who touches and who cares,
who fondles and who fancies
in these long-gone romances?

What was that all about? they are thinking
perhaps, in London –
where everything's changed and changing
in an indifferent town;
no smile, no word, no frown
from dark heads, blonde heads, red ones . . .
might just as well be dead ones.

Anthem

Our bones will all be built into the runway
with the bones of the Chinese coolies who are
                              building the runway
who are starving to death and are building the runway
so that the Japanese planes may take off over the
                              ocean.
We too shall feel faint and fall down and be built into
                              the runway
our bones will be powdered flat with the stones and
                              squashed into the runway,
the bones are an indeterminate white that go into the
                              runway,
there are no blacks or yellows or whites in the bones
                              of the runway,
they are dry and chalky as the stones we build into
                              the runway.
Each brings his stones and his bones for the path of
                              the runway,
so that the Japanese planes may take off over the
                              ocean.

Love Talk

Whatever is said,
in or on the bed
(like 'Were you
telling me a fairy story?'
or 'I want to
feel you inside me!')
is insubstantial air
circling the pubic hair . . .

From top to toe,
all the love will go
('I want to
lick you!' or 'Open
your legs a bit wider!'
or even 'I love you!'),
it will vanish away
like childhood play . . .

It stops and starts,
performing arts
(like theatre,
cinema, ballet,
there for a moment,
then slowly forgotten)
are most like this –
the insubstantial kiss . . .

Incoming Calls

They come in so happily, the incoming calls!
Stepping gaily into a room –
a room, it could be, of depression or mourning,
of someone whose sister has just died of cancer,
whose cat has been run over,
whose boyfriend or girlfriend has gone for ever . . .

The jollity of the far voices halts on the doormat,
as it were. The old friend feeling good
and wanting a long amusing chat
feels out of place, a tactless intruder.
He or she. Shut the door and stumble away –
                                ring off –
that's all they can do.

Inspired by a Simile of Roy Fuller's

Our cars were nose to tail like sniffing dogs
parked in adjacence at the rendezvous . . .
I thought of this while sitting in the bogs,
my mind stuck to your image then like glue –
although so many years have come and gone,
thick with events as any Irish Stew
(good with the bad, the Rebel with the Hon),
my Memory Lane still leads at times to you,
with coloured photos of the single bed –
the contacts made there once were not a few.
The lights were green before they changed to red
and everything was old, that once was new . . .

Doglike devotion, yes, that was the key.
It passed you by, but much tormented me!

High Potato Land

Every great poet in far High Potato Land
thinks he's the only true one –
total contempt for all those who don't reckon him,
homage is what must be done!

Thousands of poets in far High Potato Land –
every one thinks he's quite great –
man, woman, child, they all know they are geniuses,
that is their natural state!

There's a crime story by Highsmith that tells us of
quite a remarkable thing –
penises on the dried bodies in catacombs
shrivel to small bits of string.

This is their fear in that far High Potato Land:
big reputations may shrink.
They in their full ostentatious ubiquity
may not be great as they think!

Putney OAPs in 1985

They dribble down the High Street/ in dribs and
                                    drabs, on sticks,
the wrinkle-faced old women,/ the men with
                            'past it' pricks,
slow among the mums who/ wrestle with
                        push-chair kids,
they stop for 'Hello, stranger!'s/ or 'Well, I
                            never did!s',
clots in the pavement's bloodstream/ that bike-boys
                                    put at risk,
they wince at teenage swearing,/ tut-tutting or
                            tsk- tsk!

When Thatcher was a nothing/ and keen on boys
                                    or horses,
they underwent the bombing,/ and the danger of
                                    the Forces.
MPs who live for money/ and the well-being of
                                    the City
don't reckon much these old ones,/ they're a bore, a
                                    drag, a pity –
not beautiful, attractive,/ fashionable or bright,
why can't they get a move on/ into that
                                    long goodnight?

They don't appear on chat shows,/ not many ask
                                    their views,
they're has-beens of the media,/ they never will
                                    be news.
So close down the old people's/ hospitals and homes
(the Welfare State, quite clearly,/ isn't loved by well-
                                    fed gnomes),
forget the War they fought in,/ way out beyond
                                    the brink –
because it *doesn't matter*/ what such old seniles think!

Sons and Lovers: Part One

The nagging wives that drive a man to drink,
the drinking men that drive a wife to nag,
the coal scuttle, the kids, the kitchen sink,
the pregnancies that make her belly sag,
the little houses packed in, back to back,
like the poor sleeping husband and poor wife –
for those with work, a smoking chimney stack,
others stay cold, an unrewarding life
though neighbours with coarse kindness bring
                                    some help,
it's still an animal thing, like dog and bitch,
fawn to the masters, snarl, suckle and whelp,
make do and mend, clean, cook, and knit or stitch –

till Saturday's beer breaks in, hot cock and hen,
the night that starts the cycle going again.

'A Piece of Cake'

(In Memoriam Dieppe, 19 August 1942)

No, the murders left no traces on the shore,
no, the murders left no traces
on the bright and murdered places
where the murderers were active once before,

and the sun shines bright on that bright promenade
where the slayers crouched to slay them,
there was massacre and mayhem –
because, to tell the truth, it isn't hard

(though there are hundreds in the landing craft)
if you know you'll be invaded
and you have them enfiladed,
to mow them down at leisure, fore and aft.

Just the accidental skirmish out at sea
and they went to Action Stations.
All they needed then was patience,
like the spider in his web – you must agree

it wasn't hard, with strong points on the cliffs,
you could do it sitting, standing,
even though the tanks were landing
you could knock them out without the 'buts'
                                        and 'ifs'.

No, the murders left no traces on this scene;
where there once were blown-up bodies
kids with eyes like silly Noddy's
run in joy as though that war had never been.

Dieppe, August 1984

NOTE   The Dieppe Raid of 1942 had as its centrepiece a frontal
attack on the town by Canadian troops, towed across the
Channel in landing craft. The operation was compromised, not
by any security leaks, but because a German E-boat patrol
sighted the left flank of the convoy and opened fire. If

communications had been better, the raid might have been called off, even at this late stage. The whole operation depended on very exact timing (waves of fighters attacking the town) and the timing went wrong. One battleship shelling the defences would have made a lot of difference, but the Royal Navy reserved its battleships for the Atlantic War. As a result, the Canadians lost 56 officers and 851 other ranks. One Army officer at the briefing is supposed to have told the regimental commanders that the raid would be 'a piece of cake'.

All Souls

This is the room where the great poet breathed
                    his last.
His breathtaking originality is now like mist on
                    the air.
Here is the desk where he worked, and in the corner
is the old wind-up gramophone that helped him
                    when he typed.

There are photos of friends, and letters: *Cher collègue*!
In glass-fronted bookcases are his books, including his
Collected Poems translated into Icelandic.

In the master-bedroom there are photographs of
                    his wife.
She has less of an aura, but nonetheless she is there.
He is the star, the children are photo-appendages,
                    like the small
groups, quite informal, of him with the great
                    Other Writers.
He didn't have much taste in pictures, the landscapes
                    are dullish.
To show honesty, perhaps to shock, is a detailed
                    line-drawing
of the small obstinate penis that caused him so
                    much trouble.

Some love-letters survive, with the work-sheets
                                    of verse.
There are even, like sleeping beauties, curled locks of
                                    their hair.

The There Then meets the Here Now in piped
                        appropriate
music, its fixed harmonies run like lost dogs through
                                    the rooms.
His walking stick too lies doglike in a glass case.
It will never walk again, 'it has finished
                                with walking',
as his pupil expressed it in the famous
                        memorial poem.

Going into the Details

There are scholars who
get hooked on all the particulars
in Dictionaries of Slang,
e.g. 'to fist it (of a woman):
to seize the *membrum virile*
with a sexual intention'.
There are many others I could mention.

Even though it's all
stigmatised as 'low', 'colloquial'
and obsolete as well,
the learnèd lovers really like it
(though, indeed, the whole language,
one could say, is obsolescent).
Such words make a don or two tumescent.

But this is to put
a magnifying glass on every letter,
the language of love
takes in much baboon behaviour,
you don't need reams of Latin
to get the actual satisfaction.
Idiots too are in the web of thought and action.

347

Jurisdiction

I want to be a Hittite Priest-King
but the Canadian Geese on the lake are barking
                              like dogs
and over them I have no jurisdiction.

I am warm, I am comfortable, I am staying in a
                              guest-room
where Yeats once stayed in the 1920s.
It's a high-class guest-room and a charming duplex,

by the main entrance and covered with ivy,
nicknamed by the College simply 'The
                    Prophet's Chamber',
where the Bible-bashing preachers relaxed from
                              their labours

in the days when Divines were the reverend visitors –
and far more than me like the Hittite Priest-Kings.
But the geese on the lake still escaped their
                              jurisdiction.
                         Wells College, Aurora, N.Y.,
                              April 1986

Part Two *The So-Called Sonnets*

'I Didn't Have Enough Sex'

(John Betjeman in old age)

In my bad dream I paid the man in the caff.
Threepence for the tea. Then moved away.
I drank half, then came back for some sugar.
'I know your sort!' he said (or something such).
He poured my cup of tea into the sink.
'I paid for that!' I said. But he just looked,
confident, arrogant, a kind of god.
He gave no answer but a settled hate.

Dreams in which we are slighted and disliked.
And never get the things we ought to have.
Think of the millions! Betjeman's Complaint!
The beautiful, the young, the commercial sellers
are rare exceptions (and they have too much).
The sugar and the god are usual.

British Poets

We don't get jailed for criticising the Government,
or sent into exile or into lunatic asylums,
the small freezing concrete cells are not for us.
Even the avant-garde lives in bourgeois comfort,
in Polys and suchlike, teaching – part of the
    Establishment.
Hard labour, sleeping on sacks, the whips, the dogs,
we live apart from these, in limited envy.
We can even manage humour, and not always bitter.

It's really only in Northern Ireland the cracks are
    showing
(what you might call an Arab-Israeli situation);
three hundred years earlier the men were planted
like dragon's teeth. So now we have cowardly heroes
and a chance to write of political suffering,
like the genuine Russian, European, South African
    sufferers!

The Daytime Mugging in the High Street

Who would want to attack that poor little thing
walking up Putney High Street at 9.30 in the
                                    morning,
without a thought in her head except to get to
                        Putney BR Station
and then to Clapham Junction, to a sale at Arding &
                                    Hobbs,
with a view to buying a quilt, or was it a fan-heater?
Well, somebody did! Went for her purse in her
                            basket,
pushed her into the road. Severe bruising, three lower
                            vertebrae cracked.
A young chap, he missed the purse, made off into
                        Fulham.

I reckon he was a loony; or an addict, crazy on a
                        Monday morning,
needing a fix after the weekend. Who knows? She
                        didn't even see him.
Luckily for her, there wasn't any traffic. Thrown
                        into a main road,
she could have been killed. All the conventional
                            judgments
say what a terrible thing (true) and what a terrible
                                man!
But I say, too, she *might* still be better off than a
                        tormented young junkie.

Protein

I can confidently predict that very soon we shall all
    be dead.
On the telly a horrible white mantis, looking far too
    much
like something out of a ghost story by M.R. James,
has caught a great big beautiful Brazilian butterfly.
Fairly slowly, as it clasps it, it begins to eat its head.
The wings still flap pathetically. Oh, yes, we wince.

But our horror is not pure, it's two-way sympathy.
We feel those wings beating in our own mouths,
    we're omnivorous.
After all, dogs (beloved dogs) eat baby rabbits head
    first
and I expect cats do too (they certainly eat baby
    rabbits).
We do nasty things to calves and battery hens
and quite disgusting things to geese in Strasbourg.
You just have to get your protein from something.
Like the Army living rough, eating worms – also on
    telly.

The Garrotting

('It's an Old Spanish Custom')

In an Exhibition devoted to the Art of Barcelona
there is this picture of a public execution –
I marvel at the date – 1894!
But no, it's in modern dress, a crowd in a big
    square,
the seated victim, the hypocrites crowding round,
telling him Jesus loves him as the iron collar tightens,
the executioner turns the screw that's boring in
below the skull, to kill the spinal cord.
Are the men in pointed hats the Inquisition?

This is Old Spanish Cruelty. The suffering
benefits sadists only, a threat, something to show
that *status quo* has meaning in the world.

I think of Larkin's hard throat cancer death,
better than being garrotted – but not much.

February 1986

NOTE   The last public execution in Britain took place in 1866.

Making Love to Women

Auden said making love to women was 'too easy'.
I and another old man (both, you could say, lovers
   of women)
consider this statement. With laughter.
Those who don't care or who don't take it seriously
are not affected by anxiety – both Auden and
   Isherwood,
without any doubt they could go through the
   motions.
It meant nothing to them. Now with *boys* it was
   different –
here the love was less 'easy', there was infatuation.

Do lesbians think making love to a man is 'too
   easy'?
I've never heard so. But, with Yeats,
'the fascination of what's difficult'
was a potent factor; and surely all such questions
are fraught with interest? Auden also said the
   'fucking'
was the most disagreeable part of an affair.

NOTE   See p. 368 of Stephen Spender's *Journals 1939–1983*.
Auden is supposed to have said to Margaret Gardiner in 1929,
'What I hate is the fucking.'

Intermittent Claudication

I told a doctor, at a party, all about how
I kicked a football in a dream and next day
my left knee was strained and extremely painful
and how I walked about 5½ miles to a bookshop in
   Toronto
and the calf of my left leg gave up.
It comes and goes, I said.

What you have, an effect of old age, he said,
is called intermittent claudication.
You remember the lameness of the Emperor Claudius?

But what I remembered was the medical report on
   Yeats:
We have here an agèd arteriosclerotic (was his doctor
   Gogarty?)
and how Yeats said he would rather be called an
   agèd arteriosclerotic
than King of Lower Egypt.

Ah, the words! The words! They can reconcile us to
   anything!

NOTE   The name of Claudius has nothing to do with lameness.
Claudicare (= to limp) and *Claudicatio* (=limping) are both
straightforward Latin, and favourite words of Cicero's.

Into Science Fiction

When you find yourself in a spacetram
with a big tough feminid called Tnuc,
who is having it off with a small delicate feminid
called Sirotilc – on a planet called Odlid –

and there are two terrible entities called Zbog
and Vrig, and all the names of the humanoids
are anagrams or palindromes or
    unpronounceable . . .
why, then you'll know you're into Science Fiction.

Which hasn't moved since Mr Nosnibor and
    Erewhon –
although the Aliens have taken over Algolagnia
since the Time Traveller set out, since the Eloi and
    the Morlocks,
and Einstein has freaked out with the bug-eyed
    monsters.
The theories, the technologies, are sexed as adventure
    stories
suitable for green teenagers with nine purple
    arms . . .

Psychiatrist, Heal Thyself!

Once the husband of my sister who died
nearly twenty years ago. Then Consultant
in this very hospital where he is now,
the biggest loony bin in the South-West;
Sir Arthur Quiller-Couch's daughter Fowey,
they say, a fellow-patient.
Healthy and happy, but the mind has gone,
the memory doesn't really work.

Does he know *me*? It's hard to say. He doesn't
call me Gavin. He seriously says,
'I don't go to London much these days.'
All questions are asked two, three, four times.

On the wall in the ward, for these casualties, is a
notice:
YOU ARE IN ST LAWRENCE HOSPITAL, BODMIN,
CORNWALL.

354

Part Three

Shall I Die?

(A Critical Exercise)

Did the Bard try quite hard
when he wrote what they quote –
    a new-found poem?
Is it good? or dead wood?
Starched and stiff? Who knows if
    scholars know 'em,
the true joys, Real McCoys,
and worthy of Shakespeare's great canon?
    They attribute; he is mute.
So easily it might be by Anon!

Where the words fly like birds
some young ponce thinks they're nonce,
    while others, snarling,
say the Muse would refuse
to undress – it's a mess –
    or be Will's darling!
Suspicious doubt, O keep out!
The rooms in God's famous huge mansion
    aren't reserved, nor yet deserved
by dabblers in dubious scansion!

The rights and wrongs of Shaker's songs!
He's so posh – but they're tosh
    in several places.
Any fool, who's *not* choir school,
as you know, sings high and low –
    your true love's graces
aren't much praised when this is raised
as sign of remarkable merit!
    You don't remark 'Oh, hark!'
when rabbits squeal loud at a ferret.

Dons explain 'wind and rain' –
but *you* try 'When that I
              was and a little
tiny boy'! Grammar's joy
it is *not*, nor so hot!
              No jot or tittle!
It *does* prove songs that move
rely on the music, and singing –
    smooth nonsense can unnerve a man.
junk food can set dinner bells ringing!

'Cheeks', 'brows', 'hair', 'beyond compare',
and a 'dove'? Words of love
              frequent such lyrics.
Not just Will! Bad writers still
use them all, though talent's small,
              in panegyrics.
Faded now – but, somehow,
in earlier days they were voguish.
    Georgian Verse could immerse
a sex urge in terms then thought roguish.

It's bad enough, it's awful stuff;
by him, when young, what might be *sung*
              did get written.
But stand aloof (there's no proof),
you must chew words that you
              too fast have bitten!
And cheeks, instead of lips, are red!
While noses, like foreheads, can wrinkle!
    And sure as eggs, from our legs
comes an unmistakable tinkle!

NOTE The poem 'Shall I die?' included in the 'Bodleian MS
Rawl poet 160' (its jovial nickname among scholars) was
attributed to Shakespeare in or around 1630. Later commentators
have not agreed. Malone, for example, the great 18th-century
Shakespeare editor, seems not to have supported the attribution.
Mr Gary Taylor, using computer analysis of the vocabulary,
now claims that neologisms and parallels with existing work
known to be by Shakespeare make it likely that the attribution is

correct. One reason for doubting this, it has been pointed out, is
the fact that love songs of c. 1600 all share the same vocabulary
(the vocabulary, roughly, derided in Shakespeare's famous
Sonnet 130 – 'My mistress' eyes are nothing like the sun'). The
line 'Suspicious doubt, O keep out!', in my second stanza, occurs
in the original poem.

The Madness of a Headmistress

Don't be a fool, don't go to school,
don't put a foot outside –
Old Miss Oysterley
is eating bubblegum,
Sellotape, tin-tacks and Tide!

Be like a mouse, stay in the house –
her mouth is open wide –
weird Miss Oysterley
is drinking printer's ink,
paint and insecticide!

Don't go near the Head, just stay in bed –
jump in a box and hide –
Old Miss Oysterley
is fond of the little ones,
roasted or frittered or fried!

It's very sad, she's gone quite mad,
her brain is quite putrefied –
poor Miss Oysterley
munching through Infants I
that once was her joy and her pride!

The Poets' Revolt

In *Poetry Review* (Volume 75, Number 4) there is a League Table
of the living British and Irish poets, divided into four Divisions,
as in the Football League. This list begins with all the H's –
Heaney, Hughes, Hill, Harrison (in that order). This is the work
of John Sheeran, of Oxford University. Altogether, 92 poets are
'placed'.

Heaney is the only one
who'll be pleased with what he's done –
you can't say the same for Hughes,
Laureates hate being Number 2s.
You don't need a Holmes or Freud
to guess they'll *all* be quite annoyed
to see that they've been ranked below
frauds and pseuds like So-and-So.
Kit Wright numbered 89 –
put down so far he's in a mine!
One First Division woman (20) –
one woman only, and that's plenty –
that seems to be the general gist
of this dreaded donlike list.
And Wendy Cope at 91!

Surely it would be quite fun
(and poets, surely, should be able)
to make a *Critical* League Table
where all the dons who love to spout
and splash like whales and swim about
had numbers stuck upon their backs.
All open to harpoon attacks.
Guess who'd be bottom! Just guess who!
Sheeran! Like Patten (92)!

Vicar's Daughter Raped by Fiend

(Headline, the *Sun*, 7 March 1986)

Who but a Fiend would rape a Vicar's daughter?
So deaf to all appeals to Christian charity,
So blind to Love and Lust – their vast disparity –
So hot from Hell, so breathing fire and slaughter!
No need to reason or to seek out proof,
Plain as the saintliness of Saint Theresa,
He was no likely lad, she no cock-teaser,
He had the horn, he had the cloven hoof!

She was an Angel – that's quite likely too –
Folklore runs deep in every yellow press –
Each tabloid Born-Again from day to day
Loves anything that's blasphemous *and* blue,
Her shapely tits escaping from a dress
Over their minds quite obviously hold sway.

Re-assessing Modern Masters

At first they say, 'He's very wonderful!'
then they say, 'He's very wonderful but . . .'
Just a bit old-fashioned they may not say – but think.
'When he wrote that he must have been half-cut!'
'His anti-sexist immune defence system★
must have been on the blink!'

'Of course he was remarkable in his lifetime –
but we've moved on from there.'
They think his preoccupations very old hat,
like outdated slang or poems on lips or hair.
They cut no ice with them. Or melt, or soften,
each frozen critical cat!

★ Compare Acquired Immune Deficiency Syndrome

Sonnet 155

(Never Before Imprinted)

I stand as doubtful in the eye of Time,
The day unknown that fairly gave me birth,
Obscure I am and in obscurer rhyme
I hid myself, my woe, my youthful mirth,
My rustic marriage to uncertain Anne,
The years in that great city where the play
Seduced my honeyed Muse, where I began
To harvest in my wit, in the world's way.
I hid my loves, though players did report
Encounters in the deep deceitful dark,
While some were wont to say I loved the Court,
Sweet ladies deer in that high scented park.
    My life I am content should be unknown,
    So that my works to Time shall still be shown.

NOTE Shakespeare's actual day of birth remains a matter of
conjecture. The details of his marriage to Anne Hathaway, at
the age of 18, are confused. Nothing is known of his early life in
London. Contemporaries reported both that he was indifferent to
Court approbation, and that he was at ease there and welcomed
it. The 'dark lady' of the Sonnets is still not certainly identified.
Apart from signatures on documents, no specimen of
Shakespeare's handwriting exists. Shakespeare's 'honied muse'
was referred to by a contemporary.

'Sex in the Soapsuds'

(Found poem, *Wandsworth & Putney Guardian*, 30
January 1986)

Romping Romeos indulge in steamy launderette
   love-ins
while their dirty linen is washing.

As their clothes tumble in the dryer
they tumble sexily in the soapsuds.
And their lust is getting launderette owners in a
    lather.
This is just one of the vices soiling
the whiter-than-white image of our launderettes.
Laundry staff allege that customers
have sex in front of washing machines
sniff glue and smoke pot
beat up staff
intimidate managers
spit on old ladies' clean undies . . .

Mavie Nolan, who works at the Coin-op, Bedford
    Hill,
says she can hardly believe
how people abuse her launderette.
'I come in and a couple are having sex.'

Cause and Effect

Wives of drinking husbands
never stop to think
that it's anti-drinking nagging
that drives them all to drink.

A Kilkenny Cat

(The Power of Magic)

Walking up the hill past the Castle
on a cold late November morning –
on the frosted wood of a bench,
with a woolly-gloved finger,
I make the Sign of the Cunt,
a crude drawn outline . . .

Farther up the hill I meet, walking down,
a very pretty girl. She smiles
and says *Good morning*! (unaccosted by me).

Surely that Sign was auspicious!

Kilkenny 28 November 1985
Putney 23 February 1986

Hell in Putney

(mostly found, *Wandsworth & Putney Guardian*, 30
  May 1985)

There's just a little too much billing and cooing
around Sarah House, Arabella Drive!
Tenant Mrs Ruby Hattersley said:
'The entrance to the flats is diabolical.'
Any minute they're expecting
the Pigeon Prince of Darkness to arrive!

The council put up netting to stop them roosting –
'There's pigeon mess,' said Mrs Hattersley,
  'everywhere!
They go in behind the netting and it stops them
  falling off.
They love it!' Those stains are biological!
Housing Management Chairman Peter Bingle
is really tearing out his hair!

'For every bird we trap,' he's quoted as saying,
'There seems to be two or three to replace them.
I just wish this was a problem that would fly away!'
Is the answer perhaps carbolical?
'It is really giving us the bird!' says Peter.
The problems of Evil in Putney – we must face them!

Lewis Carroll's Health Rules

If you have a cold
you must eat a lot of crumpets
and blow your nose like trumpets
and do as you are told.

If you have a cough
you must drink of lot of Guinness
and drive about in Minis
and try to have it off.

If you have a corn
you must boil your feet in syrup,
teach budgies how to chirrup,
and practise the French Horn.

If you're down with flu
you must ride around on piglets
and eat mince-pies and Twiglets
till everything turns blue.

If you have a sprain
you must wrap it round with raffia,
and call Sicilian Mafia
to give you some real pain.

A Jig for John F. Deane and Poetry Ireland

The fine City of Dublin!
With joy we're all bubblin,
no toilin and troublin,
    it's there in the sun,
so happy and glorious
(the cold wind is Boreas) –
and the Emperor's Warriors★
    add to the fun!

★ An Exhibition of an early Chinese Emperor's guardian statues
at the Royal Hospital in Kilmainham.

And no Victor or Valerie
needs a great salary,
the National Gallery
    opens its doors!
No pamphlet or fascicle
can beat Neo-Classical –
whose scenes lad-and-lassical
    Poussin encores!

Our hearts go all fluttery,
prayerful and muttery –
like boys in the buttery
    sinkin their jars
we look up imploringly,
gladly, adoringly,
as Great Art unboringly
    wings to the stars!

Three-person'd God's battery
flames above flattery,
a Sligo-born Slattery
    thrills to the paint!
The Four Courts are flamin
with sun, it's quite shamin –
their beauty I'm blamin,
    I'm feelin quite faint!

O Eireann Eire,
my secretest sharer,
your Dublin shines clearer
    than Fastnet sea-fog –
or rains of the Amazon.
My headache hammers on,
bring me some Jameson,
    the hair of the dog!

Sally

'*Are you interested in knowing* when and whom you will marry?
What the year will bring you? If you will gain in a lawsuit? . . .
What are you best adapted for? If you have enemies and who? If
you can trust your friends? Why your love acts strange? What
lies in the future and what fate awaits you?'

– New York street handout

Anglo-Saxon Sally operates between Third and
    Lexington –
she makes large claims:
'Forecasts – Future – Past – Present
with Palm, Tarot Cards, Crystal Ball, Readings'.
Are her clients all dames?

Or does the SPECIAL WITH THIS AD Regular
    Card Reading
$5.00 OFF
offered to the street-passers
pull in young, confused, gullible, male New Yorkers,
chauvinist at the pig-trough?

Tune in to these thoughts: 'Why don't that Marylene
    let me
touch up her ass?'
'Why she act so strange, man?'
It doesn't seem likely, probable – or possible even.
No, a different class,

the unsure more-than-mature woman is here
    targeted.
'That Mrs Feinblatt,
she look at me in a funny way!'
'Ed don't love me any more. He think I'm done for,
    past it!'
'Mr Fink's a dirty rat.'

Or just a bit younger? When Romance can be
    mentioned,
Love that will last.
'Will Wilbur ever kiss me?'
Sally knows these thoughts like the colour of the
    dollars,
forecasting the Past.

New York, June 1985

The Damsel-Fly

'The yin that did it last time,
  A canna dae it noo!'
    The Ball of Kirriemuir

The damsel-fly
is a pretty spry
small kind of dragon-fly,
in every way it is pretty fly.

When the male makes love
it doesn't need Martinis –
and it has a very remarkable penis.

It doesn't read Sex Manuals
or, indeed, *any* books –
but its prominent pintle is furnished with hooks.

With these it hooks out the sperm
left behind by any previous lover –
and substitutes its own. It's a real undercover

secret agent in the
miraculous Courts of Love . . .
Venus ought to promote the damsel-fly.
It's far cleverer than the dove!

366

Tallness is All

Pope and Keats were nothings,
only two feet high –
all the enormous Sitwells
were towering to the sky.

Edith once told Bottrall
physical size was all –
miniature masterpieces weren't on,
by anybody small!

All long, or little, poems
by Thwaite or Taner Baybars
are bound to be a waste of time
and, you might say, lost labours.

No chance for midget madrigals –
the Muse abhors dwarf dwellings.
The palaces of giants alone,
with music's sweetest swellings,

grotesque and slightly clumsy,
but *large* and madly airy,
are where she likes to take her ease,
a fatuous fat fairy.

So little people, leprechauns,
and those the size of Japs,
need not apply as geniuses –
the fitting of the caps

goes on, and Immortality
(despising sound and sense)
will only settle on your head
if you are quite immense!

NOTE   Keats was in fact 5 ft 2 in tall, and Pope 4 ft 6 in.

Behaviour Unbecoming a Lady in a British Cultural Centre

At the Poetry Society
there were men of notoriety
saying farewell to all anxiety
and their usual sobriety –
    they had had an awful lot.
As they plunged into the liquor,
as their brains began to flicker,
they got much much drunker quicker,
    gave it all they'd got!

Yes, they needed all their talents
to maintain a state of balance –
full like mainsails and top-gallants,
they were quite uncanny callants;
    fou as any fiery Scot!
A birthday was being celebrated –
with booze bottled, canned and crated –
to stop *him* being underrated,
    like Lang Syne forgot!

Unsober night of worthy cotter
(not some starchy English rotter)!
They soaked drink like any blotter,
they could barely stand or totter
    like an infant from his cot!
Poets, yes, but also boozers –
beggars (buggers) can't be choosers,
whisky-winners, lager-losers,
    each distinguished sot!

Watching them, a poetette.
She could not play hard to get,
between her legs she might be wet –
but not behind the ears, you bet!
    For all *men* she was quite hot.
Other girls might think a lady'd
not make women so degraded –
she, for males both fresh and faded,
    had her softest spot.

She, as well, had not absented
self (or lips) from what's fermented,
till her self-control was dented –
the gayness was what *she* resented.
   So there, at once, to stop the rot,
she incontinently decided
to follow where her instincts guided!
Some have foolishly derided,
   as black kettle pot,

all that's gay, each satisfaction
stemming from same-sex attraction,
all the homosexual faction –
she preferred to take some action!
   Cowardly, oh, she was not!
Towards them she at once proceeded,
grabbed their private parts and kneaded
(it was quite *outré*, dear, what she did),
   so to frig and frot

those so gentlemanly members!
Did she hope to stir some embers
of what Adam still remembers –
Eve's hot sun in our Decembers?
   Like a sexy sans-culotte!
Envy? She could not enjoy them.
Probably just to annoy them.
They, for her, would not employ them.
   So, they were a blot

on the landscape of her thinking –
she, remember, had been drinking,
with her Super-ego shrinking,
in womanly confusion sinking
   many a stirring tot and shot.
Not one rose up like an airman
to stand up primitive, a bare man!
Instead, complaints went to the Chairman!
   That's what!

A Wee Laberlethin For the Lads Wi' the Lallans

(See *The Concise Scots Dictionary*, 1985)

Och, lackanee! alas! an' wae!
The Muse o' birse-cups an' the brae,
yon lammie-meh ye cuddle tae,
   she's aiblins left ye
an' o' the sense tae sing or say
   she's sure bereft ye!

D'ye no mind John Logie Baird,
wha rules the soun' waves lek a laird,
wha blins the sicht till nane are spared,
   an' fettles baith –
gars mak a lame, a mant, a *merde*
   wi' laidron laith?

Ye lawbour on your lawboards still,
but Telly taps Parnassus Hill,
ye hae the bensell an the will
   but still ye're waitin'
the Muse – an' she'll be missin' till
   ye write i' Laitin!

Lacklustre labsters! Lampeekoo
is a' ye're fit for here an' noo,
lawins an' lounrie when ye're fou,
   lampin' alang
wi' sic lamgabblich – as a coo
   might mak a sang!

Ye'll not owercome the pow'r o' Ringo,
or a' the glamourie o' Bingo,
or Sex, flumgummery flamingo –
   high-kiltit verse
will aye be in their lugs laich lingo
   an' Fame's reverse!

Ye laik, ye laig, ye lauch, ye lagger,
ye claut the laggin till ye stagger –
lak lacrissye they laib Mick Jagger,
    your lays stir anger,
lang lugs, ye slay lek dirk or dagger
    wi' fearfu' langour!

Knapdarlocks, in your kneggum strang,
fa' silent, ye hae sung owerlang
the Scots your kickmaleeries wrang!
    Leave th' kilfuddoch!
Ye've nae mair apitude for sang
    than th' puir puddock!

GLOSSARY

laberlethin a rigmarole, rambling discourse
    (la 19th–20thC)
lackanee alas (la 19thC)
birse-cup final cup of tea with whisky instead of
    milk (e20thC)
lammie-meh pet name for a lamb (20thC)
fettle go for (a person) (la 19thC)
lame a critical injury (15–e16thC)
mant a stutter, a stammer (19thC)
laidron rascal, loafer (16thC)
laith evil (la 14th–15thC)
lawbour = labour
lawboard (*Labrod*) lapboard, a board laid across the
    knees for working on (19th–e20thC)
bensell force, violence (la 17th–e20thC)
lampeekoo a variation of hide-and-seek
lawins a session of drinking, esp. in a tavern (16th–
    17thC)
lounrie sexual wickedness, fornication (la 16th–
    e18thC)
lamp stride along (17thC)
lamgabblich a long rambling discourse, a rigmarole
    (20thC)
glamourie = glamour (18thC–e20thC)

flumgummery any foolish or frivolous thing

high-kiltit having the skirts well tucked up, immodest, indecent (la 18th–e20thC)

laich low (la 14thC)

laik amuse oneself (15th–16thC)

laig chatter (la 19thC)

lauch laugh (la 14thC)

lagger sink in mud or soft ground (18thC)

claut the laggin drain a container of drink (la 18th–19thC)

lacrissye liquorice (la 15th–16thC)

laib lick up, lap, gobble (18thC)

lang lugs a donkey (a person with long ears) (18thC)

langour boredom (la 15thC)

knapdarlock hardened dirt or dung hanging from the tail of an animal, a dirty, cheeky person (1. la 19thC, 2. 20thC)

kneggum disagreeable taste or flavour (la 18thC)

kickmaleerie a flimsy trifling thing (19thC)

kilfuddoch a meeting and discussion (19thC)

puddock a toad (or frog) (la 16thC)

Breakfast All Day

(Notice outside a café in the Lower Richmond Road)

Breakfast all day!
What a marvellous thought!

Fresh orange juice, cereals,
eggs and bacon, toast, marmalade,
tea or coffee!
Or even pancakes and maple syrup,
buckwheat cakes, bagels, iced water!

In Heaven I bet they have
breakfast all day –
with Room Service angels –
and the taste and the joy and the appetite
stay fresh, all day!

Unhappiness Begins at Home

Horace once wrote a poem
saying that high feelings are all very well
but the most serious thing for a poet
is to have a cold.

4,000 people die in an earthquake
in Mexico City;
an old lady in her seventies
(close friend of my old dead aunt)
is told she must have a foot amputated.

But all I worry about
is that I have only one poem
in a new anthology of representative verse.

Small Ads

On the back page of a Sunday paper
are the Small Ads and the Crossword and all that
                                             caper:

'NEW AUTHORS! Tired of rejection?'
'Not vanity publishing!' (This is the *literary* section.)

'All categories considered including
war memoirs, autobiographies and poetry.' Also, the
                                    self-deluding.

Between ATTACK CANCER and TIES
                          NARROWED
these narrow roads to Fame are modestly and
                              tastefully arrowed.

So are NEXUS, SELECT FRIENDS,
                        UNATTACHED?
Somewhere there's somebody with whom you might
                    be discreetly matched.

There's no mention of orgies or binges.
Just LATEX RUBBERWEAR, VASECTOMY, and
ENEMA SYRINGES.

Nothing to excite lust or loathing –
unless you're turned on by EXPECTATIONS
('leather and rubber clothing').

Do GAY LINK INTROS hint seductions?
It says 'discretion assured'. 'Nationwide male and
female gay introductions'.

It's all a bit shadowy, what these proffer –
but there's nothing one bit shadowy about the
DUREX FREE OFFER!

Names named. Prices. Take a siesta –
lie down and dream of FETHERLITE, NUFORM,
BLACK SHADOW, FIESTA!

This is *it* for SELECT FRIENDS you dated,
quite bowled over by the charms of your
GOSSAMER LUBRICATED!

And there's something rich and strange
about the missile-worthy names of the celebrated
AEGIS RANGE:

STIMULANT OR DELAY. What joy!
ROUGH OR RIBBED, FRUIT FLAVOURED,
TIGHT FIT, BIG BOY!

High heels! Underwear! You won't look back
once you get stuck into that extra special SUPER
VARIETY SELECTION PACK!

Kingsley Has a Go at a Latin Poem

Stabat mulier beata,
omnibus conspicua, mammeata,
invidia multis iam conflata!

Praeclara tamen stat papilla,
odor fragrans in axilla,
meretrix, nomine Camilla!

Centuriones sunt amentes,
Venus flagellat omnes gentes,
cupidines non sunt absentes.

Magnitudo erectionum
optimum eis certe bonum,
plaudunt, magnum faciunt sonum.

Miraculum labia maiora
sed autem, quae sunt meliora,
dulcissima labia minora!

Amantium precationes
et ejaculationes
longae sicut orationes!

Languescunt, partem femineam
illae Camillae pensant ream.
Laudunt omnes illam deam!

Translation A happy woman was standing, in the
sight of all, big-breasted, the envy of many
straightway excited! Very beautiful, in the same
way, stands out the nipple, there is a fragrant odour
in the armput – she is a harlot, by name Camilla!
The centurions are out of their minds, Venus lashes
all the nations, desires are not absent. The size of
their erections is to them, for certain, of the highest
good, they applaud, they make a great noise. A
wonder to see her labia majora – but moreover,
what are even better, her very sweet labia minora!
The prayers of her lovers, and their ejaculations, are
as long as public speeches! They faint with languor,
they consider the womanly part of that Camilla to
be the cause. All praise that goddess!

NOTE The Rev. Charles Kingsley, best known as the author of
The Water Babies, *Westward Ho!* and a handful of poems, was
remarkable for his belief that life in Heaven consisted of never-
ending sexual intercourse – a belief not common in his lifetime
(1819–1875). His model here is the rhymed poem in Latin written
by monks in the Middle Ages, usually a hymn.

My Life in the Theatre

In 1933 I played the part of a Student
(in Greek) in Aristophanes' *Clouds* at Wellington.

In 1937 I wrote the words of a song
that was performed by the Footlights at Cambridge.

In the same year (I think) I scene-shifted *The Queen
of Spades*
and fell (accidentally) into the arms of Pat
Rawdon-Smith.

In 1979 my words to John Gardner's *Tobermory*
were sung at three performances – Royal Academy
of Music.

Of the Poetry Readings in theatres
we do not wish to speak.

Rubaiyat of the Prostate

Awake! For in the Lavatory Bowls of Night
Old Men have peed and stained the brilliant White:
    And Lo! the Yellowness of Age has dimmed
The Star of Youth that once shone bold and bright!

Ah, me, once Damsels all they had bestowed
On those Young Men who batted, bowled
                    and rowed –
    Though they to all and sundry, on their Bikes,
Their rosy Knickers in the Daylight showed!

'Tis at this age that we remember How –
But no more have we, Friends, the Strength; enow
    To lay the Loved Ones in the silken Bed!
Though HE did us so mightily endow!

Strange, is is not? That Sailors, greatly thewed,
By us with Godlike Beauty were imbued:
    And now from Sea return'd lie still in Earth,
That erst so dazzled us, when in the Nude!

The Wine, the Grape, the Visions that we saw –
And shared, it seemeth, with great Evelyn Waugh!
    Ah, these the Liver faintly doth forbid.
Once Nightingales, but now the black Rook's Caw!

I dreamed that Dawn's Left Hand was in my Fly
And lighted was the Candle, burning high!
    But, waking, saw with disappointed Gaze
That Light a flicker, and about to die.

The Roses and the Gardens, let them go!
Our Youth, our Love, that we once fancied so,
    Forget them, as the Nights of Too Much Wine
Blot out all Memory like falling Snow!

NOTES 'Dawn's Left Hand' is a phrase that actually occurs in
Fitzgerald's masterpiece. He had a very idealised love for sailors.
The *Ruba `i* is a Persian quatrain (rhyming as above), used by
Omar Khayyam in the 12th century.

The Kidnapping of the Lindbergh Baby (1932)

What a country for crime!
American criminals are the best!
Just look what these simple kidnappers achieved:
they took the child from a house full of people,
they collected a large ransom,
they escaped all consequences,
the wrong man was executed for the crime,
and lastly (not that it mattered to them)
they killed the baby.

Kipper

(Rudyard Kipling died in 1936)

I went out to a Salong – they invited me an' all –
An' a bloke in fancy dress, 'e looked down at me, so
                                                    tall;
An' 'e wouldn't tike me ulster, nor 'e wouldn't tike
                                                me 'at.
'Presoomably,' 'e says, says 'e, 'You're *known* to Mrs
                                                    Catt?'
   Ow! It's Kipper this, an' Kipper that, an' 'Wot a
                                            little runt!'
   But I'll 'ave me revenge indeed when blue-blood
                                        boys wot 'unt
   Mikes me out their bloomin' mascot! Yes, the
                                        idiots wot 'unt
   Won't think me such a runt no more – them blue-
                                    blood boys wot 'unt!

I 'eard the screamin' cows that sing (if singin's wot
                                            they do);
To me it sounds uncommon like they're bustin' for
                                            the loo!
There was funny pictures on the wall, an' a woman
                                        stiff as tin

She says to me, all ladylike, 'Why, 'ow did *you* get
                                                    in?'
    Ow! It's Kipper this, an' Kipper that, an' 'Go back
                                        to Stone'enge!'
    But I'm a Primal Tory an' I *will* 'ave me revenge,
    I'm a blasted Ancient Briton, an' I'll tike me own
                                            revenge –
    With the 'elp o' them Young Fogies I shall tike me
                                        own revenge!

Intellectuals an' reds that reads me books turns pile!
I'm especially vindictive in that Mary Postgate tile!
I'm a bully that was bullied (see the evidence in
                                            print),
    You'd best keep clear o' me, me boys, if you can tike
                                            an 'int!
        Ow! It's Kipper this an' Kipper that, an' ''E's a
                                        Philistine!'
        But I'm full o' that Hinitiative an' I knows well
                                        wot is mine,
        Yes, I knows well wot is mine, me boys, I knows
                                    full well wot's mine,
        I'm Private Enterprise 'isself, true blue, I knows
                                        wot's mine!

No, I'm not no blinkin' blossom sich as you might
                                        see at Kew,
I 'ates the rich an' idle, I'm suspicious o' the Jew –
I loves Hindians an' Irish *but* (an' 'ere's a funny thing)
I only loves 'em when they fights for me own Queen
                                        or King!
    Ow! It's Kipper this an' Kipper that – 'It's a
                                Crippen, 'is mous*tache*!'
    But I'll 'ave do*min*ion – palm an' pine, an'
                                meadowland an' marsh –
    In Tory Eras I shall rule, both meadowland an'
                                            marsh,
    Yes, the Lesser Breeds shall suffer, in town,
                                meadowland an' marsh!

As critics wilt an' fide away, wi' their jargon an'
                                        their sneers,
I shall stand them Young Conservatives a multitude
                                        o' beers!
Blind obedience is me rule, *ideas* are wot I 'ates,
It's suff'rin' soldiers wot I loves, me rough tough
                                        workin' mates!
    Ow! It's Kipper this, and' Kipper that, an' ''E was
                                        keen on Kim!'
    A *detergent* omo-sex-u-al! But I'll mike their eyes
                                        go dim,
    The ones as thinks unclean o' me, I'll mike their
                                        eyes go dim!
    'Ighbrows, fairies, socialists – I'll mike their eyes
                                        go dim!

Home, Sweet Home!

'The cyanide – it was put in her tea – didn't reach
Mrs Shaw, but killed a house-cat.'

              Ellery Queen, *The Adventure Of The Bearded Lady*

The American Language explicates everything –
a guest is a house-guest, a cat is a house-cat;
but every coat isn't a house-coat
nor every boat a house-boat.
You *could* have a house-mouse or a house-rat
but not a house-condor or a house-shark.
However much wildness and inexactitude are hated
not *everything* can be domesticated.

Sado-Masochism

(A Black Ballad)

'He lived with a prostitute of twice his age who
enjoyed being maltreated'

– Colin Wilson and Patricia Pitman, *Encyclopaedia of Murder*,
      on Peter Kürten, the mass-murderer of Düsseldorf.

There's something funny about the wimmin,
they seem to like violence of sorts
(though they don't really want to end up in the
      morgue
with all the other *mortes*).

Kürten would go out into the woods with
a simple servant girl –
he'd put his hands round her throat and say
'Why not? Let's give it a whirl!'

They didn't object, it seems, and what they
would give was a sexy giggle.
Sometimes he hit them with hammers or stabbed
      them –
no struggles. At most, a wriggle.

Heath was a drinker, and one of the boys,
the girls didn't think *him* bad.
He carved Margery Gardner, known in the
      underworld
as a notorious slapperad

and into bondage. And Doreen Marshall
was chased through the trees and slit –
she didn't want it, she was unlucky,
the female masochist bit.

But certainly German girls seemed to expect it
in the old pre-Hitler Twenties,
they thought it was normal, in no way kinky,
and they were quite compos mentis.

No one excuses these really horrible
male sadistic pigs –
but should the girls have met them half-way?
To pass them by like prigs

381

would have been safer, to say (like Puritans)
'Stuff your hammers and knives,
strangle *yourselves* if you must strangle somebody
and leave us alone, with our lives!'

NOTES 'Slapperad' is, or was, underworld slang for a female
masochist. Neville Heath was a big, strong handsome man. He
had fantastic success with women. Indeed it has been suggested
that he turned to sadism (late in his sexual career) because he
was bored with everything else. He was also a confidence
trickster and used to wear uniforms and medals to which he was
not entitled. He was executed in 1946 for the two murders
mentioned. Kürten, for murdering (at least) eight women, was
guillotined in 1931.

The Saints of the Suburbs

We are prized, we husbands – yes, we are prized.
Sometimes, when our coats are smooth and brushed,
we are allowed out.

Our arms are taken in the street, yes, we are prized.
We clean the car, we dig in the daffodils,
we photograph kids.

We are shown off in public – *Look what I got!
And he's mine, all mine, like a mortgage!*
A property, an investment.

We are boasted of, for other wives to wonder at.
Digby made the rabbit hutch and all the bookshelves!
A handyman, each of us!

We never drink too much or look at a secretary,
we are chauffeurs with sensory deprivation,
such saints of the suburbs!

Doctor Kildare

If Doctor Kildare
suddenly turned into
Doctor Darekill –
with his deadly hypodermic
and his lethal pill –
none of us would ever
dare to be ill!

Mrs Rat's Tea-Parties

(All honour to Ronald Firbank, born 17 January 1886, died 21
May 1926)

At Mrs Rat's Tea-Parties
there are (velleities)
and diplomatic ladies in delicious gowns
widening their eyes at a stone-god's big-big . . .???!!!
There is only a smattering of Hearties
(unless they have hyacinthine hair
like the more attractive Deities

or in other ways resemble a Donatello).
The 'prose' is out of Pater,
assez amusante! One might note a page or a faun
slyly 'at' the Heir Apparent's cool champagne . . .
while a vapid valse distracts a 'cello –
a weary music with a dying fall
and a 'Lost Boy' longing for Mater . . .

There *is* the sadness of the Peacocks' crying,
the last crow's-foot resting
beneath those eyes that are always-always tired.
My dear! The 'dialogue'! You can just see Evelyn,
imitative and more than a little trying,
'trying it on'! It's a (camp) comedy
no one's succeeded in besting . . .

and the mood music *can* be terrific
(about night, twilight, flowers),
it's all fabulous without a fable, mistily 'staged',
but even (Oh, the Sitwells!) on the edge of farce.
In his life, to be more specific,
he worked hard and certainly suffered
and all the pleasure is ours . . .

21 May 1986

Song: What We Are/Were Sentimental About

The Ancient World had seascapes
and very wonderful weather,
columns and architraves
and crucified slaves
and whips made of beautiful leather –
but no whisky or heather.

The Ancient World had flautists
whose music was so appealing,
dolphins and boys with curls
and qualified girls
who gave you a beautiful feeling –
but no cabers or reeling.

The Ancient World had dramas
to throw you right off your balance,
poets in togas who
until all was blue
read epics, with wine drunk in gallons –
but no ceilidhs or Lallans.

How to Write a Poem in the American Style

Use the
two-word
line, en-
jambement,
etc.
where poss-
ible &
don't forget
the ampersand!

No need
for rhyme,
not much need
for rhythm –
it's all
like trying
to touch
your toes.
Anyone
can try it.

Campoets All!

Down the lanes of Literature, leafy Spring and Fall,
Come with me and sample the blossoms on
                            the bough!
Nowhere is a leafier lane (where poets have a ball)
Than where those flowers of Cambridge show so
                            fairly now –
Milton/Byron★/Tennyson/Empson!
Lamb poets, WHAM poets! Campoets all!

Ham poets, spam poets? Never, not at all!
Gray is there and, near him, his ploughman with
                            his plough! –

Nashe and Marlowe flourishing – the flowers that
                                        never fall
Are Cambridge flowers simply, standing straight
                                        and tall –
Milton/Byron*/Tennyson/Empson!
Ram poets, BAM poets! Campoets all!

* Or substitute Wordsworth – according to taste. This poem is
   dedicated, in a way, to all Professors of Poetry at Oxford.

A Scottish Psychiatrist Considers La Bohème

Of course, this opera is pre-Freud;
in 1896, when it was first produced
and Mimi first offered herself to be seduced,
Freud's main work was *Studies on Hysteria*
(1893). In collaboration with Breuer.
Would Giacosa and Illica have made Mimi coyer

if they'd ever read it? I think not.
Mimi, you remember, says she's lost *the key to*
                                        her room.
She looks for it *in the dark, with a man* – we assume
she deserves guid Scots words of trust and praise –
as one might say, a 'douce wee body'.
But she's not so douce – or as innocent as Noddy!

Later she tells Rodolfo the losing was sham.
She's a sly puss, a schemer, and that's
interesting; *Mimi* is what the French call pussycats.
(For us there's significance in a word like pussy.)
In those days Freud was only feeling his way –
but so was Mimi, we could, without
                                        contradiction, say.

Eddie Linden

(see 'Hohenlinden' by Thomas Campbell (1777–1844), a poem
once very popular in schools)

On Linden, when the sun was low,
The Polis★ struck a bitter blow –
And from his lip the blood did flow,
    And from an eyebrow, rapidly!

Six stitches needed on the brow!
We cannot say exactly how
(The Force is quite a Sacred Cow
    And deals with suspects doughtily.)

We know they chucked him in a cell,
That he was drunk we know as well –
But why combine to give him Hell
    So bravely and with chivalry?

We've all been legless in our time,
Deep drunkenness is not a crime –
I'll bet a dollar to a dime
    That this was harmless revelry.

And if a man can hardly stand,
Why give him such a helping hand
To make him painfully to land
    In all the sleep of misery?

Of course we know the fighting drunk
Are more detested than a skunk,
But passing out, like doing a bunk,
    Is harmless stuff, like scenery.

The combat deepens. On, ye Brave,
Who rush to glory, or the grave!
But *beating-up*, what fool or knave
    thinks that's the height of bravery?

★ Scottish pronunciation, accent on first syllable.

Black eyes, romantic in old verse!
The guns, the fists, the looming hearse –
Though pigs feel better, we feel worse
        Beneath their shielding canopy!

Catflap Cats

Catflap cats are
latchkey children.
They're always
in or out –
rushing in for meals or
out to play in gardens.
That's what their life's
all about.

What Shall We Say of The British Council?

A Sea Shanty of 50 Years Ago
(Tune, roughly: *What Shall We Do With a Drunken Sailor?*)

What shall we say of the British Council,
what shall we say of the British Council,
what shall we say of the British Council
        early in the morning?

Tyrrell of Avon – then Lord Lloyd was Chairman,
he wasn't a soldier, sailor or airman –
but he really got in Lord Beaverbrook's hair, man,
        early in the morning!

That was the way with the British Council, etc.

He was as mischievous as St Trinian's
sent word to attack to his pulp dominions
(the papers that published his own opinions)
    early in the morning!

What did they say of the British Council, etc.

Remove coffee stains from harpsichords, boys,
how to – advice the Council affords, boys,
and that was *all*, said those primitive hordes, boys,
    early in the morning!

That's what they said of the British Council, etc.

Yes, Beaverbrook longed to run the Council,
as canaries long to munch up groundsel!
When you want a ton, a single ounce'll
    irk you in the morning!

So what can we say of the British Council, etc.

The Cou wants understanding, appreciation
of Britain abroad, through co-operation
(cult, ed., tech.) with every nation
    each and every morning!

That's what it wants, does the British Council, etc.

Spread the word, so that British Culture
shan't suffer premature sepulture,
the world be greedy as a vulture
    for British Life each morning!

Spread the word on the British Council, etc.

NOTE   When I worked for the British Council (1946–52) the
folklore was that when the Council was founded Lord
Beaverbrook thought the Chairmanship should have been his
and, out of envy, gave orders that the *Daily Express* should
attack the Council every year when the Annual Report was
published. The 'story' that all the Council did was to tell

foreigners how to remove coffee stains from harpsichords
actually appeared in the *Daily Express*.

Mr W.S.

You may have had syphilis
and your hair fallen out
or some of it (Verlaine
went in for such things),

did you have (Baudelaire)
a black woman for a mistress?
We guess you had a shrewlike
wife, big, a shouter,

older, a virago.

For these, your compensations:
Ben Jonson and the boys
thought you wrote the best
plays, as they were drinking,

in days when plays meant verse,
and the literary lordlings
admired your sugared
emblematic sonnets;

and of course, too,
you enjoyed the taverns,
a river not the Avon,
a large, important city

where you could be both
happy and unhappy,
be on your own,
and make by your scribbling

quite a bit of money.

The Victorian Singing

Yes, we had quite a large,
quite a large collation,
we discussed, yes, we discussed
several pork chops.
Some dozens of claret
were opened, were opened;
a pipe of port was in question,
in question.
Nobody was sober, was sober, was sober.
Lifted skirts, naked thighs, high boots.

All discussed, all discussed
in the lewdness of Latin!

But O for the oysters, oysters, oysters!

Chester

(Paean for a Perfect Idiot)

My favorite American cat is Chester –
and as a favorite he gets American spelling –
and it's in his praise that my organ is swelling!
But he's not the cat that would ever need belling* –
he's certainly not a criminal or a crumb
but he *is* a wee bit dumb!

He's genuine, not man-made or polyester
and he's mostly white, with very dark grey
                                    splotches –
if he were a fabric, you could match him, in
                                    swatches –
but he's far superior, by several notches;
raccoon-tailed, he's completely covered in *real fur*
and he sure knows how to purr!

* 'Belling the Cat'. The old nursery story describes how the mice
try to put a bell on the cat's neck, to warn of his approach.

He's never been a student – not even half a
                                        semester –
and his talent isn't for teaching or table-talking
but he's renowned everywhere for his way of
                                        walking;
with Tarquin's ravishing strides he goes by, stalking.
There's no need for brains in aristocrats –
Chester's a prize fool among cats!

New York, 16 April 1986

PENULTIMATE POEMS (1989)

Part One *The Heavier*

The Last Days of Old Poets

Many old poets are dead, that were thought of by
                                        me once as rivals,
  enemies even, deadbeats, and arrogant terrible
                                        pseuds.
  Edith Sitwell, e.g. (though of course she's an older
                                        example).
  Bandersnatches abound; on the wartime trek round
                                        the pubs
Tambimuttu was there, as they all played 'Follow
                                        My Leader',
  the Fitzroy, the Wheatsheaf, and then the *Caves de
                                        France* and the French,
  that was the evening round – but the one thing
                                        lacking was talent.
  Or so I used to think. Though Maclaren-Ross was
                                        good,
David Archer had charm, like a left-wing Bertie
                                        Wooster.
  You can't blame them – a boring war, and not
                                        much to do but drink . . .

But now as the dogs catch up, the travelling Hounds
                                        of Heaven.
  and pull us down one by one, the stag, the rat, the
                                        mouse,
I feel more mellow to them – for the death that we
                                        have in common –

companions of my youth, that people hated and
                                                loved,
tattered and torn and old, that once amazed with
                                          their brightness,
   the other side of that war – the deepest, darkest
                                                ditch
between what was young and this Now, as I begin
                                          to feel tender
   to those who survived (or not). But still are a part
                                                of me.

Byron's Problem

When they come up to you, as you're sitting quietly,
and lay their fat boobs on your knees,
and look into your eyes with their own big eyes
and wistfully caress your cheek
and so, without speaking, say 'Please!'
it's a clear invitation to come out and play
and you can't just tell them to go away!

When the wine's round and they press up against you
   gently,
it's much like a musicless waltz
as they talk about books (and they all write books) –
that's *foreplay*, nothing else, my son,
true sex; it's the talking that's false!
But you can't make a snarky and sharpish riposte,
with words like 'Forget it!', 'Get lost!'

When they stroke your hair too, and finger your coat
   slyly,
or lay a neat hand on your shirt,
they all cast you as Faust (and they all know Faust),
each one's a Gretchen, maiden, pure;
but they all want your hand up their skirt.
So men of great talent must pay this high price,
and no one will think that you're terribly nice!

Written in honour of Byron's Bicentenary (he was born in 1788).
He once claimed that he was 'raped' by the highborn
intellectual young ladies after he became famous.

Ecossaise

'The Scottish melodic idiom seems to be absent from all the tunes to which the name is given. Beethoven, Chopin and Schubert have left écossaises for piano, and there is nothing Scottish about any of them.' – Percy Scholes, The Oxford Companion To Music

Like Robert Louis Stevenson living in Samoa,
like George MacBeth living in Sheffield,
like Ian Brady living in Greater Manchester,

I am a Scotsman living in exile; my father
was the first of the family to fly south –
my grandfather stayed, a professor in Edinburgh.

My mother was of mixed blood, with some from
                                     Buchanans
who went to New Zealand, then came back again.
She was at least half English, she didn't know
                                     Lallans.

We lived in London. We went, as you might say,
                                native.
We were eating long-pig and cooking the breadfruit,
beachcombers, cast off from the as-it-were-civilized
                                whalers.

This meant that as kids or wee bairns or children
she walked us often across Hyde Park to Harrods
with her dogs which were always Scottish terriers –
                                bewildered

by any intercultural shock we were not, a change of
                                houses
would have meant more; we accepted it all, as the
Kanakas (bullied by the missionaires) gave up a kilt
                                for trousers.

After all, we were born there. Cricket seemed
                                        natural.
A tartan was just a pattern (though we did choose
                                Buchanan).
We gave no thought to Scotland – our thinking
                                wasn't lateral.

There were memories of Burns and acquaintance
                                with whisky
but our politics and newspapers and governments
had only one word, stiff-lipped, riding to hounds:
                                England.

Oh, others have done it. I think you might cite
                                Byron,
he was a Gordon. My dad, with his half-caste wife,
went after Success, the foreign and feminine Siren.

Cambridge 1987 – A Postlude

(Revisited 21/1/87)

Surely you remember Guy
with his Old Etonian tie
and that teddy bear coat,
drinking all that gin?
Yes, you took it all in.
A little country so proud
of Eton and such things
in 1935 –
muted semi-fascist, not loud,
just smug and half-alive,
a bit like now.
And Hitler in the wings,
waiting to make his bow.

You canvassed in mean streets
on behalf of the Labour Party –
and Depression streets *were* mean –
you were all of nineteen.
As rowing men were hearty,
it seemed quite *natural*, God-sent,
that we'd get between the sheets
and love and admire a Conservative
fine old true blue Government.
'Is there any chance of your voting Labour?'
you diffidently said,
to receive the confident answer:
'Not unless I go off my head!'

The lower middle class
had Cambridge in its grip,
Baldwin was never the one
to economize on the pipe-puffs
or let the stranglehold slip.
Was it a pipe of peace?
The 'bourgeois' Peace Pledge Union
swore not to fight again.
Mosley had Jews on the brain
and a kind of unholy communion
with horrible Hit and Muss.

Did we make too much fuss?
About Abyssinia, about Spain?
You didn't think so, then.
A war can be stopped – if you try –
but it's easier to give in,
to let Austria go (and Czechoslovakia).
Hitler turned out a true Boojum
and his tone grew much snarkier.
No one came to the rescue,
like Oliver and Roland.
Till we got into the soup
too far to withdraw – over Poland.

You look at the Colleges now,
so beautiful in the sun,
a life you lived somehow;
there was money for which to run,
but we didn't think so then,
our minds were all on the Doom
that sat like a ghost in the corner
of any and every room –
ready like Little Jack Horner
to pull out that war like a plum,
while we were all deaf, you might say,
or maybe just dumb!

But is it so changed? No, alas
and *oimoi* and *eheu* and the rest!
It's just the same but fissile
and every anti-red missile
and every atomic test
and every speech by a Tory
tells us the old, old story.
History repeats. And you must
be quick on your feet and box clever –
or else in that nuclear winter
you will lose all your Cambridge for ever!

'I was always there when the tortures began'

The sadists are always waiting, you never have to
                                        look far,
they've been there throughout history. The pulley,
                              the rack and the bar,

mechanical pain and contrivance, the cross and the
                                        chair and garrotte,
fire and iron maidens and so on – they've used the
                                        flaming lot.

The Greeks not so much as the Romans (though the
                                      heated brazen bull
made the tyrant's craftsman a roarer. Greek tyrants
                                      were masterful)

The Romans were experts on Christians and, later,
                                      Inquisitors too
(you might say turning the tables) put the terrible
                                      heat on the Jew.

The secret police are recruited from people you read
                                      of in Freud,
and some police that aren't secret are fellows you'd
                                      want to avoid.

A classical case – the Gestapo. And Stalin's more
                                      hidden blokes.
All ordinary, ordinary people, but murders were
                                      duties or jokes

to all of these solid citizens. It surely makes you
                                      despond
to think of neat-uniformed nasties, as mean as each
                                      strapping blonde,

and what a wonderful lease of life (or death) it was
                                      to the Japs
to practise their Co-Prosperity! Such lovable little
                                      chaps.

And so the National Front, the police, everyone fixed
                                      in a squad,
are tempted to go for the beating up, like Oxford
                                      dons in a quad

they relish the pain they give others, their chase has a
                                      beast in view
(there's malice in mashing a martyr, revolver-butt or
                                      review).

By no means are they all psychos or primitive as
                                            Stonehenge,
so often on a dirty world they're taking a dirty
                                            revenge,

the down-trodden ones are the keenest to earn their
                                          daily bread
by finding a wretched victim or two on whom *they*
                                          can tread.

Lust-murder of course (and how German!), Peter
                                    Kürten and Heath,
but if you lifted a big flat stone and unwisely looked
                                      underneath

you'd see the creepie-crawlies run, each torturer's
                                      apprentice,
bad but not so different from you, and perfectly
                                  compos mentis.

The Oracle Speaks in the Dressing Room of Mr Patrick Stewart at the Barbican, before a Performance of The Winter's Tale

The blood shall flood erectile tissue
and Lost and Found shall be an issue.
True woman, screeching like a mynah,
truth shall be spoken by Paulina.
Courtiers shall dine on rich and rare food,
Antigonus shall end as bearfood.
Mamillius shall die, mum-missing,
too young for court or country kissing.
Unwanted characters, however spot on,
shall be knocked out to help the plot on.
Dramatic irony and fitness!
A whole ship's crew goes – there's no witness!

Autolycus, no Montezuma,
shall give the thing a dash of humour,
and Love shall grow, by Chance much pandered –
for what's unlikely here is standard.
Coincidence shall stare straight at you,
the King believe his wife's a statue;
sensitive as an armadillo,
shall give Paulina to Camillo!
All shall end well, all shall be friends here,
Apollo won't allow loose ends here,
Genius shall win (Will has his way)
but it's a pretty funny play!

An Elegy

Who cares if Giles and Cuthbert
are phantoms of my brain?
Or John, who a few years ago
finished with joy and pain?
The second was my teacher,
the first my main school friend,
and John made Cambridge bearable –
but now there is an end.
Who died the last was oldest,
died after, born before –
my adolescence died with him,
it's not there any more.

They all made marks on paper
and books were left behind,
and you can see the children
exist outside the mind;
but this was not their function
where my life was concerned,
it wasn't passionate friendship
but something to be learned
and intellectual questions

were put to me by them –
ideas were what they carried
like a Maharajah's gem.

This very year it's over,
mementoes that they are
(my father kept from Cambridge
an old tobacco jar),
they chose this spring to vanish;
the last one, out of breath,
has added physical absence
to the other kinds of death.
When adolescent gloom was thick –
you'd cut it with a knife –
their ideological brightness
put some interest into life.

It's no use feeling sorrow
or saying 'It had to be!' –
if they were living now again
they'd be no use to me.
Though I had great affection,
there's no cause for regret,
and it's thanks that I am offering
and I owe a lifetime's debt,
for discipleship and friendship
lessen trouble as we live;
they helped me through those young hard times
with what they had to give.

Canadian Capers

We drive out from Toronto
to an Indian Reservation –
we see an exhibition
of the artefacts and history.
There is talk of wampum,
the guide is a top Indian.
There are photos of old chieftains.

Also there are models,
as it were a kind of waxworks,
of the people and a village
before the White Man found them.
One child, a boy, is naked –
wears only a bead headdress.
He is nine or ten, I guess, and
his genitals are missing.
He is brown and smooth and sexless.

Is this prudishness (Canadian)?
Or was there some taboo then,
or even now, with Indians,
that forbade straight sex-depiction?
I want to ask this question –
but I know it's not a question
I can ask aloud in public.

I know, without being told, that
the guide would not much like it.

A Skull in Chain Mail

He has long done with
the smelly feet
the fishy loins
the randy drinking
all kinds of horseplay

the swords
the crossbows
the dog-barking
cannon

imagine
the Battle of Towton
30,000 dead
and more

the Cock Beck
crammed with
the armoured bodies
Lancastrians

he wears a peaceable
skull–cap
recorded in History –
things have changed
but not much.

The Battle of Towton, between the Yorkists and Lancastrians,
fought on Palm Sunday, 26th March 1461, claimed more lives
than any other battle fought in England at any time.

The Revenge for Love

(for Patricia Craig and the ghost of Montague Rhodes James)

You made a good point in your *TLS* review:
no woman is ever haunted in any of the ghost
                                            stories.
And, as far as ghosts have sex, most of the haunters
                                            are male
(though there is the ghost of a woman in 'Martin's
                                            Close').

So now for my theory, which may or may not be
                                            new:
for him, heterosexual love held no glamours or
                                            glories,
his love wouldn't speak its name, it was beyond the
                                            pale,
the kind that has guilt on its fingers wherever it goes!

This kind of thing wouldn't please a stern Victorian
                                            father

(and all stern Victorian fathers were hated and
                                    feared);
you could hide it and hold high office – Lord
                                    Rosebery did,
and so, in the closed world of Academia, did he –

but perhaps it made him spiritually shifty and rather
frightened of a Jealous God with a big white beard
who knew all the secrets that he sanctimoniously hid!
Practising or not, to whatever cloistered degree,

his desires were punished, in these tales, by demons –
a legion of Fathers both horrifying and cruel
(as one might say) that tracked down and pursued,
casting their runes, with all those warnings to the
                                    curious,

more terrifying than boys on burning decks by Mrs
                                    Hemans!
For wrapped round the treasure, guarding the
                                    precious jewel,
was the ghastly toadlike Guilt, by no means a
                                    pseud . . .
and over the hills came the horrible hounds, fast and
                                    furious . . .

The Wages of Sin is Death! So pale scholarly men
have to whistle up something nasty that comes from
                                    the sea
(though in fact curiosity, the cat-killer, is a sin that is
                                    mild)
and be chased by nameless horrors till they have
                                    heart attacks . . .

But was the Eton College Scout Troop ever exactly a
                                    den
of undisclosed iniquity? And in King's over tea,
with muffins or crumpets, should there be the
                                    tremblings of a child
at God the Father driving his devils along the Backs?

Forcible Conversions

'. . . the civil and military powers were directed to obey his commands; and the cruelties exercised by this Semi-Arian tyrant in the support of the Homoiousion, exceeded the commission, and disgraced the reign, of Constantius. The sacraments of the church were administered to the reluctant victims, who denied the vocation, and abhorred the principles, of Macedonius. The rites of baptism were conferred on women and children, who, for that purpose, had been torn from the arms of their friends and parents; the mouths of the communicants were held open, by a wooden engine, while the consecrated bread was forced down their throat; the breasts of tender virgins were either burnt with red-hot egg-shells or inhumanly compressed between sharp and heavy boards.' – Edward Gibbon, The Decline and Fall of the Roman Empire, Chapter XXI

Even if your theology is rickety,
it's no good being pernickety,
if you're going to be a sadist
shout loud 'O God, Thou madest
this world! These are Thy Laws!' –
then open sharklike jaws!
Go the whole hog, don't be tender!
Though the difference may be slender
and admit of some confusion:
Homoousion, Homoiousion.★
Consubstantiality?
Trinitarian reality?

Hot erections, welcome juices!
All the theories are excuses.
Sex acts these, when all is said.
Making people dead (not red),
holy war, crusade, jihad –
none of these, of course, is bad!

They give everyone the chance
to let their Id find true romance
Tortures that are truly cruel
for *them* shine like the brightest jewel.
Red-hot egg-shells are the thing,
instinct with the joys of spring!
And the young outstanding breast
by sharp and heavy boards compressed!

The hypocrites religions breed!
It's unbelievable – and so's the Creed.

* The difference between the two (the Athanasian and Arian
viewpoints) is so small as to be invisible to anybody not steeped
in theology, as Gibbon implies in a footnote. Yet this difference
inspired the tortures.

How Love and Lust are Hard to Separate

Romance is really quite ripe and rumpish,
it bends the beauties and the frumpish
into the shapes that make good nights
for the lovely ladies and the frantically friendly
    frights –

they're all pig-willing to get stuck in,
in any posture, to try their luck in
the carnal copulatory greedy grooves
that the Church allots to doting demons with hairy
    hooves!

However high-minded and pi and pure, you
must get down to it, I assure you,
the knickers off and the flies unzipped.
for Love has always inhabited the crazy and
    crapulous crypt

as well as the choral congregation
where vows are made with ostentation,
and animals like me and you
get quite lit up with the lust that is Love's definite
    due!

So don't think True Love is so ethereal –
you hear low notes when it sticks up its aerial –
don't outlaw it like Robin Hood,
a little bit of what you freely and foolishly fancy
does you good!

The Death of a Mouse

The death of a mouse from cancer is the whole sack
                            of Rome by the Goths,
the end of the British Empire is the munching of
                            coats by some moths,
the smallness of any action doesn't stop it from being
                            the same
as anything big or bigger – it's just the scale, and the
                            name.

Living With

Liking is easy,
loving is easy –
but living with is hard.
That's the joker,
the unknown card.

That marvellous man
may be a bedroom farter
or an anecdotal tirer;
and that beautiful girl
a party show-off or a
self-admirer.

Between the four walls
they behave naturally,
like angels or ogres,
with all their moods –
like Adam and Eve in the garden,
with nothing bogus,

but boxed-in.
Like something steaming
in a pressure cooker,
they live in an atmosphere –
the intelligent witty woman
and the no-good good-looker.

Snow White

She's a widow-maker
and a credit-taker,
everything good's due to *her* –
it's not accident,
she's Heaven-sent,
she can only sit and purr

as the cream grows richer
and the culture kitscher –
and there's no dissenting voice
as the topcats scoff it
and the god called Profit
is the South East English Choice

and the Press grows hottish
as the traitor Scottish
beg to differ a bit;
while the BBC too
she must certainly see to
with her Instant Pressure Kit!

There is homeless weeping
but her Good Housekeeping
will make us happy and strong
and the Future fissile
through each new missile –
you don't get those for a song.

The Falklands Factor
or a dodgy reactor,
she takes them all in her stride,
nothing loth, nothing lother –
the Contras, Piet Botha!
She's not just there for the ride.

Queen of every chat show,
the Crystal Cat Show
never ever produced such a cat,
worshipped by Wogan,
her personal slogan:
I'm right, never wrong! And that's that!

Eyes and Pictures

See again as in childhood: the fox, the mice, the
                                          rabbits.
As our mother saw, when she read these booklets
to the two young children, avid for the pictures.
A comfortable indoor scene, excited by Tom Kitten –
sinister was the word for waistcoated Samuel
                                          Whiskers.

The pictures are the same. The eyes are closed. Not
                                          childhood's
protected sleep with the guttering of a nightlight.
But death. For one listening sister and one reading
                                          mother.

War Generations
(A Loaded Lyric)

Youth's uniform was smartish
and tartish were our thoughts,
there were too many Ought-nots;
we liked instinctual Oughts.

Thou shalt not! seemed quite boring,
like snoring, irksome too –
a thing that older people
seemed most inclined to do.

Yet six years' war came bubbling
and troubling our lives,
as hot as hell and sharper
than pointed butcher's knives.

We lost our early beauty,
so fruity and unlined,
the brave and cowardly drowned in
those seas both deep and mined.

Back forty years or fifty,
once nifty and unstained,
we gaze with eyes so moral.
The hypocrites look pained

to hear the young things singing
and clinging with a sigh
to their so brief enjoyment
before they come to die.

Classical Times

And so, in a grove, the Goddess
is masturbating some serious women,
the nymphs are filled with joy
by their intromittent boyfriends,
flutes are being played by fauns.

There are great bearded oaths from warriors –
'By Clytemnestra's clitoris!',
wooded hills are wonderful,
streams sparkle in sunlight,
Apollo trims some hexameters.

Philosophers dream of cocks,
slaves are stretched, pleasure or agony,
the couch or cross, while wine
pours into everything
in hot dry olive country.

Oxford Poetry 1916

In the year of my birth
and the death of Henry James,
at a bad time in the First World War,
edited by T. W. Earp and A. L. Huxley
and W. R. Childe (who he?).

Earp was an art critic, Aldous was Aldous.
What was it like then?
Wine and floppy ties?
The threat of the trenches
for those whose eyesight was good?

Robert Nichols, N. M. Mitchison,
L. A. G. Strong, Sherard Vines
and E. H. W. Meyerstein (Magdalen)
(who rhymes 'romaunt' with 'jubilant').

James Elroy Flecker, Ernest Dowson,
Lionel Johnson, Oscar Wilde
stand in the background,
in the foreground
a very non-aesthetic war.

Two poems mention the dead.
The best poem is by Aldous.

Of course they fade – and all our verse will fade.

War Anthology

I don't like those desert poems,
they have a hot sandy taste.

The ones about ships
are too salty, unstable and tempestuous.

Anything airborne
promotes a terrifying fear of heights.

Even on foot there's mud and dust –
and everywhere the revolting smell of death.

Cats and Women

When I say 'I like cats'
I don't count the ones that look like Zsa Zsa Gabor,
the big fluffy Persians with bad-tempered faces
or most of the cats that win prizes at Cat Shows.
The cats I like are almost always tabbies,
ginger cats or tortoiseshells – or black and white.
Pure black cats too, that were once persecuted
because they were associated with witches . . .

When I say 'I like women'
I don't mean models or Elizabeth Taylor
or any professional beauties in real fur coats
or any of the ones that are in love with themselves.
The women I like don't have elaborate hairstyles
and they're certainly not dyed blondes.
What's more, they're shaped like women
and not like coathangers or stick insects.

Leaving the Land of Cockaigne

With Cary Hunt and Corny Hock
we revelled in the pubs
that seldom knew the Queen of Hearts,
where still the Ace of Clubs
was King, and no knives gathered rust
in scenes of violence and lust.

The roystering and roaring boys
gave girls the biggest thrill,
young acrobats – and safety nets
provided by the Pill
made pleasure commonplace, with fun
just waiting for the starting gun.

Once syphilis and gonorrhoea
had waved and gone away,
we thought at last the time had come
for everyone to play;
with no more plagues on men or maids –
but we had reckoned without AIDS.

Girl Squash

In 1936 at the age of about fifteen
Alan Ross played squash with a girl
who worked at Government House –
she had some Indian, or perhaps Chinese, blood.
Her skin, he says, was 'pure ivory'.
Afterwards, in her flat in Bhawanipore Road,
they would take it in turns to shower.
'Look at me if you like' she once said to him,
letting her towel fall open.
No sex, but she was kindly (less than ten years
                                        older).

This was Calcutta.

In about 1948, when I was thirty-two,
I played squash with a girl called Nicole Onoff –
she must have been about the same age as Ross's
                                    girl.
She was partly Russian, partly (I think) French.
She was friendly, sturdy, very athletic,
played hockey for England and was also,
I believe, an Olympic diving champion.
She played to keep fit; I could just beat her,
but only if I ran like a demon.
Drop shots and lobs were no part of our armoury.
No sex, naturally. I guarded the shower
while she was using it – to forestall intruders.
Then we bicycled away, separately.
From the Oatlands Park Hotel –
because this was in Weybridge.

The Wages of Sin

'. . . *enjoying the freedom of expression his own outspoken canon first established*' – Simon Rae, *TLS*, 13 February 1987

'There's a lot to be said for being a cad!'
as H. G. Wells said to Siegfried Sassoon
in the Reform Club when Hilaire Belloc
was trying to cut him –

he simply ignored his ignoring
and shouted, 'Hello, Belloc! You're getting fat!' –
in the same way my Muse can go naked
and no one's surprised now,

even though the critics with mouths like
small Gothic slits are creating
and think the whole thing's a bit vulgar
and not academic.

But it leaves me quite free for the poems
that have fantasies about Lord Lustful –
a late eighteenth-century rakehell
in his folly-cum-fortress,

who makes his friends dress up as monks
and as reviewers and bishops and so on,
or even as sheep, and have orgies,
drinking down girlpee

and fondling a milkmaid or two
who are fastcar-driven from Sloane Street
and often use the silver chamberpots
kept behind a curtain.

Likewise a more serious love can be treated,
where a lover says, 'Your navel is pretty',
'You've got good legs', 'Your head's a nice shape',
'They're very tiptilted'

and so on. 'You're looking very kissable!'
All these things can be said and described
by lovers without a stitch on between them.
It's an advantage.

It's what you get for being sex-obsessed.
Being able to say 'cock' without a hiccup.
And since the cocks and cunts are so basic
and rule our behaviour

probably it gets us a bit nearer
to human life and what, in it, is important.
The 'naked truth'. They said it, you said it,
it shouldn't be harmful

The Marvellous Writer

He was skunkdrunk for more than a hundred days –
but nobody minded, he was such a marvellous
                                        writer.

416

He pinched the shirts of his friends and rumpled their
girlfriends –
but nobody minded, he was such a marvellous
writer.

He told some wonderful lies, he was truly inventive –
but nobody minded, he was such a marvellous
writer.

He encouraged the groupies to send him their verse
about rabbits –
but nobody minded, he was such a marvellous
writer.

He was never nice or trustworthy or kind or unselfish –
but nobody minded, he was such a marvellous
writer.

Pogroms

'Humanity is shocked at the recital of the horrid cruelties
which they committed in the cities of Egypt, of Cyprus, and
of Cyrene, where they dwelt in treacherous friendship with
the unsuspecting natives;* and we are tempted to applaud
the severe retaliation which was exercized by the arms of
the legions against a race of fanatics, whose dire and
credulous superstition seemed to render them implacable
enemies not only of the Roman government but of human
kind.

* In Cyrene they massacred 220,000 Greeks; in Cyprus, 240,000; in
Egypt, a very great multitude. Many of these unhappy victims were
sawed asunder, according to a precedent to which David had given the
sanction of his example. The victorious Jews devoured the flesh, licked
up the blood, and twisted the entrails like a girdle round their bodies.
See Dion Cassius, 1. lxviii, p. 1145.' – Edward Gibbon, The Decline
and Fall of the Roman Empire, Chapter XVI.

Always beware of anyone who hates you
because of the colour of your skin
or because they have a very highly developed
Sense of Sin.
To do you in

is the ambition of many a religion –
some preach a timeless Holy War,
their prophets are bigoted, rambunctious,
rude and raw . . .
To them, a saw

is just a tool to carpenter the faithless,
to cut them, as they say, down to size;
and the lethal gases were truly invented
by the wise
to close the eyes

of all the subhuman unbelievers
squeezed into some harsh unholy zoo,
electric fences and piano wire are
useful too –
yes, they will do

to cut them off from the land of the living.
So will axes and big wood fires;
and tortures of all kinds can fulfil
God's desires –
watch them for hours

they could, Hitler and Inquisitions,
and any old execution crowd;
in Colosseums, on holidays, they
shouted loud,
they were quite proud

and happy to see a measly Christian
sewn in an animal skin, what debauch,
what snarling joy! or pitch-smeared, lit
like a torch
over a porch!

But it's not just in the Dark Ages or
in far-off times that now seem dim;
just two centuries ago only, the witches,
sink-or-swim,
glorified Him.

And in 1915 Turks hanged Armenians
on hooks in their butcher's shops –
holocausts are commonplace
and seldom flops!
It never stops.

It is not, and was not, my intention in this poem to arouse anti-Semitic feeling (anti-Jewish or anti-Arab). But rather to show the blood-thirstiness of religious and totalitarian regimes, both of which work in very similar ways. Religious persecutions are not new; the word 'pogrom' derives from a Russian word meaning complete and swift destruction, invented by newspapers to describe the Czarist persecution of the Jews in 1905–6.

The last witch was burned, in Peru, as recently as 1888. In Scotland the last witch was executed in 1702.

Jabberwocky

Retrospect 1.
So I sit down and ask myself: what kind of a poem should this be? And I answer myself: perhaps it shouldn't be a poem at all, perhaps it should be a prose-poem if you like to call it that, and the best thing to do is to write it out straight. What *can* be said in prose is better said in prose than in verse (as Eliot himself said, in other words).

So we go back to my childhood. Would I be about five or six years old? Six probably, rather than five. To me and my sister, eighteen months younger than me, our mother is reading *Alice Through The Looking Glass*. I am terrified – not so much by the sinister appurtenances of the Jabberwocky poem –

> 'Twas brillig and the slithy toves
> Did gyre and gimble in the wabe:
> All mimsy were the borogoves,
> And the mome raths outgrabe . . .

with its atmosphere of doomful horror but because, although I do not recognize this at the time, Tenniel's drawing of the monster resembles my father – in the prominent rabbit teeth and the fact that *it is wearing a waistcoat*. My father had teeth slightly of this kind; and, in his professional capacity as a consulting surgeon, he always wore a dark suit with a waistcoat. The fact that the Jabberwock wears *only* a waistcoat makes no difference to the eye and mind of childhood. Furthermore, this fearsome animal seems to be wearing *spats*, which my father also wore in the Twenties, or at least some kind of socklike mittens, on its horrifying claw-toed feet.

So we have the perfect nightmare picture of paternal castrating vengeance (as many psychiatrists would say). Someone intent on destroying me because of my love for my mother, the very well-established rivalry between the father and the son. The monster is far bigger and more frightening than its young assailant – who, however, is armed with a disproportionately long sword (the penis and its importance?).

As a young child I took only a little comfort from the fact that the Jabberwock is killed. What I didn't like was the picture of the confrontation. In the forests of the night, in my childish dreams, I was

420

afraid to meet this baleful father-figure. And in my nightmares, as I remember, I did. I didn't know then that Carroll intended this poem to be a burlesque of dialect folk poetry and ballads; nor would it have interested me if I had. Children like being frightened by ghosts and goblins (so the experts say) but sometimes they can be frightened too much.

Retrospect 2. 1922
The drawing-room, the winter fire
that crackles with the wood and coal –
but in the book there's something dire,
the unhealth that the demons skoal,

and clearly through the funny words
a menace stalks the child that hears,
and fierce outlandish beasts and birds
crawl round the cretonne-covered chairs.

The jaws that bite, the claws that catch!
The mother reads and shows her son
the picture and the words that match –
just Tenniel's Victorian fun!

But in the long and lonely nights
the Jabberwock is out, in woods
where Jubjub birds are frumious frights –
no comforts from the motherhoods

and no protection from the rage
of the avenging awesome ug
now rampant on the frightening page –
and large as life upon the rug!

The Ordinary Joes

The people in the ballroom
Were stuffy and arty
So I began to get
Just a little bit frayed –
I went into the kitchen,
I dug me a party:
The waiter and the porter and the upstairs maid!

In Britain where the Scots are not the same as the
                        Eastenders
there have been faiths and fealties and even Faith's
                        Defenders –
though rulers find that treachery is often just the job.
A King will never keep his word when dealing with
                        the mob.
Remember old Wat Tyler and his put-down men of
                        Kent,
safe conducts count for nothing, it's the Barons that
                        are bent.
Through history the ones with hacked-off heads and
                        hands and toes
have always been the not-too-clean and ordinary
                            Joes.

In South East England where they have the very
                        special vowels
and His and Hers and Unisex is written on
                        the towels,
they love the City and the Law and hate the
                        Welfare State –
Capitalism is the word that makes *them* masturbate.
It isn't north of Hadrian's Wall, or past the Firth
                        of Forth,
for them it's north of Watford is the dangerous
                        cold North –
that's where the lesser breeds are found, and that's
                        the way it goes,
they're the élite, they never meet the ordinary Joes.

They live in separate places and their kids have
                              separate schooling.
What's 'equal opportunity'? They'd think that you
                              were fooling
if you said it wasn't good to have One Nation split
                              in two –
so long as *they're* all right, Jack, that's the very thing
                              to do!
Though the wall is made of money, it quite surely is
                              a wall –
the Southern side can hardly hear the long
                              distressing call
that is drowned out by the Yes-men – the faint or
                              angry Noes
of the homeless and redundant, all the ordinary Joes.

If you are black or brown or Welsh or look quite like
                              a miner
you're not much better, in their eyes, than a burst
                              bin-liner,
non-human like the Jews, the Reds, the gypsies and
                              the Poles,
the ones that Hitler hated and made lampshades or
                              shoe-soles.
But Old Etonians know that *they* were born to rule
                              the roost
and anything is good for us that gives *their* shares
                              a boost.
Pity and love, like polar bears aloof on swift ice
                              floes,
float past and never stop, or see, the ordinary Joes.

The Enemy Within is us – the ones the Tories govern.
To them a Greenham woman's just a crazy slut,
                              a sloven.
The warheads in their thousands simply make
                              them purr,
each one an end to Britain if the flying of the fur
goes as far as Reagan, quite complacent, thinks
                              it might.

We know that Maggie thinks so too, and into
                              Nuclear Night
she will lead men, women, children, with the stags
                              and fawns and does –
when they've sunk her in her bunker, far from
                              ordinary Joes.

Or is the Enemy a She? A tiny Right Wing platelet
but active in the bloodstream? Is a little
                              Fascist Statelet
what Britain's turning into, with no Unions and a
                              Press
that only puts one point of view? Where the old in
                              their distress
die of cold in heatless winters and disheartened
                              unemployed
look for lost jobs in industries that she herself
                              destroyed?
No need to look so very far to find Great Britain's
                              foes –
they're not among the old and young and ordinary
                              Joes!

The Cultural Ambassador

The Cultural Ambassador
and, even more, his wife
can cut through the inessentials at a party
like a knife.
You'll know when you're famous
and the first of the few
when *they* plunge through the
unimportant people
and make a bee-line for *you*!
But anybody who's an inessential
must wait in the queue.

The Cultural Ambassador's children,
from the age of about three,
have had nothing but celebrities
for breakfast, lunch and tea.
They wouldn't know how to
speak to an ordinary person
like you or me.

It's a demanding life
and never quiet
up there on the heights,
living on a rarefied diet;
where, unless you've written
the book of the year,
of the month – or the day –
they will look straight through you
or turn away.

The Ruined Cemetery on Putney Common

In the middle of the common
with no gates, no railings round it,
half an acre, less?, we guess it,
it is simply tree-surrounded
like an eighteenth-century picture
(as it might have been by Watteau)
but without the nymphs and shepherds.
Still, it's green and there are statues –
one or two are headless angels
martyred by the local vandals.
Chunky, plain, the fat stone crosses
stand on piles of fancy rockwork –
often just the base is left there.
In the middle, one tall boxlike
stone construction stands, imposing
memory on us newcomers,

and on it a mourning female
figure and the cross, as always.
On the slabs it's not the Bible,
instead pious hymns are quoted.

It is closed, if that means something.
A 1967 burial
seems to be the last, the tombstones
cracked, the headstones stagger
at some sad subsided angles.
The polished marble only keeps its
shiny confident true glitter.
'Son of the Above' and also
two children buried with their mother
(1870s, 1880s)
and small groups of close relations;
husbands, wives are sharing tombstones . . .

but the weeds have taken over
and the healthy autumn brambles
with their red and black bright fruiting;
and the vandals prising letters
from inscriptions on the tombstones
(mother of pearl inlaid in stonework,
or some very similar substance)
and initialling the uprights
have been here for rites at midnight –
witchcraft no, but sexual dalliance
in uncomfortable surroundings
is a possible for guesswork.

What a moral for the moral!
How our life is dust and ashes
and our brave words are neglected,
hardly seen, to most not known-of . . .

all that keeps on keeping on is
change, decay, and sex and mischief
and the blackberries' bright shining.

Freud

I first met Lucian when I was a friend of Spender's
at Stephen's flat (I've always been a friend of
                                            Spender's)
in 1938 or 1939 – I would be twenty-three and he
                                  would be seventeen.
In 1939 he would be seventeen.
This wasn't much of a meeting; but we were in the
                                            same room,
it has to count as a meeting, if you're in the same
                                                room
and introduced, as we were. Ah, but the next time!

There was something very different about the next
                                                time!
I remember it like a dream, I was walking by
                              Green Park –
down Piccadilly, by the summer-green Green Park,
on my way to catch a bus home at Hyde Park
                                        Corner,
and all the way from Green Park station to Hyde Park
                                              Corner
he followed me, saying *Gavin Ewart is a terrible person*
and attacking my character, saying what a terrible
                                              person
I was. I cowered. I wasn't used to such attacks,
I'd done nothing whatever to deserve such attacks,
I was innocent and unsophisticated. What could
                        I answer?
I now realize I should have stopped walking, and
                              made an answer.
Was he drunk, or on drugs – or was it a fugue?
Is that sort of thing what the shrinks call a fugue?

At about that time Stephen showed me a photo of
                        Lucian at the age of nine,
like a small beaky bird, at the age of nine –
saying how sweet he looked. That was the last time I
                                        saw him;

427

in Piccadilly was the last time I saw him.

But I heard about him, later that year, from
                              Ian Lubbock
when he had married Lys. My girlfriend. Next,
                                        Mrs Lubbock.
In 1939, I would guess. He came home one day, he
                              told me,
and found *Lys in bed with Freud* – that's what he told
                                        me.
He didn't seem worried; it was like a piece of gossip.
And the next time I heard about him it was
                              genuine gossip:
Lucian was very clever at the time of his call up!
When they interviewed him at his call up,
he told them he always had a funny feeling
in a room full of men – a very funny feeling.
And he said he couldn't leave his little cat,
he didn't think he could go into the army and leave his
                              little cat.

This may have been malicious, but it was quite
                              entertaining.

And if anybody thinks these jottings are entertaining
they're quite welcome to use them. In a *Lives Of The*
                              Great Portrait Painters
for example. I think he deserves to have his life in a
                Lives Of The Great Portrait Painters.

Goethe (Sehe mit fühlenden Aug, fühle mit sehender Hand)

Goethe was one of the boys, and in love with the
                              skirts that he lifted,
    cotton or wool or brocade – and in those dandified
                              days
women of high class or low never had heard tell of
                              knickers,

428

nothing opposed his desire (only the dancers wore
                                            tights).
Heterosexual men, and the homosexual women,
    all agreed with him there; this was the true
                                    Promised Land!

He was in love too with Rome, with all its classical
                                            ladies
    savoury as to us now the Grated Parmesan Cheese
('Italian', Sainsbury's says); they were the cake-
                                    topping icing
    too, if your tooth should be sweet. But, if we're
                                    talking of Truth,
sex has a taste and a smell that can never be
                                    packaged in plastic.
    The breasts and the backs and the bums! To him,
                                    so creakingly, beds
spoke like the poets of love, Propertius, Catullus,
                                            Tibullus;
    it was a hot Roman speech – sacred, you might
                                            say, to Pan,
Venus, etc. He called them, most fitly, Triumvirs.
    Girls in the nude, or in shifts, in Goethe's
                                    barbarian arms –
clearly he beat out the beat on the brown-skinned
                                    backs of his lovers,
    pagan and metrical both, hexapent, noble and old.
Shy are the nymphs now and shy the garden gnomes
                                            of Priapus,
    mentula is a non-word; but he from the forested
                                            North
went after the instincts, yes, the exiled and dark gods
                                            of Lawrence,
    far from the State and the Church, warm in the
                                    sun and the South.

Sailing to Byzantium
(A 61st Anniversary Version)

That's no place for oldies, where the kids
are having it off all over, and treeborne birds
(and they snuff it, each and every) sing!
The salmon fool about in the rivers, macks in the
                                            sea,
swimmers, runners, flyers through all the summer
are hyping all that's born and kicks the bucket.
And in that woozy music nobody pays heed
to the books of the highbrows and the string
quartets!

An old guy is, sure, a no-account thing,
some threads on a broomstick, if he don't
make with the soul and bust the ozone
in proportion as he's looking kinda crumby.
And they don't care for getting the joint jumping,
all they want is to admire their own star quality.
So for these reasons I booked a steerage passage
and now I'm in God's Own City – Byzantium.

You wise guys standing in God's Holy Fire
like in those mosaic things on walls,
unwind for a moment, you old honey-buzzards,
and give me a lead – I wanna make some music!
Eat my heart out, by golly! It's got the hots
for something, it's lost its identity, it's stuck with
an animal that's gonna croak! So just take me
into the make-believe they call Eternity!

Once I've handed in my dinner pail
I'll never wanna be a living man or beast,
but more like stuff some Greeks made out of gold –
gold and enamel, say, by bashing it with hammers
to keep some dopey Emperor from hitting the hay.

Or the clockwork birds they put on golden branches
to sing to the high-class guys and dolls of Byzantium
of what's been and gone, what's new, or in the
                              stars yet!

W. B. Yeats, 1927. Gavin Ewart, 1988.

A Neo-Classical Scene (1982)

Is it like a Horatian ode? Is it?
Do they think of themselves as Romans
as the slave girls pour the wine?
   In a lively Italian restaurant.

They are the managers, each has a chariot;
the world still has its dancers and flute players.
In some places, Jews are a problem.
   The more it changes, the less it changes?

I was lying with Myra under a fruit tree
and I said to her: It only *looks* the same.
We use up youth like an expense account,
   the whisky, the roses,

we are not classical, but blurred in our outlines
and a line of verse is reduced to two words:
no good. Myra opposed with
   a supersoft nipple.

The truth is, the advertising got into our bones,
it made us property-mad and purseproud, comrades,
and even the tribunes of the people
   are a darn sight keener

on remaining tribunes of the people, than
giving up the chauffeur-driven cars and the boozing –
and as for those pinstripe suits (from the Thirties)
   a principle's something

they think they have in the Civil Service.
We are either living in Ancient Rome, or out of it,
everything's so rough. Like the football?
   Myra gave a giggle.

I never can get Myra to be serious. It's like
a complacent bourgeois sentimental comedy,
where the wifely jokes are a definite put-down,
   not that Myra's a wife . . .

but she likes footballers and pop stars. Once,
oh, please don't tell me (I know), it was gladiators.
She'd vote for Hitler because she liked his moustache.
   What a world, my masters!

At least we've done without crucifixion – or have
   we?
The tortures go on in the huts and the houses,
the businessmen lunchers are simply the icing
   on a pretty horrible economic cake.

The Pilgrim's Progress
(A Board Game In 100 Moves)

Start. The City of Destruction.
   1. Christian meets Evangelist (must throw a six to
      do this. Second turn and start on Pilgrimage).
   2.
   3. Persuaded to turn back by Obstinate. Wait here
      until another six is thrown.
   4.
   5. Falls into Slough of Despond. Returns with
      Pliable to Start.
   6. In Slough of Despond. Wait one turn.
   7.
   8. Plucked out of Slough of Despond by Help. Go
      on to 12.
   9.

10. Meets Mr Worldly Wiseman, coming from the town of Carnal Policy. Turns aside to visit Mr Legality. Miss one turn.
11. Meets Evangelist again. Go on to Little Wicket Gate (14).
12.
13.
14. Little Wicket Gate. Good-Will lets Christian in.
15. The Interpreter encourages Christian with parables. Go on to 20.
16.
17.
18. The Cross and the Sepulchre. Christian loses his Burden. Go on to 25.
19.
20. Three Shining Ones give Christian a Roll.
21. Stops to talk to Simple, Sloth and Presumption. Lose one turn.
22. Meets Formalist and Hypocrite. 'If we are in, we are in'. Go back to 14.
23.
24. The Hill Difficulty. Throw a six to continue.
25.
26. Meets Mistrust and Timorous. Loses one turn.
27. Realizes he has left his Roll in Arbour on Hill. Back to 24.
28. Finds Roll and goes on his way.
29. Frightened by two Chained Lions. Lose a turn.
30.
31. Encouraged by Watchful, reaches the palace Beautiful.
32.
33. The virgins Discretion, Prudence, Piety and Charity entertain him to supper.
34.
35. First sight of the Delectable Mountains. Go on to 37.
36. Goes down into the Valley of Humiliation.
37.
38. Fights with the monster Apollyon. Wait two turns.

39. Enters the Valley of the Shadow of Death.
40. Meets two Men, who advise him to turn back. Return to 30.
41.
42. Sees the Mouth of Hell. Uses the weapon of All-prayer. On to 45.
43. Beset by Fiends.
44. End of the Valley of the Shadow of Death.
45. Sees two Giants in a Cave, Pope and Pagan. Wait one turn.
46. Catches up with Faithful.
47. Slips and falls. Wait one turn till Faithful helps him up.
48. Faithful tells Christian of his meeting with Wanton. Back to 39.
49.
50. They meet Talkative. Wait one turn.
51. Evangelist joins them. Go on to 60.
52.
53. Put in the stocks at Vanity Fair. Wait two turns.
54.
55. Tried by Lord Hate-Good, for speaking ill of Lord Lechery, Sir Having-Greedy, the Lord Carnal Delight, etc.
56.
57. Faithful martyred. Christian remanded to prison. Throw six to go on.
58. Christian escapes.
59. Joined by Hopeful. Extra turn.
60.
61. They meet By-Ends, a relative of Mr Facing-Both-Ways. Go back to 49.
62. On the plain called Ease. Move to 67.
63.
64. Turn aside to see the Hill called Lucre. Wait two turns.
65.
66. They see the Pillar of Salt inscribed 'Remember Lot's wife'. Stay one turn to wonder at it.
67.

68. Rest by the River of God. Move, refreshed, to 74.
69.
70. Turn aside into By-Path Meadow. Miss one turn.
71.
72. Captured by Giant Despair. Kept in Doubting Castle from Wednesday to Saturday. Miss two turns.
73. They escape with the Key called Promise.
74.
75. Reach the Delectable Mountains. Extra throw.
76.
77. Pass through the Country of Conceit.
78. The ways divide. They hesitate. Back to 71.
79. Caught in a net by Flatterer. Wait two turns.
80. Chastised by a Shining One.
81.
82. Listen to Atheist. Back to 74.
83.
84. Hopeful tells Christian the story of his Conversion. Wait one turn.
85.
86. They leave Ignorance behind. Go on to 90.
87. Pass over the Enchanted Ground into the Country of Beulah.
88.
89. See the Celestial City close to. Fall sick with desire. Back to 81.
90.
91. They reach the River. Disturbed because there is no bridge. Wait one turn.
92. Christian fears he will die in the River. Back to 71.
93.
94. Hopeful saves Christian. On to 99.
95.
96.
97. Other side of River. Welcomed by Two Shining Ones.
98. Escorted by a Company of the Heavenly Host.
99.
100. Christian and Hopeful enter the Celestial City.

Lawrie

It was in North Africa, summer of 1943,
I was posted to a Light Anti-Aircraft Regiment
with another officer. He was a very efficient officer
(I was not a very efficient officer) –
but this was not a very efficient regiment.

It was a converted Infantry Battalion.
None of the senior officers knew any gun drill.
One wise sergeant (a cockney) said to me:
'If you keep a crease in your trousers and a shine on
                                                  your boots
you can do what you like in this regiment.'
Later, I heard, he lost both legs from a mine.
Perhaps the War God doesn't like you to be *too*
                                                  clever . . .

Anyway, we arrived at a Battery Headquarters,
living in tents not far outside Tunis.
We were dumped at night, with our kit, in a tent.
Next morning I approached a batman:
'We're two officers, we've just been posted, can you
                                    get us some breakfast?'
He answered ungraciously, 'Well, fuck your luck!'
This was Gunner Pyne, a Catholic criminal
from the East End of London, and Lawrie's batman.

Lawrie was a homosexual actor, 'resting' in the
                                                  Army –
he must have been a very bad actor –
but he could sing a few songs to entertain the troops
and do a drag act. Like me, he was a Lieutenant.
Tunis had recently fallen, and the troops were bolshie –
all they wanted to do was to go straight back home.

The other officers in the Battery found Lawrie
                                        amusing,
and in fact, it being wartime, he *was* quite amusing,
terribly camp and very proud of his face,
('And what a face!' said my unimpressed
                                        companion).
He also had malice, he loved gossip and trouble,
telling the Battery Commander how the two new
                                        officers
were fantastic shits to the men.
In fact, it wasn't easy for us.

My batman too was a criminal, a little Irish criminal
                                        called Byrne.
When we were deployed on an airfield before the
                                        invasion of Sicily
stole my scissors and sold them to an American
                                        paratrooper,
or perhaps he just exchanged them for Jack Daniels.

I remember one of the paratroopers bringing whisky
(at Lawrie's invitation?). He started feeling up
                                        Lawrie.
My friend and I frowned
and were ticked off by Lawrie for puritan outlooks.
I remember fingers outlining khaki.
It looked like the beginning of mutual masturbation
but it didn't go so far, I think Lawrie had some sense
                                        left.

It occurred to me later: perhaps Lawrie and Pyne lent
                                        each other a helping hand?
They were certainly on very familiar terms.
Later, in Italy, the unit was split up.
I heard that Lawrie had an eye blacked by a
                                        Commando –
one that he approached with a certain proposition.

But I shan't forget that face
or his telling me how Pyne's mother
always threatened 'I'll tell the Father!'
('Not *your* father, *the* Father!' Lawrie would say).
I believe in fact he did run into trouble,
perhaps he was cashiered? He should have been in
                                        ENSA.
He loved music – opera – and spoke about Joan
                                        Cross.

11 November 1986 (Remembrance Day)

Joan Cross was one of the best British singers of that period, an
operatic soprano.

A Patient of Dr Rycroft's

Today I am feeling comatic.
After a long night with Kit.
But all love is infantilistic
and even reactionary men
have no sense of structure –
even the most sensitive are incapable
of lasting personal relationships.
I regard all sex as masturbatory,
there's no point in kissing or 'foreplay'.

I have my language, you have yours.
A lowerarchy is a hierarchy viewed from above.
You laughed when you asked me
'Were you annoyed?'
and I answered 'Annoyed? I was paranoid!'

Suffixes, prefixes? Who fixes them? I fix them.
There's iron in irony, although you smile.
Socrates? How does he come into it?

I don't understand metaphors,
semaphores and meaningless signals.
'Getting something off my chest'
means a bra or a boyfriend.
Things are things, and not other things.

You're surprised I call them 'lovers' –
I have so many of them.
Most, you say, would mistrust, distrust
such casual encounters. I have no fear,
once a teenage pillion rider on a wall of death.
Just as I have no social shyness.

At ten I decided to be Shakespeare, and a
   ventriloquist.
At seventeen I wrote a poem identical with one of
   Verlaine's
and a melody identical with one by Rachmaninov.
I could have been a great ballerina.
I have telepathic powers.
Freud, you say – 'sexual overestimation of the ego'.

But I have my effigies, and my own theory.
'Physically real internal figures'.
I worked it out myself,
with the help of two books,
one by Reik and one by Reich.
I want to be a child analyst.

Distelligent, sensationful, miswanted –
you smile at my vocabulary – but I still love cats.
If there are 'love-objects'
in this world, they are cats.
They are overstanding.
All mothers are sadistic.

I am beautiful and an actress.
I also believe I can find a way to be immortal.

See the case history 'Miss Y: The Analysis of a Paranoid
Personality' contained in *Psychoanalysis and Beyond* by Charles

Rycroft. 'Reactionary' = sensitive, in her vocabulary. People who 'have no sense of structure' do not want lasting relationships.

The Idea of Children at Houghton, Michigan (Main Street Inn, 52 Rooms, Kingbeds, In Room Whirlpool Tubs)

So I sit with my french toast and my coffee
with a view of a bridge that has as it were
an upward-travelling crossbar to let the shipping
                                              through
and some guy with a synthesiser is playing 'Un Bel
                                              Dì Vedremo',
a choir sings 'Always'.

But the food, the view and the radio
are only the background.

The background might seem complex
but the thought is simple.
As I grow older, my concern is the children.

The parents, it's true, each loves a partner –
but our lives are very nearly, you could say, over.

The young man, the young woman,
how will they do – without us?
The Governments are pleading: Oh, just *one* more
                                              missile!
piling on the agony.
Will they go forever into that nuclear winter?
How will they do, will they both be happy?

It's a simple thought, you could call it sentimental.
It has something in common with 'Un Bel Dì
                          Vedremo' –
which contains in a way a hope and a promise
although it has its pathos, through dramatic irony;
the audience knows that the end will be bitter.
And 'Always' too (and the choir made it schmaltzy)
is a promise imbued with deluded sadness,
it's not a happy tune.

Strangely enough, they both share an emotion.

This is what I feel, as I move from juice to
coffee and more coffee.

It's a wish and a prayer and a hope for their future.

Part Two *The So-called Sonnets*

Sonnet: Children

In middle age and in old age the partners realize
that however fond they may be of one another
the thing they worry about most is: the children.
Everybody must die, but how will the children get on
when we are no longer there to watch, to help, to
  advise?
In such a world, there must be great anxiety –
a nuclear war, a kind of fascist state
and/or Direct Rule from the Oval Office?

These are possibilities, if you're going to be anxious.

Children in the past have fought their way through.
Children become adults. They have talents and
  qualities.
They don't think of themselves any more as children.
As we have been, they are grown men and women,
able to take the new responsibilities: children.

Sonnet: People who love Abstractions

All people who say they love abstractions
must be cold people – people who say they love God,
                                    for instance,
must be cold. If you say you love Truth
or Justice, it's a bit more reasonable.
Everybody knows, roughly, what's true and what
                                    isn't;
and people also know, more or less, what's just.

But nobody knows very much about God –
or, rather, too many people think they know about
                                    God.

All that a human being can really, truly, love
is flesh and blood – men, women, children.
You could add dogs, cats, horses to the list.
But we're not designed to adore intangible nothings
whose attributes and desires are so variously
                                        interpreted
and whose existence even can be seriously
                                        questioned.

Sonnet: 'Rarely, rarely comest thou, Spirit of Delight'

So you come into the kitchen one morning
(the only room with cat-flap access)
and you find the larger cat, covered in blood, on a
                                        chair
and patches of blood on the chair and the floor.
His left foreleg is limp, he can't move it
from the wrist, as it were. A car, a tom-cat?
A dog, or even a suburban fox?
Pathetic, when you stroke him he still gives a very
                                        faint purr.

He limps about, on drugs. Two weeks, the damaged
                                        nerve is healing.
Our Alleluias go up. Because we're there and see it
it's like the end of a famine in Ethiopia –
more real, for us! The genuine rejoicing
that shakes the people at the end of wars –
crowds drinking, singing, splashing in the fountains!

Sonnet: The Scene at 29 Ratcliffe Highway in 1811

Inside the shop, the body of James Gowen (14),
                                        apprentice –
his head battered to pulp, brains on the ceiling, blood
                                        everywhere –

444

by the door, Mrs Marr (24). The same.
Behind the counter, the body of Timothy Marr (24).
                                        Ditto.
In the basement the baby (3 months), face battered,
                        throat cut through.
'Most inhumanly and barbarously murdered,' said
                    the Home Secretary.

'A sickly sweet smell of blood and brains,' say the
                            crime writers.
General panic. Fear and hate for Portuguese and Irish.

Next, all four corpses laid out on beds. But no
restrictions on sightseers. Neighbours. Fine ladies.
                    The stench of Wapping,
the press and mill of stinking living bodies,
'the first sickly-sweet intimations of decay',
the inquest four days later. Horror would
                        overpower –
but what would shake *us* most would be the smell.

See *The Maul and the Pear Tree* by P.D. James and T.A.
Critchley. Another similar murder in the same district only
twelve days later had tremendous effect. This was the cluster of
murders that De Quincey wrote about in his essay 'Murder
Considered as One of the Fine Arts'.

Sonnet: Ghost Stories

They're about something nasty in a room with a
                            locked door.
Or about the locations of old wickedness, cruelty,
                            violence.
Or about how the dead come back, in their
                        frightening disguises
as decomposing bodies, skeletons. But they move.
                    It's against nature.
Or how a man sees the paw of the fiend on the table
                        before him
and realizes, slowly, that it is standing behind him.

Or how in a hotel room there are two beds –
and the empty one has an occupant . . .

The dead want to get back into life: that's a very
                                        ancient thought.
And it may be we have guilt for not having treated
                                        them well.
But the guilt is, too, from a personal persecution
                                        mania
and we haunt ourselves with the memories of evil
real or imagined. And the evil we have done
comes back as the lonely-road demon that is walking
                                        behind us.

Sonnet: Fear

Isn't it in *Lady Chatterley's Lover*
that Mellors and Connie are watching the pheasant
                                        chicks
as they face the world with perfect confidence and
                                        lack of fear?

Young life, as Lawrence says, is not suspicious.
It doesn't know about the guns and foxes,
how so many things are bad on an earth where
a superpower lives off the Third World
and all the dictators are prosperous and happy . . .

Even the defenceless, born in baby-bashing families,
are not (to begin with) conscious of fear.
It's a way of life, though they learn early
to duck or run when he hits them.
It's boring to say it's fear that leads to the missiles.
Everybody knows. But fear *is* terribly boring.

446

Part Three *The Lighter*

Modest Proposal

Good light verse is better than bad heavy verse
    any day of the week.
Of course it's not the greatest thing in the universe
    but it's able to speak
clearly of the ironies – not dull or solemn
    or proud or stuck-up.
It needn't be frivolous, or dodging the column,
    or selling a pup.

Responsible, insouciant, and civilised too,
    it ought to be calm,
not at all hysterical and not well advised to
    tickle Love's palm,
it's not good at rhapsodies, heartaches or yells,
    it's partial to rhyme –
for the egotistical sublime, or church bells,
    it hasn't much time.

Loving Unsuitable People

All lovers love unsuitable people –
a Moslem loves a Jew,
a Protestant loves a Catholic,
and I'm in love with you!

A Capulet, from the whole of Verona,
will choose a Montague,
Housman loved Moses Jackson,
and I'm in love with you!

Noel Coward adored Jack Wilson
(straight as a ruler too),
and Don José loved Carmen –
and I'm in love with you!

Auden loved Chester Kallman,
Adam loved You-Know-Who,
Bohemians all loved Mimi –
and I'm in love with you!

Some Saints loved God only
(a funny thing to do),
while Bonnie loved Clyde Barrow –
but I'm in love with you!

Ah! Tristan loved Isolde,
and Byron's head of the queue
was prim Teresa Guiccioli –
but I'm in love with you!

Frankie, they say, loved Johnnie,
and stuck to him like glue
till it came unstuck in a shoot-out!
But I still love you.

Millions loved Shirley Temple –
what sentimental goo! –
in love, I'm afraid, with a minor,
as I'm in love with you.

It's always unsuitable people
that seem the first of the few –
and that might be the reason
that I'm in love with you!

Perfect love is a phantom,
a dream that won't come true –
but lots of us are in love with love
and I'm in love with you!

Heaving Drinking
(A Secret Narrative of the Fifties)

'A few months later Guy Burgess was dead. The years of hard living, heaving drinking and chain-smoking had wrecked his body.' – Penrose and Freeman, Conspiracy of Silence

He was a gent and an agent,
devoted to heaving drinking
and to fags and rough trade.

His wife used to reproach him,
raising her little tea-stained face,
fingering his Old Etonian tie.

She lived in the lip of luxury,
lounging like a lizard,
eating mink chocolate. . . .

But he was away, interfering
with the intelligentsia,
obsessed by forbidden boys.

She was Ludmila, he was Russian.
Or so you *might* say. The secrets!
He was definitely a tractor.

And all the police dogs
were not on his trail – the slavering
Chipmunk-Pinchers

and the Press were howling
and sniffing; so finally
his flat was bugged and

his flies were searched.
It was Apocalypse! The Apostles,
All Soul's, Christchurch!

Not to mention Trinity!
His wife! Her teats were unavailing!
Distraught! Her heavy bosom!

Lots of spivs end like this,
caught by the Three Wide Men . . .
set a thief to catch a

Dear Old Esmé
(A Late Victorian Letter)

It really was awfully bricky of you to write me such
                              a long yarn,
when in the midst of such gaiety and pleasure!
And now you are off on a good old spree to Holy
                              Island (or Lindisfarne)
where the monks laid up so much spiritual treasure!
You are a lucky beggar and no mistake! Here all is
                              very quiet.
Just now Roderick and Leonard are outside the
                    window, rotting on the lawn.
Sometimes we play tennis; but there are no scenes of
                              debauchery and riot.
There are no dances of nymphs and satyrs, not even
                              a laughing faun
to disturb us as we stroll in our nearest approximation
                    to a woodland glade.
Thank you so very much for sending me the
                    charming head flannel.
What a lot of tommy rot I write! But I carry on,
                              undismayed!
I believe, to get to Lindisfarne, you have to cross a
                              very small channel.
I hope you're a better sailor than I am. I hate those
                              beastly boats.
What rot not being allowed to go for a walk alone
                              with Theo!
We may be rabbits, but some of these mothers
                                        are stoats!
(What a thing to say!). I'm glad to hear he's a Leo.
I'm a Capricorn. I'm sure he will be broad-minded.
                              I'm afraid Jack
has lost all interest in poor little Gwenfrewi.
He's terrifically chummy with Cyprian and Hilarion,
                              and as for Mac,
he won't let him out of his sight! Julius is a bit jewy
for my taste. He doesn't somehow seem right for
                              kissing and babies:

though his moustache is nice his way of walking's a
                              bit rum!
He and Febronia! As the village people say, 'They be
                         great gabies!'
I hear Mother calling. So I must stop. Goodbye for
                 now, your very loving old chum

                                             Vicky

The Gordians

*'When he reluctantly accepted the purple, he was above
fourscore years old; a last and valuable remains of the
happy days of the Antonines, whose virtues he revived in
his own conduct, and celebrated in an elegant poem of
thirty books. With the venerable proconsul, his son, who
had accompanied him into Africa as his lieutenant, was
likewise declared emperor. His manners were less pure, but
his character was equally amiable with that of his father.
Twenty-two acknowledged concubines, and a library of
sixty-two thousand volumes, attested the variety of his
inclinations; and from the productions which he left behind
him, it appears that both the one and the other were
designed for use rather than for ostentation.★*

Whatever else then, this was not
to do with any Gordian knot!
One Gordian was a fearful swot –

the other knotted (in his way)
with broads in beds (this was OK).
Entwining limbs by night and day,

enticed by girls (and their good looks).
No poems came in thirty books;
for only dedicated cooks

★ *By each of his concubines the younger Gordian left three or four
children. His literary productions, though less numerous, were by no
means contemptible.'* – Gibbon, The Decline and Fall of the Roman
Empire

can serve great dishes. His excuse
was good enough: to shine in use
is best, and here he could adduce

as proof of bestness 88
kids that could serve the Roman State
and make it bigger and more great!

The Gods put tools into our hands;
Imperial purple, life expands.
And this the wise man understands!

When the Cats Leave
(Victorian Values)

We shall miss the little faces
in the long-accustomed places.
Yes, it will be so.
There'll be empty chairs and tables
like the long-left-empty stables
when the horses go.

All the jumping up and purring
will no longer be occurring;
and the plaintive miaows,
irritating and endearing,
will not persecute our hearing
like a lover's vows –

catstyle lobbying and pleading
when the time comes round for feeding.
Silence there instead.
We are overlords, cats peasants.
Their fertile furry feline presence
meant that time, like lead,

never hung too heavy for us.
Cats like that could never bore us.
Ali Bongo, Funk.
Funk could open fridges. Ali
had the highest birdcatch tally.
Sober cats or drunk,

feral cats or cat show beauties,
scratching spitters or calm cuties,
couldn't equal *them*.
It was character that counted,
attributes that all amounted
to *crème de la crème*

honoured cathood! Day of sadness!
We shan't see them go with gladness –
each an honoured guest –
we, at waving tails departing,
will find our eyes just slightly smarting,
we shall feel depressed.

History

Of course AIDS is awful but
think of all those centuries

when syphilis was awful too
and there was no cure and

men worried about whether
they had cuts or other small

lesions on their cocks you could
get infected so easily. Now

they ought to invent small
French letters or condoms

to fit on people's tongues
for anyone keen on the widespread

well-known *cunnilingus*.
How did it start? It may be

it was AIDS that wiped out
the dinosaurs can't you just

see them lying on their backs
in the swamps being sucked or

licked? Ah life was very
naughty in the days before

history!

Nominal Hexameters

Smith, Brown, Robinson, Jones! No, the names of
                              the English aren't lovely.
Was it Matthew Arnold who said that, for ugliness,
                              no other nation
could ever quite equal their Bloggs? The French
                              would regard it with horror.
'Wragg is in custody' too struck him as so typical,
                              blatant,
inhumane, the no-sex putting-down of a criminal
                              woman.

Are they much better, those names that come
                              running up at the double?
Montgomery-Massingberd? And thousands of
                              Robinson-Forsytes,
or even a Robinson-Jones? Where a name-change
                              inherits some money!
If the great name dies, the legacy goes to a cousin.
What about Cave-Brown-Cave? Like a marvellous
                              Beethoven trio,
there is sonorous silliness here of the kind that the
                              French and Italians
surely would hardly believe; though I know that there
                              once was a singer
called Meneghini-Callas (till she lost both the name
                              and the husband)
and shone forth as Callas alone. The Germans have
                              von, and *zu* also,
the Spanish an 'and' (just an *y*). The *Conde de Coca y
                              Cola*

was Cyril Connolly's joke, just a *blague* but it
                                    indicates something.
like the Bishop of Bath and Wells, or the title a
                                    friend once invented:
the Earl of Newhaven and Dieppe – and that
                                    something is pompous.
'I am a SOMEBODY' is the clear message to every
                                    Pooter.

But among all the multiple names, and the names
                                    that are solemn or trivial,
Hovell-Thurlow-Cumming-Bruce* thunders by like a
                                    martial quadriga!
Even to think that it's real gives the ordinary street-
                                    man a headache.
But it is! It's quadrivial (Joyce used this word, as *he*
                                    would) but it's mighty!
On the horizon no sail of a quinquereme threatens its
                                    beauty!

* Francis Edward Hovell-Thurlow-Cumming-Bruce and Baron
Wolfgang zu Putlitz, are both mentioned in *Conspiracy of Silence*,
the book about Anthony Blunt by Barrie Penrose and Simon
Freeman.

The Reason Why (for Love read Lust)

A Crisp Cole Porter Confection with a Delicious Extra Topping of Internal Rhyme

. . . and that's why bats do it, cats do it,
in warehouses and whorehouses the rats do it!
Let's do it! Let's fall in love!
Some gays in plays on hot days do it,
cowhands in a thousand different ways do it!
Let's do it! Let's fall in love!

Those folks with jokes in the bars do it
when the alcohol bites,
hordes of bored broads do it
in the nights without tights!

Young Teds with oil on their heads do it,
reds in the obscurity-security of beds do it!
Let's do it! Let's fall in love!

Love made Mae West with great zest do it,
the worst and best and all the rest do it!
Let's do it! Let's fall in love!
Love made staid Edward the Eight do it,
with his refined and re-designed great mate do it!
Let's do it! Let's fall in love!

The Janes with champagne do it
and that old Tarzan call
is an invite each night to it –
boy, what joy! What a ball!

Love makes each he and each she do it,
Sir Stephen and, believe it, even *me* do it!
Let's do it! Let's fall in love!

Advice to Wendy Cope on Touring the USA

When you're on the Chicken Circuit★
where the worst is like the best
it's not wise to mutter 'Firk it!'
or in any way protest –
make no Cockney observation
on a language's inflation!

Suffer mildly 'meeting up with',
'Burglarized' and 'as of now'
(long spoons, devils you must sup with) –
don't exclaim, astonished, 'Wow!'
for this is the very nation
that made transport transportation.

★ Strictly speaking, the Chicken Circuit is the round of
diplomatic functions in Washington, where chicken (being bland
and neutral from a religious point of view) is very frequently
served. This poem was written when on a reading tour of the
United States.

456

Every statement looks a dollar
that in truth is just a dime,
every whisper is a holler –
'at this moment' (say) 'in time'
books are 'authored'; mutilation
is the wordsmith's occupation!

Presidents and Generals waffle –
don't mindboggle if they do!
It's alfalfa and falaffel,
'expletive-deleted' too!
O 'disinterested' Station
of that Cross – Disinformation!

The Story of the Gadsbys
(Rudyard Kipling)

Captain Gadsby ignored the basic rules of chivalry
and rode about mashing – married woman devilry!
Till he married a chit,
lost his nerve – and devil a bit
was he any more use in the Cavalry!

The Premature Coronation

'AD 310 September. *Although Sapor was in the thirtieth
year of his long reign, he was still in the vigour of youth,
as the date of his accession by a very strange fatality, had
preceded that of his birth. The wife of Hormouz remained
pregnant at the time of her husband's death; and the
uncertainty of the sex, as well as of the event, excited the
ambitious hopes of the house of Sassan. The apprehensions
of civil war were at length removed, by the positive
assurance of the Magi that the widow of Hormouz had
conceived, and would safely produce, a son. Obedient to
the voice of superstition, the Persians prepared, without
delay, the ceremony of his coronation. A royal bed, on
which the queen lay in state, was exhibited in the midst of*

457

the palace; a diadem was placed on the spot which might
be supposed to conceal the future heir of Artaxerxes, and
the prostrate Satraps adored the majesty of their invisible
and insensible sovereign.' – *Edward Gibbon*, The Decline
and Fall of the Roman Empire, *Chapter XVIII*

It's all in Gibbon. It is. The cruelties, the tortures, the
                                                             battles.
   Intrigues of the eunuchs, the lot! The heresies,
                                            martyrs, the wars
stirred up from time to time by invidious competitive
                                                 bishops.
   Barbarian hairy campaigns, the luxury life of the
                                               East,
rampant theology too, the Arians and Athanasians,
   the thick Praetorian Guard with Emperors made
                                         by the sword!
Then as now cry Alas! for History's dismal agenda!
   But you find little nuggets of gold, such as scholars
                                 enjoy with their wine,
laced with the Latin and Greek, the rumours, the
                                      quite anecdotal.
   Gibbon's humour is dry, and it's that of a rational
                                           man;
the things that he didn't believe are recorded with
                                 admirable balance.
   See the story above. It's a smile, not a laugh, up
                                       his sleeve.

                 ★   ★   ★

Surely he relished the scene! As the queen lies in state
                                        on a day-bed,
   there are psalms and musicians, perhaps; learnèd
                                men, all the sages and priests,
a solemn hullabaloo, in the rich coloured silks and
                                      the satins
(Constantine dyed his beard – in the East, where
                                 anything goes –
in parti-coloured bright stripes, all the lords and
                               ladies were lustful),
   and there at the centre, the queen – jewelled and
                                 perfumed and fat –

veiled, I expect; with a crown; and her nails painted
                                            red as a ruby.
    Likewise her lips, is my guess. Her skin is a
                                    beautiful brown,
oiled and exciting and soft, a prominent jewel in her
                                            navel –
    naked, I think, below this. For the ceremony's
                                    there to be seen,
a cloud of witnesses round, and everything solemn
                                            and proper.
    Incense and hymns. A High Priest intones with a
                                    world-shaking bass,
some cymbals are struck, as he bends with the
                                    diadem over the sexparts,
    curled and crisp pubic hair, oiled and anointed
                                            with nard,
an odour of sanctity! He lays on the crown, an
                                            orgasm
    of ritual climaxing there. And we have another
                                            Great King!

                    ★   ★   ★

Long pipes, wine glasses with stems, the most they
                                    will do is to chuckle.
    They are the civilized men. Such stories are not for
                                            the mob.
Long coats, long waistcoats too. Long views are
                                    what History teaches.
    Long-headed men, and of them Edward Gibbon
                                    most fit to be loved
for his long-term attachment to truth, and the style
                                    that's so clear and Olympian.

    Rien n'est beau que le vrai. Rhetoricians, avaunt! (he
                                            implied).
Let all those born-again boys who fancy themselves
                                    as God's Sales Force
    look on this man who worked years, not valuing
                                    money, but Fame!

The first volume of Gibbon's *Decline and Fall* appeared in 1776.
The last two in 1788. Gibbon was born in Putney in 1737, and
died in 1794.

'Simply Supply Us with a Good Photograph'

'Whether it be a portrait of you, a loved one, a faithful pet, your home, boat, etc. There is nothing like the look of vibrant textured oils.' – Leaflet mailed in January 1987

CLASS & ELEGANCE NO ONE SHOULD BE
    WITHOUT
Have you ever commissioned a genuine oil painting?
It stands out from the wall like a defiant shout –
class & elegance no one should be without –
it makes your friends' prints look shabby; without
    doubt
their envy will have them furious or fainting!
CLASS & ELEGANCE NO ONE SHOULD BE
    WITHOUT
Have you ever commissioned a genuine oil painting?

'Condom Man Loses Finger'

'An executive of the London Rubber Company had his finger bitten off when a group of men attacked delegates at a sales conference for condom makers in Brighton.' – The Guardian, *8 May 1987*

When a condom man loses a finger
there's a lot to be pondered upon!
And the thought that's most likely to linger
is: *Quite what the hell was going on?*

For a condom itself's not immoral –
like the beer that runs out of the spigot.
With the condom most men have no quarrel,
except for a rare kind of bigot,

and when AIDS is a serious threatener
and makes everyone sexy think twice
and can blow us all up like an Etna
and completely make nasty what's nice,

then the condom's indeed quite a saviour
and important to national health,
a safeguard when loving behaviour
is overt and not governed by stealth.

So was that executive taunting
the men in that violent group?
Was he teasing, flamboyantly flaunting?
A dirty great hair in the soup?

Did he waggle a condom-clad finger,
admonitory, just to annoy?
Like a falsetto North Country singer?
Was he gay? Were *they* gay? *Attaboy!*

– did he shout out loud? – *Come and get it!*
Or were there Mariolaters there?
Who saw Satan arising, and let it
get too deeply involved in their hair?

Was it *Birth Control – No!* they were shouting,
with their own self-control lost and gone,
on that punitive passionate outing?
So yobbish, a cad's carry-on!

I will bet you that biter was oral –
the whole thing was a Freudian thing –
they were acting it out, it was choral,
in a Sussex-like Highlandish fling!

And in *Brighton*! Once famed as the Mecca
for everyone's dirty weekend!
The wencher! The smuggler! The wrecker!
Where all rubber was once a good friend!

The Peter Reading Poem

Rūmpĕtў̆|- tūmtĭttў̆|- tūm ‖ tĭttў̆|tūm, tĭttў̆|tūm,
                                  ŭkŭl|ēlĕ
  Rūmpĕtў̆-|tūm, hăngĭng | dōgs ‖ rūmpĕtў̆
                                  |tūmtĭttў̆-|tūm.

Bāshĭng thĕ | bādgĕrs ăb|oūt ‖ tĭttў̆-|tūm ăll
                        thĕ | rāpĭsts aňd |yōbbŏs.
  Rūmtĭttў̆ | tūmtĭttў̆ | tūm ‖ gāngs ŏf
                        ŭn|spēakăblĕ |ў̄obs.

Tēenāg|eřs rūm|tūm ‖ tĭttў̆|tūm-tĭttў̆ | ħead-
                        băshĭng |bābiĕs
  Tūm-tĭttў̆, | ūmtĭttў̆, | ūm ‖ hōmĭnoĭds, |
                        ālĭĕns, |oĭcks.

Two Poems for Bad Children

1 Fairies

When the fairies say 'toadstools'
and jump about and wriggle
it's because they're not thinking of 'toad stools'
but actually of 'toads' tools' –
and that's what makes them giggle.

2 Fairy Story

The Hooded Clitoris
is Little Red Riding Hood –
which some pure ladies aren't aware that they've
                                got.

Sometimes a Wolf
will turn up to tickle it –
and sometimes not.

Soft Contacts Turn Brown Eyes Blue

(Notice in shop window, 14th Street, New York City)

Soft contacts turn brown eyes blue –
and that's your one desire if you're Hispanic –
no other contacts are much use to you,
it's *blue* eyes make the boys so male and manic!
Likewise if negritude obstructs your view.
Hook, line and sinker, like the old *Titanic*,
under your charm they'll founder. It's the blue
that makes them ethnicize and act organic!

New York, 1 May 1987

To the Young Wives

When you've got your Mr Right
you must hold him very tight –

or he'll quietly slip away
when the girls come out to play.

When the gin is in the glass
he will want a piece of arse.

He'll end stiffer than a board
in the arms of some big broad.

His eyes, and then his feet, will roll.
Like the common garden mole

he will come up somewhere else,
far away from wedding bells!

Talking French
(Three Easy Pieces)

1 Ideas of Order

The French like turning things round
(for them it would be a horse-cart
and not a cart-horse).

For example:
A push button is a *bouton poussoir*.
If there were something called
a handkerchief-sheep
it would be a *mouton mouchoir*.

2 Please Come to My Assistance!

'Love' sounds less romantic than *l'amour* –
but the three syllables of *Au secours!*
can't be as effective as the Anglo-Saxon yelp:
'Help!'

3 Anglo-French Clerihews

Il n'y a rien d'ignoble
dans notre vignoble –
mais, au contraire, un vin
délicat et fin!

'There is nothing ignoble in our vineyard – but, on the contrary,
a wine that is delicate and fine.'

Sèvres-Babylone
has a very high tone –
but Denfert-Rochereau
sounds like the Rocky Horror Show!

Sèvres-Babylone and *Denfert-Rochereau* are stations on the Paris
Métro. *Denfert* sounds a little like *d'Enfer* (of Hell) and *rocher*
means a rock. 'The Rocky Horror Show' was a highly successful
musical.

Eight Little Ones

1 Basic English

You could get through the States
from start to finish
with *Hi!*, *Wow!*, *Right!* and *Okay!*
and you wouldn't do too badly with just
Have a good day!

2 Dr Leavis

Dr F.R. Leavis
thought Oxonians were all Miniver Cheevys,
dining out in sleek gentility –
with no sensibility.

3 Found Poem of Edna O'Brien

(Quoted in an interview with Miriam Gross,
The Observer, *14th April 1985)*

Secretly I think how wonderful it would be
not to be separate and alone, to have a mate.
And yet there must be some deep and complex
                                        reason
for choosing this solitary fate.

4 Beginning of a Ballad: At the Literary Party

It is an Ancient Poetess
And she stoppeth one of three.
Oh what, oh what, oh what, oh what
But yestreen did I see?
Could it have been a BAD REVIEW
That thou didst write of me?

5 The Gift

To some of the races of the earth
God gave myrrh, frankincense and (to a few) nard;
but to all the blossoming black men
He gave Nancy Cunard.

6 The Great Women Composers

Sybil Sibelius! Yes, Belinda Brahms!
Harriet Haydn! And even Mary Mozart!
Have all been invited to tea
by the indomitable Beatrice K. Beethoven!

7 Betjeman at Oxford

Dons are big Henry James données
like fat Old-Fashioned Humbugs –
but give me Susie with her little sinbin
to keep her sexy savours in!

8 On Proposed Legislation to Prevent British Women Importing Foreign Husbands

A thing of which we do not speak –
the Queen is married to a Greek!

Semantic Fragment: The Start of a Victorian Ballad

(*According to the* Oxford English Dictionary *of 1971*)

She had few or no material possessions, she wanted
the means to procure the comforts, or the necessaries,

466

of life, she was needy, indigent, destitute; but she was held in honour, holding an honourable position, respectable, marked by uprightness or probity, of good moral character, chaste. She was also one who suffers severely in body or property through cruel or oppressive treatment occasioned by the amusement, delight, sport of a person belonging to the sex which begets offspring, or performs the fecundating function of generation, he being endowed with large possessions, wealthy, opulent. For she came across, lit upon, came face to face with, arrived in the presence of, the country gentleman or landed proprietor who was the principal landowner in her village or district; and as a consequence she incurred the privation of, parted with through negligence or misadventure, was deprived of, the particular combination of sounds employed as a designation of herself, mentioned by others with admiration or commendation, with a reputation for being a virgin!

It is identical with what is indicated in the following context, in every country of the terraqueous globe: it is those with few or no material possessions, wanting the means to procure the comforts or necessaries of life, who are needy, indigent, destitute, that incur the imputation of demerit on account of a fault or blemish, that are subject to reproof, censure, reprehension. It is on the contrary those who are endowed with large possessions, wealthy, opulent, who have the enjoyment or anticipation of what is felt or viewed as good or desirable, enjoyment, delight, gratification, the opposite of pain. Is it not, the entire and unabated amount and quantity of it, a disgrace, ignominy (improper and matter for severe reproach) that is sanguinary, losing or emitting blood, running or suffused with blood, full of anguish from suffering?

On Being Criticized for Categorizing Rochester's 'A Ramble in St James's Park' as Light Verse

Of course, I know it's serious.
He says what's deleterious
about his girlfriend's character.
He doesn't mince his words with her.
It's furious satire, hot and strong,
and, as it tears its way along,
a negative and sexy hype,
the true harsh Restoration type,
the details of the tricks and stunts
of all the foppish pricks and cunts
laid open, plain, for all to see –
and very bitter jealousy!

But Satire is a No Man's Land,
not heavy, solemn, dull (or bland) –
perhaps you can't *quite* call it light
but most descriptions seem not right.
The anger may be sub-atomic,
the *style*, however, still stays comic –
exaggeration plays its part
in this most spiky hybrid art
(do mandrakes spring from lovers' sperm?).

Professors argue, term by term,
but for the daily me and you
maybe 'Light Verse' will have to do.

'The Body Casts Aside Its Vest and Sings'★

'The body casts aside its vest and sings'
and ludicrous poetry rises on lead wings.

'The body kicks its panties off and screams,'
enough to give a Troop of Scouts wet dreams.

'The body pulls its seaboots off and swears'
and tremulous virgins can't believe their ears.

'The body throws its bloomers on a chair' –
mustachios rise on end at all that hair.

'The body dumps its shako in the river'
and merry milkmaids start to twitch and quiver.

'The body hurls its raincoat in the sea'
and leaves the world to bathos and to me!

★ A line from a book of verse published in 1981

Victorian Hangover in 'The Duke's Head'

With trembling hands he moves the precious liquid
across the tabled, chaired and peopled floor –
a holy fluid, not mundane like chickweed,
and elevated like a solemn Host the night before!

Held to the light and worshipped, an elixir
so dear – too dear – to the initiate!
A social solvent and a marvelled mixer
leading to Love! Fair-fondlers freely fornicate!

Talkers will amputate the legs of donkeys!
Inspired by this! The wine as red as blood!
Unlocks the Soul – it never has the wrong keys –
and Genius flows fast as Thames in freespeed flood!

The Lovesong Waltzes

Goodnight, Mozart! Angels will watch o'er you!
Goodnight, Mozart! All my dreams are for you!
I'll be in the arms
Of Johannes Brahms –
So goodnight, Mozart, goodnight!

– Popular song

469

Cocks and cunts are churning past,
turning and turning, the music's fast –
the tits are so soft
as they're carried aloft,
nothing, oh, nothing is at half-mast!

Cloven, with cleavage and hair in buns,
they're whirled around by the crested ones
and all morals are bent
by the serious scent
that would not be permitted to nervous nuns!

Eyebrows arching, as hands are held,
bosom to bosom, a woman-weld,
with eloquent eyes
and sensational sighs,
it's a marital mixture, a mimsy meld!

A red-hot ritual, a chance
to simulate sex in a daring dance,
where powder and paint
make duennas faint
with the schmaltzy smell of Romance, Romance!

Dressed so dreamy, the dread dragoons
are tantalized by the torrid tunes
as the breasts sing loud
and are standing proud
in curvaceous corsets like honeymoons!

Galloping round like a filly foal
the beauty glows like a glowing coal
and the stallion snorts
as the pair cavorts –
classical chariots racing for goal!

Sweat in the bodices, bloomers wet
with all the sweetness of swinky sweat –
that swims and swoons
in the pantaloons!
Oh, what they want, they may well get!

Polished wood in marble halls,
manly and marvellous the balls,
breeches are tight
in the candlelight –
till Love bursts out like Niagara Falls!

The 'popular song' is a private version of Ray Noble's
'Goodnight, Sweetheart'. Brahms' *Liebesliederwalzer* is a set of
songs for singers and piano, recently performed as a ballet by the
New York City Ballet. When it was first danced, the waltz was
regarded as disgusting, because of the close embrace of the
partners.

The Rivals

*'You have W.W. Gibson over there I hear. Have you met
him yet? I hope he's not being the success he expected to be.
De la Mare I hear talks of nothing but America and is
keen on going out again. He made a lot of money I think
and got a lot of adulation too I think. I suppose Gibson
might make some money, but I can't imagine anyone
giving him adulation – there's something so very small and
mean about the man. Davies I hear is mad with rage that
de la Mare and Gibson have been out and getting rich
before he's had his "go" at the Americans, and is planning
to go and read his poems at 500 dollars a time. So you'll
get the whole brood of English poets out there before long.
All the ones not helping in the war that is, tho' Gibson
has written several "moving" poems from the trenches
damn him.'* – Letter from Helen Thomas (widow of
Edward Thomas) to Robert Frost, 2 March 1917

Holt and hanger and hill,
Beacon and barton and byre,
Mill-race and river and rill
And charcoal-burner's fire!

All the sweet meadow flowers,
Bryony, Old Man's Balls,
Call them with Pan-like powers
Out of the milking-stalls!

Loosestrife, bladderwort, vetch,
Hazel and hay and holly –
Tiny hands they outstretch
Make them juvescent and jolly!

Georgian Poets all,
All of them up to their necks
In country matters – but small
Is ever their mention of Sex!

Nature is censored and tame –
Picturesque is the word –
A bull and an ox are the same
For this land-literate herd!

Money excites them a bit –
Like the inns and the pints of old ale –
As they write, as they dreamily sit.
There aren't many cheques in the mail,

So it isn't surprising at all
That a chance to cash in stirs them up
To an envy by no means small,
And the bitterness of Life's cup

Overflows. And they itch to be off
To a land where the readings are long,
Where the hearers don't fidget and cough
and the singer is paid for his song!

Dear John

*(A 'Dear John' was what the American troops serving
overseas in World War II called the letter from a wife or
girlfriend announcing that the relationship was over)*

Every morning I expect it.
The envelope addressed in the round feminine
    handwriting,
and, inside, the letter from the Muse
saying 'We must break it off, I've met somebody
    else . . .'

The young men come up to her at parties
(the young women too),
they put an arm round her neck and lead her away
to sit and talk on a sofa (or it might be a
      davenport) –
and I am forgotten,
an old wooer whose performance was never very good.

'Dear Gavin, I am writing to tell you . . .'

At least when this happens (reviewers too will warn me
and the critics who are like nosey neighbours
and write saying 'We're sorry to have to tell you
she's been seeing a lot of X and too much of Y!')
it won't come as a complete surprise.

Beryl's Second Poem (and Trevor's Second) – 1981

A man on the television was saying
how there was always a great sense of occasion
at Lansdowne Road

He was announcing the line-up.
He informed everybody that this was somebody's
                              first English Cap.
He suggested that conditions were perfect.
He predicted a close thing, he speculated on the
                              outcome.

He remarked that someone was about to start the
                              game.
He came out with some statements about ragged
                              play.
He made known his doubts about the Irish pack.
He declared that the wind was extremely puzzling.
He mentioned the importance of good possession.
He revealed his opinion of shortening the line-out

He proposed that the whole of the West Country
                        would be pleased about a replacement
He expatiated on the difficulties of a loose-head prop
                        playing as a tight-head prop.
He insinuated that the change might benefit the Irish
                        scrummaging.
He inferred that the Irish had their tails up.
He stated that the whole of Ireland was rampant and
                        full of inventiveness.

He certified the merit of a little chip ahead.
He expressed admiration for a piece of running.
He implied that one of the players had got a knock.
He averred that a captain was telling them to cool it.
He reported that the referee was not a very big
                        fellow.

He claimed that a player had sold a beautiful
                        dummy.
He gave it as his opinion that a dropped goal was
                        possible.
He alleged that the age of one player was 24.
He proclaimed that someone was the most capped
                        Irishman of all time.
He intimated that something must surely be the
                        chance of a lifetime.
He testified that we had seen the try of the
                        Championship.
He imagined that there would be joy all over
                        England.
He predicted a certain amount of celebration in
Lancashire.

Pepys Into the Past

Last nighte did dreame a Dreame that was mighty
uncomfortable. For indeede I did dreame that I was
at a Meetinge of ye Poetry Society: and there were
gathered Sir Jeff Nuttall, Sir Thomas Pickard, Lord

474

Bob Cobbing, Mister Laurence Upton, and others of
note. And they didde confoundedly tease and annoie
Lord George Wightman, heaving at him from all
sides Beere Cans (these being empty) so that he,
poore wretch, was fain to fend them from his Head
and Bodie. And in their Utterances also they were
very hot against him, to the extent that my Lord
Wightman, trie as hee might, cd not have his Voyce
heard. Indeed, as ye Schoolmen speake of Hell, so I
found this to bee, these Enthusiasts shewing so like
Demons in their Intemperate Violence of Demeanour
that trulie it was a *Pandemonium* or Concourse of
Devils for noise and Unrulinesse; so that I was
heartily glad when I awoke, being in no small Fear
that they should turn their Hatred and Loathing
against my Own Self . . .

Show Ban for Peke Breeder's Contempt

(A McGonagall Sonnet based on a Guardian
report, 4 June 1985)

A wee ban has been placed, by the Kennel Club
                    General Committee,
on Mrs Barbara Lashmar, aged 63, of Redhill,
                              Surrey,
because she 'discredited the canine world'. They
                    showed no pity –
she's banned from all dog shows for ten years because
                              in a flurry
of temper she told how Miss Adele Summers (who
                    fled from the judging ring in tears
with her dog 'Modesty Permits') had slept with gay
                              or stud judges.
She said Miss Summers' dog was an effing cripple,
                              and (it appears)
she shouted out, without any winks or nudges:

'Anybody that gives that dog a ticket is an
                              effing crook!'
Miss Summers was very embarrassed and asked if
                              she had to stay.
Mrs Lashmar was calling the other breeders every
                              name in the book.
She shouted loud: 'Good. You're an effing
                              big-head anyway!'
as Miss Summers went. Major General Martin Sinall,
Kennel Club Secretary, added an afterthought:
'We regard ourselves as very much the gentle end
                              of Sport.'

American Fatties

American fatties are
wonderful people, they
take up two seats in a
train or a bus.
It's the junk food and the
constantly eating it
makes them so large and much
bigger than us.

See them so great as they
roll down the Avenues,
each with a vast and tre-
mendulous tum.
They are so huge and quite
marvellous dinosaurs –
it's hard to distinguish a
thigh from a bum!

American fatties are
best in the world and they
certainly know they're the
ones with the most!
God bless America!
Biggest – and more of them –
that is their constant and
sizeable boast!

Lesbian Laughter

Liz laughed with her, a knowing laugh. Did it sound like a lesbian laugh? She hoped so. – Valerie Miner, *Blood Sisters*

Did it sound like a lesbian laugh?
Or was it more like a gay giggle?
Like water poured from a carafe?
Did it sound like a lesbian laugh
or too high, like a tickled giraffe,
or like a straight girl who'd man-wriggle?
Did it sound like a lesbian laugh
or was it *more* like . . . a gay giggle?

'Noisy Love Romp Row'

(Found poem, Wandsworth & Putney Guardian, *18 December 1986)*

A Putney girl is in danger of
losing her home – because neighbours

claim she makes love too noisily
Residents of Kinnaird House complained

when they became fed up with the
sound of bedroom romps. But pretty

Linda Carew 23 said the majority
of people make a noise when they

make love it's natural but I
don't scream my head off I would

never shout do this do that at
my boyfriend or anything

like that I feel totally
embarrassed about this . . .

So We'll Go No More A-Roving

So we won't go wandering about any more,
into the wee small hours,
though I'm still terrifically keen on you
and the moon still looks very shiny.

For the penis wears out the vagina
(*This doesn't seem very likely – Ed*)
and the soul bursts through the tits
and the heart has to take a tea–break
and love itself take some time out.

Though the night was intended for sexual intercourse
and the day starts in before we're ready for it,
we still won't go wandering about any more
in the bright lunar illumination.

The Merlin/Vivien Situation★

My athletic grandfather, the one who played rugger
                                    for England,
in the mid–Twenties got himself into a Merlin/Vivien
                                    situation
vis-à-vis a young lady at a School of Ballroom
                                    Dancing.

Let's say in 1925, when he would be 65.
She would be a third his age perhaps, his favourite
                                    partner.

He'd been a widower since 1922. I'm sure he loved
                                    her.
Her photo was prominently displayed in the flat in
                                    Hove.
My eldest aunt said, 'We were afraid he'd marry her!'
a conversation overheard by me – but not then fully
                                    understood.

Of course Merlin was magic, and had magic potency.
Among all the facts and figures, I can't help wishing
                                    my grandfather well.

★ See Tennyson's *The Idylls Of The King*

For Translation Into Latin

The sailors love the beautiful girls.

The wise poets love the sailors.

The girls often love the sailors.

The bad poets love the beautiful girls.

The bad girls love the farmers.

All the poets hate the farmers.

The bad girls hate the good girls.

The good girls love all the sailors.

The bad girls love the bad girls.

The farmers hate all the poets.

The good girls love the bad poets.

The bad poets hate the good poets.

Note for Demotics. The Latin words for sailor, poet and farmer (*nauta, poeta* and *agricola*) are all examples of masculine nouns that have a feminine form. *Puella* (a girl) is the standard example of such feminine nouns.

Radio Cricket

Can't you just see them,
sitting there in the Commentary Box,
drinking tea, passing round the sweets,
eating the big cakes their admirers send them?
Blowers, Fred, Trevor, the Alderman,
The Bearded Wonder?

Prep School boys with nicknames,
sitting there in their shorts,
wearing their little school caps –
wool stockings up to their knees,
with elastic garters!

Literary Problems

Cyril and Evelyn
were both of them winos –
and that's the way it goes –
their prominent bellies
wobbled like jellies,
they couldn't touch their toes!

Wystan went cruising
with no underpants on
through dangerous New York,
Christopher got into Yoga
in his philosophic toga –
allomorphic pigs were pork.

Edith got high on
her own list of Geniuses,
so high she was out of sight.
'A person,' she enunciated clearly,
'There is a person,' she said austerely,
'A person called *Enright* . . .'

Stephen cried loudly
'Who is Peter Porter?',
there was confusion all round!
To know what was *chic*
and *in* for that week
you needed one ear to the ground!

It's never been really
terribly easy,
it's quite like Musical Chairs;
an Ian, a Craig, Andrew or Clive
can creep up and silently dive
and kick you quickly downstairs!

A Critic Speaks

Ewart is very frivolous and brittle.
Ewart can do very little –
though every once in a while
he might raise a weary smile.

A stallion neighing at a filly?
His best poems are silly.
Some find them not very nice.
Perhaps they're *just* worth the price.

But *only* just. It must be said,
the first thing that comes into his head
is what *he* writes about,
with rhyme and rhythm, or else without.

What, no insects? And no flowers?
No Heavenly or Earthly Powers?
No pike, no plaice, no crabs, no cod?
No fish at all! And, worse, no God!

Where is the secret narrative, the myth?
The mysticism? The concentrated pith
of Martian Arts? The learnèd story
of the proud High Tory?

The surrealist touch, quite gay
when the boys come out to play?
Animals, landscapes? Not a hint.
One wonders wanly: *Why, why print*

all this sad old-fashioned stuff?
It was once new enough –
but now, as fresh modes come in,
we drop it, fastidiously, in the bin!

Index

483

485

486